The Middle East: Thinking About and Beyond Security and Stability

GLOBAL POLITICS AND SECURITY

Volume 5

Edited by

Prof. Lorenzo Kamel,
University of Turin's History Department,
and Istituto Affari Internazionali (IAI)

PETER LANG
Bern • Berlin • Bruxelles • New York • Oxford

Lorenzo Kamel (ed.)

The Middle East: Thinking About and Beyond Security and Stability

PETER LANG
Bern • Berlin • Bruxelles • New York • Oxford

Bibliographic Information published by the Deutsche Nationalbibliothek
The Deutsche Nationalbibliothek lists this publication in the Deutsche Nationalbibliografie; detailed bibliographic data is available in the internet at http://dnb.d-nb.de.

Library of Congress Cataloging-in-Publication Data
A CIP catalog record for this book has been applied for at the Library of Congress.

The publication of this book has relied upon the cooperation and support of the Compagnia di San Paolo, the Istituto Affari Internazionali (IAI), the Italian Ministry of Foreign Affairs and International Cooperation, the German Marshall Fund (GMF) of the United States, and The Organization for Security and Co-operation in Europe (OSCE). The opinions expressed in this volume are those of the editor and the authors, and do not necessarily reflect the official policy or position of any of the above mentioned institutions or think tanks.

Cover Image: Exterior wall of the mud brick tower house in Shibam, Hadramaut valley, Yemen. Photo by Dmitry Chulov

ISSN 2624-8905
ISBN 978-3-0343-3876-9 (Print) • E-ISBN 978-3-0343-3891-2 (E-PDF)
E-ISBN 978-3-0343-3892-9 (EPUB) • E-ISBN 978-3-0343-3893-6 (MOBI)
DOI 10.3726/b16053

This publication has been peer reviewed.

www.peterlang.com

Contents

Nicolò Russo Perez

Foreword

This edited book is the result of some of the reflections shared on the occasion of an international conference – held in Beirut on 7–8 February 2019 – that was hosted by the Department of Political Studies and Public Administration of the American University of Beirut (AUB). The meeting, entitled 'The Middle East: Thinking About and Beyond Security and Stability' and co-organized by Lorenzo Kamel (University of Turin and Istituto Affari Internazionali) and Karim Makdisi (AUB), took place within the frame of the New-Med Research Network and addressed the two deeply intertwined issues of 'stability' and 'security' from non-Western perspectives.

Established in 2014, New-Med is a research network of Mediterranean experts and policy analysts with a special interest in the complex social, political, cultural and security-related dynamics that are unfolding in the Mediterranean region. The network is developed by the Istituto Affari Internazionali (IAI), in cooperation with the Organization for Security and Co-operation in Europe (OSCE) Secretariat in Vienna, the Compagnia di San Paolo foundation, the Italian Ministry of Foreign Affairs and International Cooperation, and the German Marshall Fund of the United States.

A priority of the network is to promote a non-Eurocentric vision of the region, featuring as much as possible views from all shores of the Mediterranean basin. The network also seeks to provide a platform where emerging researchers can put forward new perspectives about regional cooperation. By undertaking research and outreach activities, this 'track II' initiative aims to foster scholarly reflection on the changing scenarios in and around the Mediterranean and provide key input to the political dialogue taking place in international forums, including in the context of the OSCE Mediterranean Dialogue. Since its inception, the New-Med research network has organized several international conferences – many of them in Middle Eastern and North African countries – and published more than forty edited books and research studies on various themes tied to Euro-Mediterranean relations.

New-Med was therefore conceived from the very beginning as an open, inclusive platform for dialogue on a variety of Euro-Mediterranean issues. It aims to leverage the expertise of practitioners, researchers and academics from different 'Mediterranean spaces' to promote a truly 'two-way dialogue' on Mediterranean cooperation beneficial to a plurality of actors, particularly featuring non-Western perspectives.

In this framework, the New-Med conference hosted by the American University of Beirut provided the opportunity to analyse the historical dimension of the concept of 'security' and 'stability' in the Middle East and North Africa. The increasingly common – across academic and journalistic publications – description of this region as an inherently violent area was framed in a historical perspective, where these perceptions were explored and deeply challenged, also in the light of the role played by external powers in the establishment of 'sectarian', and thus often destabilising, institutions in the region.

Another topic of great relevance developed both during the conference and in the present volume is the analysis of how the intensification of political violence in the region and the rise of populism and Islamophobia in the West requires a deep re-evaluation of the meaning of security and insecurity for the people living in the Middle East, in the Mediterranean and Europe, on both the regional and local levels. At the same time, the production of (in)security, stability and order, as this volume demonstrates, needs to be framed within broader security-related topics, such as conflicts in the region and the role of global and regional powers in them, arms flows, securitization of refugees, the use of demographic movements, the politicization of identities and the role multilateral institutions can play in the production of security (international law, the UN, the ICC, UNRWA, UNHCR, the GCC, the JCPOA, a proposed 'Arab NATO' and others).

The Beirut conference and this volume provide the opportunity to look at the region and its stability as seen from within. A critical approach in thinking about (in)security in the region, in fact, means that we need to better understand the perspective of the people living in the Middle East and North Africa. For decades, global actors such as the

US, European states and Russia have supported authoritarian regimes for 'security' reasons. Together with some regional powers, they have invested enormous amounts of resources in opposing the rise of any government or party/movement that could have represented a credible alternative to authoritarian regimes. For the large majority of people living in these areas, this has provided a context of insecurity in their daily lives, including political, social, economic or identity insecurity.

The New-Med research network, with its original, fresh and sometime 'lateral' perspectives, provides precisely this: a tool that can be useful for shedding some light on all these aspects and better defining the contours of a stable and legitimate order that responds, first and foremost, to the needs of those living in this ancient region.

LORENZO KAMEL

Introduction

> A country does not have to be deemed fit for democracy; rather, it has to become fit through democracy.[1]

According to data provided by the US State Department, 'incidents of terrorism' increased globally by 6,500 per cent (199 attacks in 2002; 13,500 in 2014) since the beginning of the 'war on terror' in 2001 and half of them have been registered in Afghanistan and Iraq. The number of casualties resulting from terror attacks has increased by 4,500 per cent over this same time period.[2]

Washington is responsible for about 33 per cent of global arms sales and the Middle East is the primary destination of a large majority of US-made weapons (with Saudi Arabia and United Arab Emirates topping the list and Iraq and Egypt making the top ten).[3]

French arms deliveries to Egypt jumped from 39.6 million euro in 2010 to 1.3 billion in 2016 despite the EU's Foreign Affairs Council declaring (August 2013) that member states had to suspend export to Egypt of any equipment that could be used for domestic repression.[4]

1 Amartya Sen, 'Democracy as a Universal Value', in *Journal of Democracy*, Vol. 10, No. 3 (July 1999), p. 4.

2 Kit O'Connell, 'Deaths from Terrorism Increased 4,500 % Since Beginning of War on Terror', in *MintPress News*, 22 December 2015, https://www.mintpressnews.com/?p=212244.

3 US arms sales to foreign governments increased by 33 per cent under the administration of US President Donald Trump. See Peter Castagno, 'The Arms Trade Is Intensifying Under Trump', in *Truthout*, 20 February 2019, https://truthout.org/?p=255001.

4 FIDH, *Egypt: A Repression Made in France. Exports of Weapons and Surveillance Technologies*, Paris, FIDH, June 2018, pp. 8–9 and 27, https://www.fidh.org/IMG/pdf/egypt_report_english.pdf.

German arms exports doubled in 2015: Saudi Arabia and Qatar were two of the major markets[5] and German-built weapons and technology are still today (2019) used in the context of the war in Yemen.[6] Similar data apply to Great Britain (Saudi Arabia is the UK arms industry's biggest customer) and a number of other European countries.

In 2019, Italian defence company Leonardo expects to boost its annual Middle East sales beyond 1.5 billion US dollars as it pursues deals for its naval combat systems, cybersecurity and helicopters and aims to sell large part of them to Saudi Arabian Military Industries (a state-owned company launched in 2017) and Egypt,[7] where human rights abuses and 'zero-tolerance policy towards dissent' have been documented by all major international organizations.[8]

1.35 billion euro in rifles, rocket launchers, heavy machine guns, mortar shells and anti-tank weapons are currently exported from Europe (especially the Balkans) to the Middle East and North Africa; a meaningful percentage of them is used by terror groups in Syria and Yemen.[9]

This short list represents only a tiny fraction of a much broader and more articulated 'structure' that goes well beyond weapons. Despite this, a common claim that any interested observer can often hear or read in Brussels and other 'Western capitals' is that 'peace in the Middle East

5 German arms exports to Saudi Arabia have been halted since October 2018, but plenty of other countries, including Egypt and Qatar, continue to receive massive amounts of German weapons. See 'Germany Approves Export of Weapons Systems to Qatar', in *Middle East Monitor*, 24 January 2019, https://www.middleeastmonitor.com/20190124-germany-approves-export-of-weapons-systems-to-qatar. It should also be noted that French authority strongly 'resents Germany's tight export rules' regarding arms exports. See 'Sticking to Its Guns', in *The Economist*, No. 9132 (2 March 2019), p. 42.

6 Keith Walker, 'Inside Europe: Saudi Coalition Uses German Arms in Yemen', in *Deutsche Welle*, 1 March 2019, https://p.dw.com/p/3EGr9.

7 Dania Saadi, 'Italian Defence Firm Leonardo Eyes Middle East Sales Exceeding $1.5bn', in *The National*, 18 February 2019, https://www.thenational.ae/1.826910.

8 See for instance Human Rights Watch, *World Report 2018. Events of 2017*, December 2017, p. 185, https://www.hrw.org/node/312556.

9 Ivan Angelovski, Lawrence Marzouk and Miranda Patrucic, 'Making a Killing: The 1.2 Billion Euro Arms Pipeline to Middle East', in *Balkan Insight*, 27 July 2016, https://balkaninsight.com/2016/07/27/making-a-killing-the-1-2-billion-euros-arms-pipeline-to-middle-east-07-26-2016.

[cannot] be imposed from the outside',[10] as if (many) European/Western countries did and do not play an active role in the destabilization of the Middle East and in supporting authoritarianism in the region.[11] No less common is the claim that the Middle East is somehow inherently violent and thus conducive to extremism. A number of well-renowned scholars, for instance, are shedding light on this by resorting to sociological analyses focused on goals and values. Peace, in the words of McGill Professor Philip Carl Salzman, 'is not possible in the Middle East because values and goals [such as 'kinship'] other than peace are more important to Middle Easterners'.[12]

Indeed, in a number of articles published in many Western media in recent years, the Eastern and Southern Mediterranean appear as somehow distant and obscure areas. The sense of a largely artificial region, characterized by conflictual and 'sealed off' minorities (or a 'mosaic of minorities'[13]) has become widespread, to the extent that the word 'stability' continues often to be paired with concepts such as 'division', 'partition' or 'natural borders' (that is, the adjustment of border features to mirror ethnic or religious differences).[14] Yet, what most of the region is experiencing should not in any way be perceived in these terms, or as someone else's history. This not (or not only) in light of a relatively distant past, but, as this volume confirms, in consideration of a present that hinders the construction of a sustainable future.[15]

---

10 European External Action Service, *Speech by High Representative/Vice-President Federica Mogherini at the Final Conference of the MENARA and MEDRESET Projects, 'The Middle East and the EU: New Realities, New Policies'*, Brussels, 6 March 2019, https://europa.eu/!xG87vM.

11 See for instance 'UAE Arming Yemen Militias with Western Weapons – Amnesty', *BBC News*, 6 February 2019, https://www.bbc.com/news/world-middle-east-47143068.

12 Philip Carl Salzman, 'Why There Is No Peace in the Middle East', *Gatestone Institute Articles*, 14 October 2017, https://www.gatestoneinstitute.org/11117.

13 Bernard Lewis, *The Shaping of the Modern Middle East*, New York/Oxford, Oxford University Press, 1994, p. 14.

14 See Lorenzo Kamel, *The Middle East from Empire to Sealed Identities*, Edinburgh, Edinburgh University Press, 2019.

15 Too often 'we' tend to approach the dramatic present of the Eastern and Southern Mediterranean as something that pertains peoples and countries that are largely

The authors of the chapters of this volume share the belief that it is necessary, today more than ever, to overcome this segregated interpretation of 'our history' and 'their history', paving the way for a more humble approach toward the peoples' region and their sufferance. In doing so, they address the issues of 'stability' and 'security' from non-Western perspectives. More precisely, each contributor sheds light on different security-related issues, connecting all of them to one main research question: *What does (in)security mean from the perspective of people living in the Middle East and North Africa?*

It would be a serious mistake to *deny agency* to the local populations, or to downplay the role of intra-regional issues and problems while debating 'security' and 'stability' in the Middle East. This is why each chapter takes into account, in various degrees and forms, these two aspects.

In Chapter 1, Nader Hashemi, Director of the University of Denver's Center for Middle East Studies, places human security at the centre of his analysis. The author notes that debates on security in the Middle East have typically revolved around a narrow set of concerns that overlap with Western interests in the region. Common topics are countering terrorism, nuclear nonproliferation, maintaining stable oil supplies and ensuring the stability of friendly regimes. His contribution focuses on a largely underexamined security problem in the Middle East – sectarianism – and offers an alternative way of framing it, by drawing on the literature on ethnic mobilization and the politics of authoritarian regimes. The conclusions examine the theme of de-sectarianization both conceptually and practically. Arguments are advanced with the goal of de-escalating Sunni–Shia conflict and advancing conflict resolution and peacebuilding processes.

---

detached from their political, historical and economic past and present. This mindset is often part of an ongoing 'medievalization of the region', or the tendency to juxtapose an allegedly medieval Middle East and a modern, secular, normative West. On the 'medievalization' see Ussama Makdisi, 'The Problem of Sectarianism in the Middle East in an Age of Western Hegemony', in Nader Hashemi and Danny Postel (eds), *Sectarianization. Mapping the New Politics of the Middle East*, London, Hurst, 2017, pp. 23–34.

In Chapter 2, Coralie Pison Hindawi, Associate Professor of International Politics and Law at the Department of Political Studies and Public Administration at the American University of Beirut, reflects on a specific aspect of Western policies regarding the Middle East, namely the overall pattern of provision of military assistance to certain actors (whereas support to others is strictly prohibited) and analyses how such practices affect the region. Taking the massive supply of arms to the Saudi-led coalition in Yemen and the various forms of military support to Israel as primary case studies, the chapter highlights the inconsistencies of a large number of Western countries' policies. According to Coralie Pison Hindawi, they simultaneously contribute to the construction of norms designed to promote respect for human rights worldwide, notably responsible arms trade, and to the undermining of these very norms on frequent occasions. The author concludes by reflecting more broadly on how important these questions are when thinking about security in the Middle East region.

The issue of security in the Middle East region is also the focus of Chapter 3, written by Waleed Hazbun, Richard L. Chambers Professor of Middle Eastern Studies at the University of Alabama. The author argues that a critical approach to security studies in the Middle East requires a questioning of the normative understandings in existing scholarship based on a US-dominated regional order that prioritises the interests and security of the US and its allies. In contrast, the chapter outlines an alternative agenda that seeks to recognize how different actors across the region understand and experience insecurity and suggests adopting a normative understanding of a pluralist regional order. Waleed Hazbun concludes by suggesting the need to expand and pluralize the scholarly infrastructure of global security studies' knowledge production with new institutions that better reflect the concerns and experiences of scholars affiliated with the Global South.

In the chapter that follows (Chapter 4), Elijah J. Magnier, *Al-Rai* chief correspondent and veteran war correspondent, argues that the unprecedented violence that has gripped the Middle East for most of this century has promoted irrational views about Islam and given rise to misconceptions about the origins of terrorism. Over-militarization, foreign military intervention and the struggle for dominance over the region have spawned violent groups, shedding blood throughout the region and threatening the stability and security of the Middle East, Europe and beyond.

Elijah J. Magnier argues that religious terrorism, recent wars and general insecurity throughout the Middle East result from regional, Western and superpower over-militarization, intervention and struggles for dominance. It emphasises the responsibility of scholars and reporters to offer objective analyses of these events to promote public understanding. According to the author, as US hegemony fades, it is time for Europe to play a more effective role in the region. This should be as an agent and partner, and not as yet another dominant power. Such an engagement will best serve the Middle East and contribute to Europe's own security and prosperity.

In Chapter 5, Arshin Adib-Moghaddam, Professor in Global and Comparative Philosophies at SOAS, identifies 'psycho-nationalist' identity formations as a major source for insecurity in the region. Psycho-nationalism refers to invented and exclusionary national identity formations that are distinctly divisive. Through an exploration of counter-discourses taken from the rich tradition of the region's philosophical traditions – for instance the political and sociological thought of Ibn Khaldun – Arshin Adib-Moghaddam deconstructs contemporary forms of identity politics that underlie and compound problematic notions of sectarianism and/or tribalism. With particular reference to the making of imagined communities in the Arab and Iranian context, the chapter concludes that appreciating the distinct hybridity and interdependence of the peoples of the region in this part of the world has to be the starting point for a regional peace dialogue based on tolerance and respect.

In Chapter 6, Abdullah Al-Arian, Associate Professor at Georgetown University in Qatar, seeks to problematize the question of regional insecurity, exploring it through the prism of the conflict between the forces of political Islam and those of the Arab counter-revolutions. The author dissects this conflict by deconstructing some of the analytical frames that commentators have employed in debates regarding contemporary political developments. The most significant of these concern questions surrounding the role of religion as a root source of conflict, the uprisings as responsible for the production of instability, and the contradictory representations of violence that inform most analyses surrounding events in the Arab region. Ultimately, Abdullah Al-Arian contends that discussions around regional instability that make use of these frames are fundamentally flawed and tend to reflect the hegemonic discourses advanced by local authoritarian rulers, regional powers and their international backers.

Youssef Cherif, who runs the Columbia Global Centers in Tunis, tackles in Chapter 7 the issue of 'regional (in)stability' by focusing on the role of media and narratives. He contends that the 2017 Qatar Crisis amplified the Arab war of narratives, contributing to deepening political polarization in most Arab countries. The two warring camps of the 'Arab Sunni Cold War', Saudi Arabia and the UAE from one side, and Qatar from the other, are waging a media war that spans across the Arab world. In North Africa, this has led to an acute political polarization between political Islam adherents (and anyone close to their side) and the advocates of a secular state. Youssef Cherif looks at how Tunisia and Libya's public sphere was affected, by means of media content analysis.

The so-called 'Arab Cold War' is also at the centre of the analysis developed in Chapter 8 by Morten Valbjørn, an Associate Professor at the Department of Political Science at Aarhus University. The author starts his analysis by noting that it has become popular to use historical analogies in discussions about how to grasp regional politics – and particularly security-related issues – in the wake of the Arab uprisings. Against this background, he explores whether, and if so how, it makes sense to use the 'classic' Arab Cold War as an analytical lens to grasp regional dynamics in a 'sectarianized' new Middle East. Morten Valbjørn argues that the value of the exercise depends on what you expect to gain from making historical analogies. On the one hand, the Arab Cold War analogy is of limited use if one is searching in the past for firm answers about the present or future based on an (implicit) assumption that history will repeat itself. Thus, one should not expect some kind of 'replay' of the 'classic' Arab Cold War. On the other hand, historical analogies and studies based on insights from the past may still carry some value. By highlighting three takeaways from the traditional debate about the Arab Cold War, the chapter shows how historical analogies can be useful in the sense of introducing novel (or forgotten) questions and through this draw attention to potentially important but ignored aspects of the contemporary situation.

The final chapter (Chapter 9), written by me, aims to deconstruct the role of Iran, often described as 'the main source of instability' in the Middle East. The analysis starts by addressing two main research questions that have much to do with the past and the present of the country and the broader region: What are the historical roots of 'political Shi'ism' in Iran? Which historical dynamics have contributed the most to trigger the involvement of the Iranian clergy in politics?

Around the fortieth anniversary of the Iranian Revolution, academic answers to these questions appear to me more relevant than ever. To this end, the chapter provides a detailed historical framework by focusing on four interrelated historical junctures: (1) the Tobacco Revolt of 1891–2, which triggered the conditions 'to the emergence of Shi'ism as an insurrectionary movement against colonialism'; (2) the dynamics which prompted London to foster the rising of Reza Shah (1921) as the penultimate Shah of Persia and the first of the Pahlavi dynasty; (3) the coup d'état of 1953, which ended Iran's drive to assert sovereign control over its own resources and (4) the 1979 'Islamic Revolution', whose causes and implications are still very much visible in the lacerations that affect the region. Fernand Braudel noted that even an apparently minor event may be the mirror of a long-term reality, or of a 'structural conjuncture'. The four 'moments' on which the chapter focuses are themselves the components of a larger and more complex 'structure' that, in different ways and forms, continues to echo in Iran, as well as in a large part of the Middle East. The *qablan* (before), *alan* (now) and *ayandeh* (future) of Iran – as well the rest of the region – are and will remain inextricably bound together.

Nader Hashemi

Chapter 1: From Sectarianization to De-Sectarianization: How to Advance Human Security in the Middle East

Discussion and debate on security in the Middle East has typically revolved around a narrow set of political concerns. Most of them pertain to advancing security for Western strategic and economic interests in the region. According to a Rand Corporation study, Middle East security entails 'countering terrorism, countering [weapons of mass destruction] WMD proliferation, maintaining stable oil supplies and prices, ensuring the stability of friendly regimes [and] ensuring Israel's security'.[1] In the Western policy and academic debate on the topic, the broad concept of security and stability in the Middle East can be encapsulated within this framework. But what does security and insecurity mean from the perspective of people living in the Middle East?

This chapter answers this question by focusing on one source of instability in the Middle East – the problem of sectarianism. According to data on Shia–Sunni conflicts drawn from the Religion and Armed Conflict (RELAC) dataset, violence across the Sunni–Shia divide has grown exponentially in recent years. In 1989, 0.03 per cent of all deaths in armed conflicts occurred in disputes that had a Sunni–Shia dimension. By 2017, this figure had risen to 44 per cent.[2]

---

1 Promoting democracy and human rights is also part of this list but it is mentioned last and this is not by accident. See Nora Bensahel and Daniel L. Byman, 'Introduction', in Nora Bensahel and Daniel L. Byman (eds), *The Future Security Environment in the Middle East. Conflict, Stability and Political Change*, Santa Monica, Rand Corporation, 2004, p. 2, https://www.rand.org/pubs/monograph_reports/MR1640.html.

2 Isak Svensson and Desirée Nilsson, 'Disputes over the Divine: Introducing the Religion and Armed Conflict (RELAC) Data, 1975 to 2015', in *Journal of Conflict Resolution*, Vol. 62, No. 5 (May 2018), pp. 1127–48, https://doi.org/10.1177/0022002717737057.

Over thirteen years ago, Vali Nasr presciently predicted this development. In his critically acclaimed book *The Shia Revival*, he observed that traditional concepts and categories used to explicate the Middle East – such as modernity, democracy, fundamentalism and nationalism – no longer adequately explain the politics of the region. It is 'rather the old feud between Shias and Sunnis', he argued, 'that forges attitudes, defines prejudices, draws political boundary lines and even decides whether and to what extent those other trends have relevance'.[3]

The importance of Sunni–Shia sectarianism to the politics of the Middle East is not matched by a commensurate understanding of the topic. In this chapter I will argue, contrary to the mainstream Western view, that the roots of this problem are located in contemporary politics, not in ancient theology. Arguments that seek to explain sectarianism as a function of primordial blood feuds that can be traced back to the dawn of Islam do not stand up to critical scrutiny.[4]

Having noted this, it is also important that we do not romanticize the past. It is erroneous to contend that there was no conflict and group tension between Sunnis and Shia and that intra-Muslim relations were perfectly harmonious prior to the onset of European imperialism in the Middle East. Similarly, dismissing the problem of sectarianism as a function of Orientalist depictions of the Middle East does not advance our understanding of this issue.

In this chapter I would like to accomplish two goals. First, I want to summarize the arguments of three schools of thought that have sought to explain the problem of sectarianism in the Middle East. None of them, I will argue, provide an adequate explanation of the problem. Alternatively, I will advance an alternative theoretical framework that can better explicate this problem. Second, I want to reflect on the concept of de-sectarianization. How might we begin to think about reducing

3 Vali Nasr, *The Shia Revival. How Conflicts within Islam Will Shape the Future*, New York, W.W. Norton, 2006, p. 82.

4 Ofra Bengio and Meir Litvak (eds), *The Sunna and Shi'a in History. Division and Ecumenism in the Muslim Middle East*, New York, Palgrave Macmillan, 2011; Mehmet Sait Özervarli, 'Between Tension and Rapprochement: Sunni-Shi'ite Relations in the Pre-Modern Ottoman Period, with a Focus on the Eighteenth Century', in *Historical Research*, Vol. 90, No. 249 (August 2017), pp. 526–42.

conflict between Sunni and Shia Muslims in practical ways that can advance security for both communities, and by extension, the broader Middle East? What can we learn from other conflicts that have involved deep tensions and violence between communal groups that once seemed intractable but were eventually resolved?

1.1 Three schools of thought

There are three schools of thought that have informed the public, policy and intellectual debates on sectarianism in the Middle East.[5] Two of these schools of thought are located in the West; one in the Middle East. All of them misdiagnose the problem and advance solutions that are unhelpful in reducing sectarian conflict between Sunni and Shia Muslims.

The first school of thought has sought to explain the current instability in the Middle East as a function of ancient blood feuds rooted in primordial hatreds between Sunnis and Shias. These conflicts, we are told, have been brewing beneath the surface since the dawn of Islam. Authoritarian strong men had managed to keep a lid on these enduring rivalries, but with the unravelling of their control as a result of the 2011 Arab uprisings, this perennial feature of Muslim societies – rooted in unyielding intolerance – has surfaced to the top, producing the current chaos and turmoil afflicting the region.[6]

---

5 For a solid categorization of the scholarly debate on sectarianism, also in three groups, see Morten Valbjørn, 'Studying Sectarianism While Beating Dead Horses and Searching for Third Ways', in *LSE Middle East Centre Blog*, 17 September 2018, https://wp.me/p3Khxv-1Mw.

6 This echoes a thesis heard twenty years ago in the context of the Balkan wars: that a strong dictator kept control of 'ancient hatreds' but with Tito's death these forces have become unleashed. *New York Times* columnist Thomas Friedman observes that sectarian tensions in the Middle East had 'long been managed by iron fists from above'. But after longstanding dictators were toppled, 'a horrifying war of all against all has exploded'. See Thomas Friedman, 'Contain and Amplify', in *The New York Times*, 27 May 2015, https://nyti.ms/1cYSIaf.

One of the most prominent proponents of this view has been former US President Barack Obama. On several occasions, Obama has spoken of 'ancient sectarian differences' as a means of explaining the instability in the Middle East, Syria in particular.[7] These 'ancient divisions', he asserts, propel instability in the Arab world, which is 'rooted in conflicts that date back millennia'.[8] Before leaving office, Obama observed that in the Middle East today, 'the only organizing principles are sectarian'.[9]

Other prominent American politicians, both Republican and Democrat, have made similar claims. Senator Ted Cruz has suggested that 'Sunnis and Shiites have been engaged in a sectarian civil war since 632 [. . .] it is the height of hubris and ignorance to make American national security contingent on the resolution of a 1,500-year-old religious conflict'.[10] Mitch McConnell, the Minority Leader in the US Senate, has observed that what is taking place in the Arab world today is 'a religious conflict that has been going on for a millennium and a half'.[11] In expressing his support for Donald Trump's announcement that US troops would be removed from Syria in 2019, the influential Republican Senator Rand Paul made the following observation about the Arab world: 'The place is a mess. I mean they've been fighting each other for a thousand years. Sunni and Shia have been fighting each other since

---

7 White House, *Statement by the President on Syria*, 31 August 2013, https://obamawhitehouse.archives.gov/the-press-office/2013/08/31/statement-president-syria.

8 White House, *President Barack Obama's State of the Union Address*, 28 January 2014, http://go.wh.gov/2MZ8Ld. Like his predecessor Bill Clinton, these arguments were advanced to deflect calls for intervention to stop mass atrocities in Bosnia/Syria.

9 Jeffrey Goldberg, 'The Obama Doctrine', in *The Atlantic*, April 2016, https://www.theatlantic.com/article/471525.

10 Ted Cruz, 'How U.S. Can Stop ISIS', in CNN, 10 September 2014, http://www.cnn.com/2014/09/10/opinion/ted-cruz-how-us-can-stop-isis.

11 Andy Borowitz, 'Pressure on Obama to Quickly Resolve Centuries-old Sunni-Shiite Conflict', in *The New Yorker*, 18 June 2014, http://www.newyorker.com/humor/borowitz-report/pressure-on-obama-to-quickly-resolve-centuries-old-sunni-shiite-conflict.

Battle of Karbala 832 A.D. [sic]'.[12] Former Vice-Presidential nominee (and Alaska governor) Sarah Palin offered a more straightforward proposal for US policy toward the Middle East: 'Let Allah sort it out'.[13]

Mainstream journalists and political commentators on both the left and the right have advanced similar arguments. *New York Times* columnist Thomas Friedman asserts that the 'main issue [in Yemen today] is the 7th century struggle over who is the rightful heir to the Prophet Muhammad – Shiites or Sunnis'.[14] Commenting on the rise and expansion of ISIS, the comedian and liberal television host Jon Stewart took to his popular *The Daily Show* to observe that the last time Sunnis and Shias co-existed was in 950 AD. This is 'the only time it has ever happened, over 1000 years ago'.[15] The popular TV host and liberal commentator Bill Maher argued that the sixteenth century was a more accurate reference point for understanding contemporary conflict in the Middle East, in that Muslims were experiencing the equivalent of the Christian wars of religion in early modern Europe. 'This seems to be like the moment when the Muslims are having their 16th century', he quipped. 'The Sunnis and the Shiites are going to have this out and we just have to let them have it out'. The right-wing TV pundit Bill O'Reilly similarly observed that 'the Sunni and Shia want to kill each other. They want to blow each other up. They want to torture each other. They have fun [. . .] they like this. This is what Allah tells them to do, and that's what they do.'[16]

---

12 Transcript: Rand Paul on 'Face the Nation', in *CBS News*, 23 December 2018, https://www.cbsnews.com/news/transcript-rand-paul-on-face-the-nation-december-23-2018.

13 James Arkin, 'Palin: Let Allah Sort It Out', in *Politico*, 31 August 2013, http://www.politico.com/story/2013/08/sarah-palin-let-allah-sort-it-out-096128.

14 Thomas L. Friedman, 'Tell Me How This Ends Well', in *The New York Times*, 1 April 2015, https://nyti.ms/19CF3Uw.

15 Jon Stewart, 'Now That's What I Call Being Completing F**king Wrong about Iraq', in *The Daily Show*, 17 June 2014.

16 Bill Maher, *Real Time with Bill Maher*, 13 June 2014, http://www.realclearpolitics.com/video/2014/06/14/maher_the_sunnis_and_shiites_are_going_to_have_this_out_and_we_just_have_to_let_them.html. National security/terrorism expert Richard Clarke and MSNBC journalist Krystal Ball, also guests on this show, both invoked the 'ancient sectarian hatreds' thesis. See Bill O'Reilly, 'O'Reilly: Sunni

More respectable voices in the academic and policy communities have put forward variations of this thesis. According to Richard Haass, president of the Council on Foreign Relations, a key factor that explains the instability in the Middle East today is that this 'is a deeply flawed part of the world that never came to terms with modernity'.[17] Others, such as historian Joshua Landis, have suggested that the Middle East is going through a 'great sorting out' similar to central Europe during World War II, where national borders shifted to create more ethnically homogenous states. In the Arab world, by contrast, after the collapse of the Ottoman Empire and the 1919 Paris Peace Conference, the new borders that emerged produced a situation where you have 'all these different peoples living cheek by jowl, many of them not wanting to live together; not knowing how to live together'.[18]

The second school of thought traces the roots of sectarian conflict not to the seventh century but to the early twentieth century. They locate the problem in the colonial and imperial carve-up of the Middle East from the Arabic-speaking provinces of the Ottoman Empire. They are critical of the origins of the Middle East state system that resulted from the Sykes–Picot Agreement (1916) and the subsequent political arrangements that followed World War I, the terms of which were negotiated at the San Remo Conference (1920) and codified in the Treaty of Sèvres (1920).[19]

---

and Shiite Iraqis "Have Fun" When They "Kill Each Other"', in *Media Matters for America*, 26 January 2007, http://mm4a.org/1TkAZKQ.

17 'Where ISIS Was Born: Iraq's Long Road to Hell', in CNN, 25 June 2016, http://edition.cnn.com/TRANSCRIPTS/1606/25/se.01.html.

18 Joshua Landis' comments at forum on 'Sectarianization: ISIS, the Syrian Conflict and the Future of the Middle East', University of Denver, 1 October 2014: https://youtu.be/CQ-CaglfQms. See also Joshua Landis, 'The Great Sorting Out: Ethnicity and the Future of the Levant', in *Qifa Nabki*, 18 December 2013, https://wp.me/pitIS-1P4; and 'Joshua Landis on ISIS, Syria & the "Great Sorting Out" in the Middle East', in the *Middle East Dialogues* series produced by the University of Denver's Center for Middle East Studies: https://youtu.be/_-roW5Y7vbw. In a similar vein, Bernard Lewis described the genocide in Bosnia as a case of 'internecine chaos'. See Bernard Lewis, *The Middle East. A Brief History of the Last 2,000 Years*, New York, Scribner, 1995, p. 387.

19 David Fromkin, *A Peace to End All Peace. The Fall of the Ottoman Empire and the Creation of the Modern Middle East*, New York, Holt, 2009, pp. 403–14.

The key proponents of this school are journalists, public intellectuals and some political activists who, in contrast to the first school of thought, are genuinely sympathetic to the problems and political aspirations of the people in the Middle East, especially the Kurds.

The journalist and author Robin Wright is one representative of this school of thought. She has written extensively, sympathetically and influentially on the Middle East during her forty years as a reporter, commentator and author. Reflecting on the turmoil in the region in 2013, she wrote an essay on 'Imagining a Remapped Middle East'. New forces were 'pulling apart a region defined by European colonial powers a century ago and defended by Arab autocrats ever since'. She wondered that perhaps 'over time, Iraq's Sunni minority – notably in western Anbar Province, site of anti-government protests – may feel more commonality with eastern Syria's Sunni majority. Tribal ties and smuggling span the border. Together, they could form a de facto or formal Sunnistan. Iraq's south would effectively become Shiitestan, although separation is not likely to be that neat.'[20]

Scott Anderson, a journalist, author and contributing writer for the *New York Times*, also falls into this second category. In 2016 he wrote a 20,000-word essay for the prestigious *New York Times Magazine* on 'Fractured Lands: How the Arab World Came Apart'. It was later turned into a book. In this essay he sought to answer the following question: why did democratic transitions of the Arab Spring revolts fail, producing sectarian conflict and instability across the Middle East?

His answer was that the 'nations [of the Arab world] were essentially artificial constructs'. The 'inherent instability of the Middle East's artificial states' can be traced back to the 'end of World War I, when two of the victorious allies, Britain and France, carved up the lands of the defeated Ottoman Empire between themselves as spoils of war'.[21] Echoing sentiments that overlap with the first school of thought, Anderson went on to assert that underneath it all, at the core of the

---

20 Robin Wright, 'Imagining a Remapped Middle East', in *The New York Times*, 28 September 2013, https://nyti.ms/18bGCnl.

21 Scott Anderson, 'Fractured Lands: How the Arab World Came Apart', in *The New York Times Magazine*, 10 August 2016, https://nyti.ms/2aXJ8nP.

Middle East, there lie 'extraordinarily complex tapestries of tribes and subtribes and clans, *ancient social orders* that [remain] the populations' principal source of identification and allegiance'. These '*ancient* forces of tribalism and sectarianism' are reasserting 'their own centrifugal pull' due to the weakness of authoritarian rule that resulted from the Arab Spring revolts.[22] He went on to surmise that perhaps redrawing the borders of the Middle East might help contain sectarian conflict.

The third school of thought on sectarianism can be called the 'Muslim folklore school of thought'. The ideas that animate its proponents are rooted in myth, stereotypes and prejudices that are byproducts of communal relations and tensions which have developed over time and are passed down from generation to generation at the grassroots level. Sometimes these views are legitimized and promoted by state media and authority figures in the religious establishment. Rarely is there a state-backed effort to challenge these views in the public domain or in school curriculums.

In the Arab-Islamic world today, there is a perspective among some Sunnis who maintain that Shia Islam was always a threat. This heretical movement, it is believed, from its inception has sought to corrupt the core message of Islam, lead believers astray and create disunity among the community of Muslims, sometimes in alliance with outside enemies. For example, a common trope is that Arab Shias are more loyal to Iran than to their own countries. The rise and expansion of Salafism in the Arab world has perpetuated this problem, as has the regional rivalry between Iran and Saudi Arabia.

Similarly, Shia Muslims hold prejudicial and stereotypical views of Sunnis. Common themes are that Sunni Islam is fundamentally oppressive, theologically misguided and prone to extremism. Wahhabi puritanical Islam and Sunni Islam are believed to be deeply intertwined and the decline of Islamic civilization is blamed on Sunni leadership; if Shias were in power, it is believed, the global condition of Muslims would collectively be better.

All three schools of thought are misguided in explaining the problem of sectarianism. The ancient sectarian hatred thesis (school number

---

22 Ibid. Emphasis added.

one) fails to answer the critical question 'why now?' Why has there been a significant increase in sectarian tensions today as opposed to earlier moments in time? In this context, Shadi Hamid asks: 'If there is something constant about a culture and its predisposition to violence, then how can we explain stark variations in civil conflict over short periods of time?'[23] There is also the related question of geography that this school fails to answer. Why is sectarian conflict more intense in some areas with a mixed Sunni–Shia population but not in others?

The second school of thought is flawed for two reasons. First, it ignores that identities evolve and change over time. While it is true that the borders of the Middle East are colonial borders, it is also true that over the past century the states of the region have managed to create new national identities that have sunk deep roots and which enjoy broad legitimacy today.[24] Several generations of Middle Easterners have been born, bred and educated in these new nation-states. Many have comfortably travelled on passports issued by these states. Even in the countries that have been most effected by state breakdown – Syria, Iraq, Yemen, Libya, Lebanon – the majority of the people wish to remain citizens. What some may want are new internal political arrangements, along the lines of federalism or consociationalism, which give representation and a voice to marginalized groups and regions. There is little support in the Middle East, however, for redrawing the borders and the creation of new states with new borders. The cases of the Kurds and the Palestinians are notable exceptions to this rule.

More broadly, this school of thought fundamentally misdiagnoses the roots of Middle East instability, especially as it relates to sectarianism. There is an implied suggestion that if we could only separate Sunnis and Shia from each other, political conflict could be contained and the region stabilized. The social, political and economic problems of the modern Middle East, however, cannot be explained by pointing to where the borders have been drawn. The better explanation lies in what has been

---

23 Shadi Hamid, 'The End of Pluralism', in *The Atlantic*, 23 July 2014, https://amp.theatlantic.com/amp/article/374875.

24 Shibley Telhami, *The World Through Arab Eyes. Arab Public Opinion and the Reshaping of the Middle East*, New York, Basic Books, 2013, pp. 17–35.

happening politically *within* these borders over the past century. The failure of good governance and expansion of political authoritarianism during the post-colonial era is a better entry point to understand this topic.

As for the final school of thought, the problematic views on sect that persist among Sunnis and Shias can be understood by the following concept: communal groups that occupy a common geographic space and have a shared history of interaction typically produce and perpetuate stereotypes and prejudicial views of the other. If these views are not challenged, they can proliferate and can be used as a source of mobilization during times of conflict. There is nothing uniquely Muslim or Middle Eastern about this fact. This phenomenon applies to how Irish Protestants have historically viewed Irish Catholics, white Americans versus African-Americans, northern Italians versus southern Italians, and so on. Biased views of societal groups can be deeply rooted in cultures and can be difficult to alter. These attitudes, however, carry no explanatory value in terms of illuminating the problem of group conflict, in this case Sunni–Shia sectarianism. An alternative analytical framework is required.

1.2 The sectarianization thesis

The problem with the term 'sectarianism' is that it acts as a catch-all word that purports to explain many of the ills afflicting the Middle East today. Alternatively, I would like to propose the term *sectarianization* and its verb cognate *to sectarianize*, which has better explanatory value.[25] Sectarianization suggests an active process shaped by political actors operating within specific contexts, pursuing political goals that involve the mobilization of popular sentiments around particular identity markers. Class dynamics, fragile states, geopolitical rivalries

25 Here I am drawing on the introduction to a book I co-edited with Danny Postel, *Sectarianization. Mapping the New Politics of the Middle East*, New York/Oxford, Oxford University Press, 2017, pp. 4–8.

and great power politics also shape the sectarianization process. The usual term 'sectarianism' is typically devoid of such reference points. It tends to imply a static given, a trans-historical force – an enduring and immutable characteristic of the Arab-Islamic world from the seventh century until today.

The theme of political authoritarianism is central to the sectarianization thesis. This form of political rule has long dominated the politics of the Middle East, and its corrosive legacy has deeply sullied the polities and societies of the region. Authoritarianism, not theology, is the critical factor in the sectarianization process. Authoritarian regimes in the Middle East have deliberately manipulated sectarian identities in various ways as a strategy of deflecting demands for political change and perpetuating their power. This anti-democratic political context is essential for understanding sectarian conflict in Muslim societies today, especially in those societies that contain a mix of Sunni and Shia populations. To paraphrase and adapt from the famous aphorism from the Prussian General Carl von Clausewitz, about 'war being a continuation of politics by other means', in my reading, sectarian conflict in the Middle East today is primarily about the perpetuation of political rule by ruling elites via identity mobilization.

1.3 Religious sectarianism and political mobilization

To make better sense of the politics of sectarianization, the literature on ethnic mobilization is helpful. In the social sciences, at least three schools of thought compete to explain ethno-nationalist mobilization: primordialism, instrumentalism, and constructivism.[26]

Constructivism adopts a middle ground between primordialism and instrumentalism. Its proponents argue that ethnicity/religious identity is

26 Ashutosh Varshney, 'Ethnicity and Ethnic Conflict', in Carles Boix and Susan Stokes (eds), *The Oxford Handbook of Comparative Politics*, New York/Oxford, Oxford University Press, 2009, pp. 274–94.

not fixed, but is rather a political construct based on a dense web of social relationships that form in the context of modernity.[27] Like primordialists, constructivists recognize the importance of seemingly immutable features of ethnic/religious identity, but they disagree that this inevitably leads to conflict. On the other hand, constructivists share with instrumentalists the view that elites and leadership play a critical role in the mobilization process. Disagreement emerges, however, over the degree to which these identities can be manipulated. In brief, constructivists do not believe that ethnicity/religion is inherently conflictual, but rather that conflict flows from 'pathological social systems'[28] and 'political opportunity structures' that breed conflict from multiple social cleavages beyond the control of the individual.

With this framework as a backdrop, sectarianism in the Middle East today becomes more intelligible. Sectarian identities could not be mobilized unless differences in beliefs and historical memory compelled religious groups into collective action around particularistic identities. Therefore, two critical questions emerge: why are these conflicts intensifying now and why in this particular region of the world? In other words, what explains the flaring of sectarian conflict at specific moments in time and in some places rather than others? Sunni–Shia relations, for example, were not always conflict-ridden, nor was sectarianism a strong political force in modern Muslim politics until recently. How did Syrians, Iraqis and Bahrainis with different sectarian identities manage to coexist for centuries without mass bloodshed? How did these pluralistic mosaics come unglued so precipitously? What are the key forces driving sectarianization?

---

27 Benedict Anderson, *Imagined Communities. Reflections on the Origins and Spread of Nationalism*, New York, Verso, 1983; Crawford Young (ed.), *The Rising Tide of Cultural Pluralism. The Nation-State at Bay?*, Madison, University of Wisconsin Press, 1993. For a comparison and contrast between instrumentalism and constructivism, see Ashutosh Varshney, 'Ethnicity and Ethnic Conflict', cit., p. 285–8.

28 David A. Lake and Donald Rothchild, 'Spreading Fear: The Genesis of Transnational Ethnic Conflicts', in David A. Lake and Donald Rothchild (eds), *The International Spread of Ethnic Conflict. Fear, Diffusion and Escalation*, Princeton, Princeton University Press, 1998, p. 6.

The level of intensity of sectarian conflict also varies geographically where both Sunni and Shia populations coexist. What factors explain this variation? While the role of religious leaders and political entrepreneurs is particularly salient in answering these questions, Vali Nasr has suggested that we must examine the agency of state actors in identity mobilization.[29]

In the past, theories of ethnic conflict have generally treated the state as a passive actor in identity mobilization. The standard narrative held that competition from within society among contending ethnic groups would inevitably shift to the arena of the state as these sub-state actors vie for control of various state institutions as a means of enhancing their power over rival groups. The intensification of these struggles would eventually lead to the weakening, collapse and failure of the state. Drawing on research from south and southeast Asia, Nasr has suggested, however, that 'far from being passive victims of identity mobilization', states have a logic of their own and 'can be directly instrumental in [. . .] manipulating the protagonists and entrenching identity cleavages. Identity mobilization here is rooted in the project of power of state actors, not of an elite or a community. These actors do not champion the cause of any one community but see [political] gain in the conflict between the competing identities'.[30]

Nasr's insight helps deepen our theoretical understanding of identity mobilization in that it pushes the conversation beyond primordial differences and manipulation by religious authorities to focus attention on state behaviour and state–society relations.

Primordialist explanations of sectarian conflict fail to explain the current disorder in the Middle East. This widely popular view, based on alleged enduring Sunni–Shia antagonisms with roots in the seventh century, clouds rather than illuminates the complex realities of the politics of the region which are better understood as series of deep and expanding

---

29 Vali Nasr, 'International Politics, Domestic Imperatives, and Identity Mobilization: Sectarianism in Pakistan, 1979–1998', in Nader Hashemi and Danny Postel (eds), *Sectarianization. Mapping the New Politics of the Middle East*, New York/Oxford, Oxford University Press, 2017, pp. 77–100.

30 Ibid., pp. 81–2.

developmental crises (both political and economic) that the region has been facing since World War II. The policies of leading Western states toward the Middle East have only exacerbated these political and economic problems. Donald Trump's embrace of Saudi Arabia's deeply sectarian reading of the Middle East is a perfect illustration of this point, but the problem is much deeper and far precedes the Trump presidency.

While it is true that religious identities are more salient in the politics of the Middle East than before, it also true that these identities have been deliberately politicized and lethalized by state actors in pursuit of political gain. The politics of authoritarian regimes is the key context for understanding this problem. In other words, there is a symbiotic relationship between pressure from society below, which demands greater inclusion, respect and representation, versus the refusal by ruling elites from above to share or relinquish power. This produces a crisis of legitimacy that needs to be carefully managed. The politics of sectarianism or *sectarianization* – the deliberate manipulation of religious identities – is a result of this political dynamic. The response of the regimes in Syria and Bahrain to demands for political change during the Arab Spring are case studies of how the process unfolds.[31]

Notwithstanding the rhetoric we hear from Sunni monarchies in the Middle East or from presidents-for-life in the various Arab republics, ruling elites are not truly embedded into a particular sectarian identity. The driver of politics is a not a defence of theological doctrine or loyalty to the collective interests of a religious sect. The core allegiance for ruling elites is to their political thrones and their various clients, whether Sunni or Shia, who can help sustain their power. What is really salient here is not religious piety, but political power.

As Madawi Al-Rasheed has observed, sectarianism 'is not an inherent historical quality of the Arab masses'. There are 'sectarian entrepreneurs and religious scholars [who] continue to flourish' in the present by manipulating these identities in the interest of ruling

31 See chapters by Paulo Gabriel Hilu Pinto and Toby Matthiesen on Syria and Bahrain in Nader Hashemi and Danny Postel (eds), *Sectarianization. Mapping the New Politics of the Middle East*, New York/Oxford, Oxford University Press, 2017, chapters 7 and 11.

regimes, often at their request. 'Sectarianism, in other words, is a *modern* political phenomenon that is nourished by persistent dictators whose rule depends on invoking these old religious identities that become lethally politicized'.[32] In short, sectarianism does not explain the current turmoil in the Middle East – the toxic brew of authoritarianism, kleptocracy, developmental stagnation and state repression is far more salient.

1.4 De-sectarianization

There is now a serious body of scholarship on sectarianism in the Middle East. Its converse, de-sectarianism, has been understudied.[33] How might we begin to think about this concept with the goal of reducing conflict between Sunnis and Shias? In this section I offer a set of broad guidelines that can advance this goal both theoretically and practically.

A pre-condition for de-sectarianization is a firm rejection of the 'ancient sectarian hatred' school of thought. If it is believed that the roots of this problem lie in ancient history or deep theology – and not in contemporary politics – then it becomes impossible to advance solutions that can ameliorate sectarian conflict. In others words, a firm rejection of primordial approaches is required and an appreciation for instrumentalist and constructivist analytical frameworks is necessary.

Given that sectarianism in the Middle East is fundamentally a political problem, the solutions also lie in politics. In broad terms, the

---

32 Madawi Al-Rasheed 'Sectarianism as Counter-Revolution: Saudi Responses to the Arab Spring', in Nader Hashemi and Danny Postel (eds), *Sectarianization. Mapping the New Politics of the Middle East*, New York/Oxford, Oxford University Press, 2017, p. 158.

33 Scholars who have written insightfully on sectarianism include Fanar Haddad, Morten Valbjørn, Bassel Salloukh, Toby Matthiesen, Ussama Makdisi and Simon Mabon. On de-sectarianism, the research project at Lancaster University, headed by Simon Mabon, on 'Sectarianism, Proxies and De-Sectarianization', is breaking new intellectual ground on the topic, especially in studying the dynamics on how de-sectarianism can be advanced in the Middle East.

challenge is to understand the social, political, economic and intellectual conditions that have given rise to sectarian conflict and then try to reverse them. The following is required.

Armed conflict and active hostilities must end. It is difficult to envision Sunni–Shia reconciliation when people are dying and blood is flowing in the streets. This suggests some form of a political settlement that involves key stakeholders and buy-in from significant sections of the warring communities.

Some semblance of political order is also required. Sectarian identity mobilization benefits from state breakdown/collapse. When the central government no longer has the capacity to exercise sovereignty nor provide basic physical security for its citizens, other sub-national entities (militias, para-military groups, sectarian entrepreneurs) will fill the vacuum.

De-sectarianization is dependent on democratization. As discussed above, the two are deeply linked. Authoritarianism is the key political system that shapes the context that facilitates sectarianization. In many of the major cases of Sunni–Shia conflict today, playing the sectarian card is a strategy of regime survival that ruling elites employ. The political opportunity structures and incentives that allow for the instrumentalization of sectarian conflict must be changed. Only a political system that demands transparency and accountability from politicians and governments can accomplish this goal, hence the importance of democratic transitions and democratization.

New constitutional arrangements and institutions can also help advance de-sectarianization. Sectarian conflict often involves competition for access to state resources and demands for political representation. Historical grievances can impede national reconciliation. Power-sharing arrangements that are enshrined in constitutional law along the lines of federalism, consociationalism and confessionalism should be considered. In terms of historical injustices and grievances, truth and reconciliation commissions are an option. This is especially paramount in cases where mass atrocities on the level of war crimes and crimes against humanity have taken place. It is impossible to conceive of national reconciliation without the creation of these institutions and political arrangements.

Principled leadership is also required. It is difficult to think of examples of successful conflict de-escalation without the existence of visionary leadership that is willing to take risks and reach across the political and ideological divide. In the case of sectarian conflict in the Middle East today, one example of this form of leadership is Ayatollah Sistani in Iraq. The antithesis of this model would be Mohammad bin Salman, the Crown Prince of Saudi Arabia.[34]

Learning from communal conflict in other regions and religious settings can be helpful in advancing de-sectarianization in the Middle East. Ashutosh Varshney's influential book *Ethnic Conflict and Civic Life* is particularly relevant.[35] The broad research question that shaped this study was the following: why does communal conflict occur in some parts of India but not in others? The answer, he concluded, lies in civil society.

Varshney found that the most stable Indian cities and towns that managed to avoid violence were those where Hindus and Muslims had joint economic, educational and political associations. These cross-communal linkages, such as local manufacturer and trader associations, political parties, unions, professional associations, NGOs, clubs and festival organizations, played a critical role in reducing violence and maintaining peace.

Varshney's argument is that in seeking to reduce conflict between communal groups, scholars have historically focused on the role of the state and state actors. This emphasis is misplaced, he contends. There is much to learn from civil society that can help contain conflict during critical moments of communal tensions. In the context of India, he found that integrated civil networks and relationships that are cross-communal can make a critical difference.

By examining the history of communal violence in post-partition India, Varshney observes that states (national and provincial) do not

---

34 In January 2014, former Iranian president Hashemi Rafsanjani, in an attempt to reduce sectarian tensions, argued that the Sunni–Shia discord on the first caliph is just a historical matter and has no political significance. 'Who cares who was the first?' he famously said. This bold statement by Rafsanjani, which undermines the entire *raison d'être* for Shia Islam, is helpful in advancing de-sectarianization.

35 Ashutosh Varshney, *Ethnic Conflict and Civic Life. Hindus and Muslims in India*, New Haven, Yale University Press, 2002.

always behave in a neutral or legally correct way, especially when it comes to upholding the rule of law. They have a political and strategic logic of their own that shapes their behaviour. This general rule also applies to the Sri Lankan state and Sinhalese–Tamil relations, the Malaysian state and Malay–Chinese relations, and historically the US state on race relations.

Given this more realistic understanding of how states function, Varshney observes that we should not totally ignore the state nor absolve it from criticism when it fails to uphold human rights or the rule of law in an equitable manner. Varshney's prescription is more modest. Rectifying state behaviour in terms of containing communal conflict is a long-term project. In the meantime, there are things that can be done to reduce violence and communal conflict at the societal level.

In short, Varshney argues that 'an integrated organizational and civic life' makes all the difference, including forcing the state to 'behave much better than intellectual and political exhortations' do.[36] Here there are lessons to be learned for the case of sectarian conflict in the Middle East.

In a recent study, Salma Mousa found that Iraqis who participated in religiously mixed soccer leagues were likelier to see religious coexistence as possible (an attitude that favours pluralistic politics) and to mix socially with members of other faiths.[37] It is a remarkable finding in a country with such severe conflict across sectarian lines. Her study echoes the work of Varshney and suggests that social trust can be engendered when people interact with members of different social groups in the context of civil-society organizations.

De-sectarianization of the Middle East is also heavily dependent on a Saudi–Iranian detente. It is wishful thinking to believe that in the short term these two regional powers can have friendly relations. As long as the current structure of power in Riyadh and Tehran remains in place, regional rivalry is to be expected. But diminished hostilities based on a willingness to share their neighbourhood is a realistic goal.

---

36 Ibid., p. xi.

37 Salma Mousa, *Overcoming the Trust Deficit: An Experiment on Intergroup Contact and Soccer in Post-ISIS Iraq*, 13 December 2018, https://www.salmamousa.com/s/iraq-draft-5-84h5.pdf.

This would require an agreement based on respecting mutual spheres of influence in the Middle East and a deeper willingness to co-exist. In this context it is important to point out that since the 1979 Iranian Revolution, the Iranian–Saudi rivalry was not always this acrimonious. During the 1990s, there was a warming of relations between Tehran and Riyadh. Understanding the factors that brought this about is deeply instructive if the international community seeks to reduce tensions between these regional rivals. What is also required is a credible mediator that can facilitate an Iranian–Saudi detente. Oman might be a possible candidate but it lacks the power and gravitas that this task requires.

Summarizing these themes, Tim Sisk, a leading authority on ethnic and religious violence and post-conflict peacebuilding, outlines five 'principal conditions for de-sectarianization [in the Middle East]: elites committed to an inclusive political settlement; cross-cutting civil society and economic relationships; confessionally-balanced public policy and natural resources wealth-sharing agreements; regional stability and evolution of regional organisations; and a continued and expanded UN and regional organizations' role in fostering social cohesion'.[38]

Conclusion

This chapter sought to examine a key security problem afflicting the Middle East today – the problem of sectarianism. In doing so, three interpretative frameworks on the roots of Sunni–Shia relations were scrutinized and critiqued. An alternative theoretical framing was advanced, rooted in the politics of authoritarian regimes and drawing upon the literature on ethnic identity mobilization.

38 Timothy D. Sisk, 'Peacebuilding in Sectarianized Conflicts: Findings and Implications for Theory and Practice', in Nader Hashemi and Danny Postel (eds), *Sectarianization. Mapping the New Politics of the Middle East*, New York/Oxford, Oxford University Press, 2017, p. 263.

The latter part of this chapter sought to advance conceptual clarity on de-sectarianism. This is an understudied aspect of sectarian conflict in the Middle East that is critically needed today. It is hoped that the arguments advanced will be of special interest to those in the international community who are interested in conflict resolution and peacebuilding initiatives.

It is important to delineate several limits to the above discussion on sectarianism. The framing and interpretation that has been suggested applies to many of the major cases of sectarian conflict, but not all of them. Specifically, it applies to those countries where a strong authoritarian regime is in power, where there exists a mix of Sunni and Shia populations, and, in response to demands for political change, ruling elites pursue a sectarianization strategy to advance their political interests both domestically and regionally. Thus, the cases of Syria, Bahrain, Kuwait, Pakistan, Iran and Saudi Arabia fit within this framework, while Iraq and Lebanon are distinct cases that need to be understood on their own terms.

Moreover, sectarianism is a much more complicated phenomenon than what has been discussed here. In this chapter sectarianism *from above* has been the focus – state-generated manipulation of sectarian identity mobilization in the pursuit of political power. It is important to also appreciate sectarianism *from below*, which is also a driver of conflict. This type of sectarianism also overlaps with and is reinforced by patron-cliental relations, patronage networks, class divisions and rural/urban splits.[39]

Sectarianism in the Middle East also manifests itself in different ways. While many of the drivers of this process are the same, how Sunni–Shia differences are exploited can take place in different ways. For example, Iran and Saudi Arabia both engage in a sectarianization process that has similar goals but the content and application is very different. Anyone seeking a deeper grasp of this topic must appreciate these nuances and differences.

---

39 Fanar Haddad, *Understanding 'Sectarianism'. Sunni–Shi'a Relations in the Modern Arab World*, London, Hurst, 2019 (forthcoming).

A final comment on Donald Trump and sectarianism highlights how identity politics can be instrumentalized for political gain. Since the last presidential election, there has been a significant increase in group conflict in the United States. While this is not sectarianism per se, it is a form of communal conflict the dynamics and drivers of which can be understood by the arguments advanced in this chapter.

Tensions between African-American and white communities have spiked in recent years. In cities such as Ferguson, Missouri and Charlottesville, Virginia, conflict over police brutality and the discriminatory treatment of racial minorities has led to a polarizing public debate. This has been augmented by controversies over kneeling during the playing of the US national anthem at sporting events and the existence of statues from the US Civil War that honour the Confederacy. Polling reveals that African-Americans and white Americans have very different readings of these disputes. How can we explain these rising tensions in the United States today?

While there is no mono-causal explanation, the figure of Donald Trump looms large over these developments. Both as a presidential candidate and as president, Trump has pursued a political strategy aimed at mobilizing a white national identity against minority populations (African-Americans, Muslims and Latinos). A recent study revealed that in counties where Trump held a political rally there was a 226 per cent increase in hate crimes.[40]

This suggests that leadership, rhetoric and speech profoundly matter when trying to explain group conflict. The politics of Trump also applies to other authoritarian leaders, and all of this helps us appreciate the very political nature of identity conflict in our world today and how it can be overcome.

---

40 Ayal Feinberg, Regina Branton and Valerie Martinez-Ebers, 'Counties that Hosted a 2016 Trump Rally Saw a 226 Percent Increase in Hate Crimes', in *Monkey Cage*, 22 March 2019, https://www.washingtonpost.com/politics/2019/03/22/trumps-rhetoric-does-inspire-more-hate-crimes.

Coralie Pison Hindawi

Chapter 2: Selective Arms Flows and Arms Control: Producing Insecurity in the Middle East . . . and Beyond

Movies such as *Lord of War*, featuring Nicholas Cage as a Ukrainian arms dealer and inspired by the real stories of several arms dealers, present a picture of our world that is frightening in many ways: that of a largely uncontrolled black market of conventional weapons providing the planet's villains with the means to kill and oppress civilians as they increase their political power. High-level protection from powerful political figures prevents the prosecution of the unscrupulous arms dealer despite the best efforts of a tireless Interpol agent, played by Ethan Hawke. The movie ends powerfully, with the camera flying over what appears to be an endless sea of small arms that, we know, are waiting to be traded through illegal yet protected channels and then used, worldwide, to abuse defenceless people.

The actual world of arms flows and arms control, however, is frightening in many additional ways that *Lord of War* largely eludes. The poorly controlled Russian and Ukrainian stockpiles are but a fraction of weapons traded globally. Official, apparently legal, transfers of freshly produced arms flood the planet with lethal means and democratic countries of North America and Western Europe are the leading players: for the 2014–18 period, they were behind 64.5 per cent of the world's major arms exports.[1] Moreover, despite the attempts to better regulate the arms trade through the adoption of legal instruments designed to prevent transfers to 'irresponsible' actors, exports have continued to equip states accused of

1 Pieter D. Wezeman et al., 'Trends in International Arms Transfers, 2018', in *SIPRI Fact Sheets*, March 2019, https://www.sipri.org/node/4766. Russia's share of global arms exports reached 21 per cent over the same period.

grave human rights violations and attacks on civilians or on neighbouring countries.

This is notably true in the Middle East region, the only part of the world where arms imports increased significantly over the past decade in a context of multiple military conflicts. The primary military partners of the West, in particular Saudi Arabia, the UAE, Egypt or Israel, have an extremely questionable record in terms of respect for the laws regulating armed conflict (international humanitarian law) and broader human rights. Furthermore, there is confirmed evidence of arms exported by Western countries finding their way to the very non-state actors that those countries claim to be determined to fight (al-Qaeda, ISIS and the like).[2] Overall, there appears to be quite an obvious connection between arms flows to the Middle East and the production of insecurity for large portions of the region's inhabitants. Perhaps counter-intuitively – as arms control and disarmament processes tend to be generally seen as increasing human and regional security – this chapter will also question if and for whom the selective processes that have led successive Middle Eastern states to dismantle their biological, chemical and nuclear weapons programmes (alternately labelled non-conventional weapons or weapons of mass destruction, WMDs) have generated security.

Against this background, this chapter will reflect on a specific aspect of Western policies regarding the Middle Eastern region: it will review the overall pattern of provision of military assistance to certain actors whereas support to others is strictly prohibited. It will analyse how such practices affect the region, not only as a result of the quantity of arms transferred, or controlled, but also due to the selective nature of these policies. Taking the massive supply of arms to the Saudi-led coalition in Yemen and the various forms of military support to or collaboration with Israel as primary case studies, the chapter will highlight the inconsistencies of a large number of Western countries' policies: they simultaneously contribute to the construction of norms designed to promote respect for human rights worldwide, notably responsible arms trade, and to the undermining of these very norms on frequent occasions.

---

2 Amnesty International, *Taking Stock: The Arming of Islamic State*, December 2015, https://www.amnesty.org/en/documents/mde14/2812/2015/en.

Concluding remarks will reflect more broadly on how important these questions are when thinking about security in the Middle East region.

One last preliminary remark is in order: throughout the chapter, the emphasis on Western policies should not be taken to suggest that these countries are less principled than others. But it is precisely because Western, particularly West-European, countries pretend to be more principled, even when conducting arms deals, that this chapter chose to focus on their role in arms control and arms transfers policies to the Middle East. The strong involvement of these countries in the region is the other, quite obvious, justification.

2.1 Transferring and controlling arms in the Middle East: A Western-led and highly selective activity

While possession and transfer of arms tend to be uneven and imbalanced worldwide, the Middle East is surely the region where imbalance and selectivity are the greatest.

Non-conventional arms control processes

On the one hand, the region has witnessed over the past two-and-a-half decades quite remarkable processes of arms control and disarmament, essentially focused on non-conventional weapons.

First on the list of targeted countries, in the early 1990s, Iraq was forced to dismantle its biological, chemical and nuclear weapons programmes through the most intrusive and coercive process ever adopted.[3] Libya followed suit post-2003, with the dismantling of its nuclear and chemical weapons programmes, whereas Syria's chemical

---

3 Coralie Pison Hindawi, 'The Controversial Impact of WMD Coercive Arms Control on International Peace and Security: Lessons from the Iraqi and Iranian Cases', in *Journal for Conflict and Security Law*, Vol. 16, No. 3 (Winter 2011), pp. 417–42.

weapons programme was dismantled within less than a year in 2013–14.[4] Unfolding over more than a decade, the so-called Iranian nuclear crisis led to the involvement of the UN Security Council (UNSC) and to the adoption of sanctions in 2006–7. The 2015 Joint Comprehensive Plan of Action (JCPOA) agreement designed a way out of the conflict, while subjecting Iran to the most stringent form of monitoring ever designed for a nuclear programme.[5]

In all the aforementioned cases, the UNSC was involved – with its Western permanent members playing a leading role. Moreover, except for Syria, the processes relied on the Council's coercive powers under Chapter VII of the UN Charter.[6] In most cases, the processes were accompanied by further restrictions on ballistic missiles and conventional arms.

Conventional arms transfers[7]

Conventional arms transfers to the region as a whole, however, have increased significantly over the past decade. The trend is in no way unique: the 2014–18 period saw an overall increase in arms transfers worldwide, with the top six exporters (the United States, Russia, France, Germany, China and the United Kingdom) accounting for close to 80 per cent of the world's arms exports. On the receiving end, the Middle East

---

4 Karim Makdisi and Coralie Hindawi, 'Creative Diplomacy amidst a Brutal Conflict. Analyzing the OPCW-UN Joint Mission for the Elimination of the Syrian Chemical Weapons Program', in *Issam Fares Institute Research Reports*, September 2016.

5 Kelsey Davenport 'The Joint Comprehensive Plan of Action (JCPOA) at a Glance', in *ACA Facts Sheets*, May 2018, https://www.armscontrol.org/node/6372.

6 Interestingly, however, although the process in Syria did not rely on the UNSC's coercive powers under Chapter VII of the UN Charter, some key actors of the disarmament process erroneously thought that it did. See Karim Makdisi and Coralie Pison Hindawi, 'The Syrian Chemical Weapons Disarmament Process in Context: Narratives of Coercion, Consent and Everything in Between', in *Third World Quarterly*, Vol. 38, No. 8 (2017), pp. 1691–1709.

7 Unless stated otherwise, all facts and figures referred to in this subsection are based upon Pieter D. Wezeman et al., 'Trends in International Arms Transfers, 2018', cit., and upon the SIPRI Arms Transfers Database, accessed on 11 March 2019.

has been a particularly prominent region. It accounted for 35 per cent of global imports of weapons, and four of the world's ten largest importers of arms for the 2014–18 period were in the region. If one considers Arab countries beyond the Middle East, it appears that half of the ten largest weapons importers were Arab countries: Saudi Arabia ranks first, with 12 per cent of the global arms imports, followed by Egypt, Algeria, the United Arab Emirates (UAE) and Iraq, ranking respectively third, fifth, seventh and eighth.

Looking at the Middle Eastern countries that figure among the 40 largest weapons importers for the 2014–18 period, it is striking that only Egypt and Iraq received substantial Russian exports (in both cases, Russia provided them with about one-third of their overall imports). Markedly, over the past five years, it is primarily Western countries that have massively increased their exports to the Middle East: the region accounted for 52 per cent of total US arms exports, with Saudi Arabia as the main recipient (the kingdom accounted for 22 per cent of total US arms exports during the 2014–18 period, compared with close to 5 per cent in 2009–13). Also, four of the top five West-European arms exporters – France, Germany, the UK, Spain and Italy – had their highest growth in exports in the Middle East: France's exports to the region increased by 261 per cent between 2009–13 and 2014–18; German exports to the region rose by 125 per cent, Italian exports by 75 per cent and British exports by 30 per cent. Although the UK had a less substantial rise than its West-European counterparts, it is remarkable that close to 60 per cent of the country's exports for the 2014–18 period went to the Middle East, to a large extent combat aircraft provided to Saudi Arabia and Oman.

Over the past five years, Saudi Arabia thus was among the top clients of the United States, France, the UK, Spain, Switzerland, Sweden and Canada. The UAE was a key client for the US, Sweden and Canada. As for Israel, although it is a more prominent exporter than importer of weapons, its imports increased by 354 per cent between 2009–13 and 2014–18, with the United States as the country's principal supplier (64 per cent), followed by Germany and Italy.

While they are less visible, the exports of a number of additional Middle Eastern countries have been experiencing an exponential rise as well: Oman's imports (ranked sixteenth worldwide for the 2013–17 period) increased by 655 per cent between 2008–12 and 2013–17, with the US, UK and Norway as primary providers; Qatar's imports (ranked twentieth) increased by 166 per cent with the US, Germany and Switzerland as main providers, whereas Kuwait's purchases (twenty-seventh) increased by 488 per cent with the US as leading provider.[8] Despite the lack of reliable data on recent military expenditures in Qatar, Syria, the UAE and Yemen, SIPRI (Stockholm International Peace Research Institute) concluded that seven of the ten countries with the highest military burden worldwide for the year 2017 were located in the Middle East: Oman (12 per cent of GDP), Saudi Arabia (10 per cent), Kuwait (5.8 per cent), Jordan (4.8 per cent), Israel (4.7 per cent), Lebanon (4.5 per cent) and Bahrain (4.1 per cent).[9]

Selective processes

Along with the prominent role of Western countries, selectivity is another remarkable feature in both arms transfers and arms control processes.

Quite significantly, the massive exports to Saudi Arabia, Egypt and the UAE are accompanied by a UNSC's arms embargo on Iran, a country that accounted for only 0.9 per cent of imports to the region during the 2014–18 period.[10] Western providers have taken a very clear side in the competition for regional dominion that has been opposing Saudi Arabia and Iran. Qatar is the only country that has benefited from transfers of Western military equipment despite a deteriorating relationship with its Saudi neighbour.

As for the non-conventional arms control processes, the dismantlement of one arsenal after the other has left out one state, Israel – which has not been subjected to any substantial pressure to disarm although it is the only Middle Eastern state to possess the

8 Pieter D. Wezeman et al., 'Trends in International Arms Transfers, 2017', in *SIPRI Fact Sheets*, March 2018, https://www.sipri.org/node/4420.

9 Nan Tian et al., 'Trends in World Military Expenditure, 2017', in *SIPRI Fact Sheets*, May 2018, pp. 7–8, https://www.sipri.org/node/4485.

10 Pieter D. Wezeman et al., 'Trends in International Arms Transfers, 2017', cit.

most destructive and frightening of all non-conventional military means: nuclear weapons.[11]

2.2 Producing security through selectivity in the transfer and control of arms: A normative argument

To what extent can these policies, including their selective nature, be explained by a concern for security, understood in common, regional and human terms? Or can they be explained by a concern for security understood as emanating from the Middle East region and benefitting countries outside the region, in particular Western countries?

The disarmament processes that have rid the region of all but one non-conventional arsenal have been justified in precisely such terms. In the Iraq case, the entire disarmament system combining a set of extraordinary obligations imposed upon the Iraqi state with very coercive forms of international supervision and pressure, was based upon a particularly broad understanding of security: the UNSC considered that in order to durably restore international peace and security after Iraq's invasion of Kuwait and the following Gulf War that forced the Iraqis out of their neighbour's territory, the Iraqi regime had to be deprived of its most dangerous weapons and weapons programmes.[12] Against this background, disarming Iraq was presented as having the obvious effect of enhancing the security of neighbouring countries, and of the region as a whole, along with its population. By repercussion, this was considered to improve international security, thereby justifying the involvement of the UNSC, whose primary task consists of the protection and promotion of international peace and security.[13] A similar argumentation was

11 Hans M. Kristensen and Robert S. Norris, 'Status of World Nuclear Forces', in *FAS Articles*, updated November 2018, https://fas.org/?p=12747.

12 UNSC Resolution 687 (1991) of 3 April 1991, https://undocs.org/S/RES/687(1991).

13 Article 24 of the Charter of the United Nations, 1945.

used in the case of Libya, Syria and Iran. Ridding authoritarian regimes with poor human rights records and an appetite for regional domination of their non-conventional military potential seemed like a natural way to improve security at the human, regional and international levels.

As for the transfer of military means, there is a growing body of international norms and regimes designed to ensure that arms or dual-use technologies are not transferred to actors likely to use them to commit serious human rights violations or to undermine peace and security. From the Middle East Arms Control Initiative (1991) to the Wassenaar arrangements (1995), the European Code of Conduct on Arms Exports (1998) and the Arms Trade Treaty (2013), Western countries have, over the past two decades, been involved in a number of initiatives purposely designed to promote a more ethical approach in the transfer of military and dual-use goods and technologies.[14]

Taken at face value, arms control processes and the development of norms intended to better regulate the arms trade convey the impression that Western states' transfers of arms or military means to the Middle East region are increasingly influenced by concerns of ethics or responsibility, and an overall ambition to restrict 'irresponsible' actors' access to the means to harm their own constituencies or neighbours. This presumption is naturally reinforced by the fact that Western countries are liberal democracies that profess to care about human rights, good governance and diplomatic conflict resolution.

14 Edward J. Laurance, '1991 Arms Trade Control Efforts and Their Echoes', in *Arms Control Today*, 7 July 2011, https://www.armscontrol.org/node/4947; Coralie Pison Hindawi, 'Western Arms Transfers and Arms Control Policies towards the Middle East: Constraining Regional Actors or Fueling Regional Wars?', in Rasmus Alenius Boserup et al. (eds), *New Conflict Dynamics. Between Regional Autonomy and Intervention in the Middle East and North Africa*, Copenhagen, Danish Institute for International Studies, 2017, pp. 123–33, https://www.diis.dk/en/node/7186.

2.3 From selectivity to security? Practice in the Yemen war

The military conflict that has been raging in Yemen since 2015 – in which Houthi rebels, allied with Iran, are fighting against the official Yemeni governmental forces and a coalition of countries led by Saudi Arabia and the UAE – is certainly an instructive case in this regard. On the one hand, the war has been largely fuelled by massive exports of arms by Western countries to one side of the warring parties. But on the other, evidence of indiscriminate attacks and abysmally deteriorating living conditions as a result of the war – which, despite the lack of an accurate death toll,[15] is widely considered to have resulted in a massive cholera outbreak that affected over a million people, and brought large proportions of the Yemeni population to the brink of famine[16] – have generated a broad public outcry, much discussion, and legal and political actions. In some instances, these have led to an actual change in the arms transfers policies of exporting countries.

Evolving discourse and practices: Towards an ethically driven arms trade?

One year into the conflict, in 2016, the European Parliament voted in favour of a (non-binding) EU-wide arms export embargo on Saudi Arabia. The Netherlands was the first country to implement the measure in 2016, whereas Norway suspended exports of arms and ammunition to the UAE (the most significant military partner of Saudi Arabia in Yemen)

15 Patrick Cockburn, 'The Yemen War Death Toll is Five Times Higher Than We Think – We Can't Shrug Off Our Responsibilities Any Longer', in *The Independent*, 26 October 2018, https://www.independent.co.uk/voices/yemen-war-death-toll-saudi-arabia-allies-how-many-killed-responsibility-a8603326.html.

16 At the time of writing, UNOCHA estimated that 20 million Yemenis were food insecure, with 9.6 million people 'one step away from famine' and close to a quarter of a million people facing 'catastrophic levels of hunger'. See UNOCHA website, 'Yemen - Crisis Overview', March 2019, https://www.unocha.org/node/944999.

in December 2017.[17] Finland and Denmark have also restricted their arms transfers to Saudi Arabia.[18] In many other countries, discussions have been taking place, sometimes with judicial or legislative bodies asking for arms sales to Saudi Arabia to be suspended. This happened in the Walloon region of Belgium in June 2018,[19] and, most importantly, in the United States, Saudi Arabia's primary arms provider: following the murder of US-based Saudi journalist Jamal Kashoggi in October 2018, calls for a halt to US transfers of weapons to the Kingdom and other forms of military cooperation with the Saudi-led coalition amplified. The pieces of legislation proposed by US law-makers could not be turned into law so far, and they are unlikely to be in the near future, as bypassing a predictable presidential veto would require two-thirds majority support in both the House of Representatives and the Senate.[20] Kashoggi's murder also had a trigger effect in Germany, yet with immediate implications in this case: the country decided to ban all military exports – including German parts – to Saudi Arabia, initially for a two-month period which was then extended until March 2019.[21]

An evolution was also noticeable in the United Kingdom, the second-largest provider of arms to Saudi Arabia. Whereas the UK High Court rejected a legal challenge initiated by the Campaign Against Arms Trade (CAAT) movement in July 2017, ruling that weapons sales to Saudi Arabia were lawful,[22] a February 2019 report from the Select Committee on International Relations marked the first time an all-party parliamentary

17 Control Arms Secretariat, *ATT Monitor Report 2018*, August 2018, p. 14, https://attmonitor.org/en/?p=1216.

18 Pieter D. Wezeman, 'Saudi Arabia, Armaments and Conflict in the Middle East', in *SIPRI Backgrounders*, 14 December 2018, https://www.sipri.org/node/4711.

19 Control Arms Secretariat, *ATT Monitor Report 2018*, cit., p. 14.

20 Jeff Abramson, 'Senate Bucks Trump's Saudi Approach', in *Arms Control Today*, January/February 2019, https://www.armscontrol.org/node/10168; Patricia Zengerle, 'U.S. Lawmakers Criticize Saudi Arabia, Ask About Weapons Restrictions', in *Reuters*, 6 February 2019, https://reut.rs/2WJ0QDS.

21 Matthias Gebauer et al., 'German Ban on Arms Exports to Saudis Spurs Pushback', in *Spiegel Online*, 6 March 2019, https://spon.de/afqQq.

22 Roy Isbister and Elizabeth Kirkham, 'Reflections on the UK High Court Decision on Arms Sales to Saudi Arabia', in *Saferworld Comment and Analysis*, 7 August 2017, https://www.saferworld.org.uk/resources/news-and-analysis/post/727.

committee unanimously considered that 'the volume and type of arms being exported to the Saudi-led coalition' are 'likely to be the cause of significant civilian casualties in Yemen, risking the contravention of international humanitarian law'. The committee also considered that 'relying on assurances by Saudi Arabia' 'is not an adequate way of implementing the obligations for a risk-based assessment' of arms exports, as set out in the Arms Trade Treaty, suggesting that the UK may be violating the recently adopted treaty.[23] The committee also, almost imperceptibly, remarked on the paradoxical role of the UK in the Yemen conflict: purporting to be concerned over the humanitarian crisis, providing humanitarian aid and supporting the diplomatic attempts to end the war on the one hand, while on the other continuing to back the Saudi-led coalition through massive arms sales.

Such a paradox has been at the heart of civil-society critiques of Australia's Yemen policy. In early 2019, aid groups notably condemned Australia's decision not to increase its 23 million US dollar aid package to Yemen amid revelations that the government had given 36 million US dollars in taxpayer subsidies to a defence company exporting weapons systems to Saudi Arabia and the UAE.[24]

The aforementioned debates and restrictions in the export of weapons to countries involved in the Yemen war suggest that, within exporting countries, there is a growing sense of concern and responsibility over the impact of transfers. Governments, legislative bodies and civil-society actors refer to the existing legal instruments developed over the past decades, in particular the Arms Trade Treaty, to call for more ethical and more selective arms transfers. Ethical concerns, in other words, should lead exporting states to be more selective in order to ensure that 'arms sales strengthen, rather than undermine' human rights, democratic values and international norms, to borrow the concluding words of

---

23 House of Lords Select Committee on International Relations, *Yemen: Giving Peace a Chance* (6th Report, HL Paper 290), 16 February 2019, paras 72–3, https://publications.parliament.uk/pa/ld201719/ldselect/ldintrel/290/290.pdf.

24 Lisa Martin, 'Aid Groups Urge Australia to Do More for Yemen After Saudi Arms Export Revelations', in *The Guardian*, 26 February 2019, https://gu.com/p/ap5jy.

Jeff Abramson's call for a stronger oversight of arms sales by the US Congress.[25]

Resistance to change

Yet for all those efforts, resistance to change is strong, both within and between countries. As described above, civil-society groups and legislators in major exporting countries are struggling against well-vested interests in the military-industrial branch as well as the executive. This explains the inability of concerned citizens to achieve significant change in the UK and US export policies to Saudi Arabia and the UAE.

Even Germany, the only state among the most prominent weapons providers worldwide to have radically changed course and ceased sales of weapons and parts to Saudi Arabia, has been subjected to considerable pressure. Not only have arms manufacturing companies expressed their discontent and threatened legal actions.[26] Close allies, such as France and the UK, have been extremely critical of the German move. Being involved in the joint production and export of military goods, France and the UK are indeed affected by the German exports ban. They have, as expected, argued that Germany's policy change was putting their economic and military partnerships at risk: a leaked letter from British foreign secretary Jeremy Hunt to his German counterpart Heiko Maas, for example, expressed the secretary's concern over 'the impact of the German government's decision on the British and European defence industry and the consequences for Europe's ability to fulfil its NATO commitments'. Hunt further warned against Germany's loss of credibility and insisted on its obligation to honour agreements with partners.[27]

---

25 Jeff Abramson, 'How Congress Can Exert Responsible Oversight on Trump's Dangerous Approach to Arms Sales', in *ACA Issue Briefs*, Vol. 11, No. 1 (15 January 2019), https://www.armscontrol.org/node/10188.

26 'Wuerth-Konzern wehrt sich gegen Ruestungsexport-Stopp', in *Spiegel Online*, 18 February 2019, https://spon.de/afqjI.

27 Patrick Wintour, 'Germany Resists UK Plea to Resume Arms Sales to Saudi Arabia', in *The Guardian*, 20 February 2019, https://gu.com/p/anpbn.

French and British leaders have also, more audaciously, justified their own position on weapons exports to Saudi Arabia and the UAE in ethical terms: French president Emmanuel Macron decried the German decision to halt its sales to Saudi Arabia following the Kashoggi murder as 'pure demagogy', arguing that there is no connection between weapons sales and the journalist's assassination.[28] The French president further rebuked accusations of French unprincipled exports policies as opposed to Germany. He claimed in October 2018 that Saudi Arabia was no longer one of France's major partners in terms of arms transfers. This is quite a surprising claim given that according to the latest SIPRI figures, Saudi Arabia was the third-largest recipient of French exports for the 2014–18 period, with an increase over the last three years. In 2018, France was the second-largest exporter to the Saudi kingdom, even if French exports paled in comparison with the largest exporter, the United States.[29] For his part, the British foreign secretary tried to argue that the conditional transfer of arms gives exporting countries more leverage on Riyadh than a ban on such deals.[30]

At the time of writing, the pressures exerted on Germany seemed to have an impact on the country's determination to be more selective in its transfers of weapons systems and parts. The German press reported notably about a January 2019 French–German secret agreement in which the two partners committed not to oppose the transfer or export of jointly produced weapons systems to third countries, a substantial compromise from a German perspective. Furthermore, a number of German representatives, such as defence minister Ursula von der Leyen, insisted on the need to compromise with European partners in order

---

28 Jean-Baptiste Chastand and Marc Semo, 'Ventes d'armes à l'Arabie saoudite: Macron se dissocie de Merkel', in *Le Monde*, 27 October 2018, https://www.lemonde.fr/proche-orient/article/2018/10/27/ventes-d-armes-a-l-arabie-saoudite-macron-se-dissocie-de-merkel_5375467_3218.html.

29 Pieter D. Wezeman et al., 'Trends in International Arms Transfers, 2018', cit.; Data on arms exports to Saudi-Arabia, 2016–18, in *SIPRI Arms Transfers Database*, generated on 11 March 2019.

30 Patrick Wintour, 'Germany Resists UK Plea to Resume Arms Sales to Saudi Arabia', cit.

to develop joint ethical standards, rather than stick to a more radical German position.[31]

As a result, for all the discussions about the impact of massive arms sales on the Yemen war, and for all the talk about the need for arms transfers in general to be more selective, more transparent and more ethical, things have not yet changed much. The countries that have stopped their transfers to Saudi Arabia or the UAE do not belong to the most prominent weapons exporters. The only country among the world top six arms providers that decided to cease exporting weapons and parts to Saudi Arabia as a result of the Yemen war and of Saudi's overall contempt for human rights, Germany, was not its most significant military partner. It has nonetheless been facing massive pressure since it stopped its exports, especially from European partners benefitting from German participation in the joint production of military goods. Far from following Germany's initiative, European partners have made it extremely difficult for this country to genuinely promote more selective and ethical arms transfers policies, if it ever wanted to. Or, more accurately, arms transfers policies to countries involved in the Yemen war continue to be quite selective, as they exclusively provide the Saudi-led coalition with massive military power. This particular form of selectivity, however, is not conducive to much security, at least from the perspective of the Yemeni people stuck between the front lines.

A similar observation could be made in another case, that of the seventy-year-old conflict over the territory of historic Palestine. While not as impressive as the Yemen war in terms of loss of life and outright destruction, this other case allows us to explore further the nexus between selective arms transfers or control and the production of very exclusive forms of security in the Middle East region.

---

31 'Deutsch-französisches Geheimpapier regelt Waffenexporte neu', in *Spiegel Online*, 15 February 2019, https://spon.de/afqeb.

2.4 From selectivity to very exclusive forms of security: The case of Israel–Palestine

The case of Israel–Palestine differs from that of Saudi Arabia–UAE in Yemen in many ways. Unlike the two Gulf countries, Israel has a solid arms manufacturing industry. Accordingly, it is not only far less dependent on arms imports from abroad than its Arab neighbours, but it also is a prominent weapons exporter, engaged in various military partnerships with a wide range of countries. Its main clients, for the 2014–18 period, were India, Azerbaijan and Vietnam.[32] At the same time, Israel is a country that has been benefitting from exclusively Western arms exports and partnerships, and it has been for decades the unrivalled recipient of the highest amount of US military assistance worldwide. As such, its military strength and deriving ability to impose its will upon the dispossessed Palestinian population is closely connected to Western support.

Selective military support

Overall, Israeli imports of arms increased by 354 per cent between 2009–13 and 2014–18 according to SIPRI figures. For this latter period, Israel ranked fifteenth among arms importers worldwide, with the US, Germany and Italy as its primary providers, whose shares of Israel's total imports reached respectively 64, 27 and 8.9 per cent.[33]

While it only partially appears in the SIPRI data on arms transfers, US military assistance to Israel is remarkable in many regards: not only is it the highest of its kind in terms of global amounts, but it also translates into a wide range of diverse and close partnerships that have increased the level of US and Israeli integration notably in terms of military research and development, or production. Since 1999, under the Clinton administration, the United States has outlined its planned bilateral

32 Pieter D. Wezeman et al., 'Trends in International Arms Transfers, 2018', cit.

33 Ibid.

military assistance to Israel in 10-year Memoranda of Understanding. Although non-binding, these documents have largely been followed by Congress in its appropriation of aid to Israel. Under the terms of the latest such Memorandum (approved in 2016), the United States pledged to provide 38 billion US dollars in military aid to Israel from fiscal year 2019 to 2028 (an increase by 8 billion US dollars, in current dollars, compared to the previous decade).

These funds have notably helped Israel to purchase large numbers of F-35 Joint Strike Fighters, making it the first international operator of the aircraft, which it then customizes. The F-35 deals even benefit Israel twice, as they entail business offsets (that is, US engagement to make reciprocal purchases of Israeli military equipment) that reach several billion US dollars.[34] US funding has also allowed for US–Israeli cooperation in several missile defence programmes (Iron Dome, David's Sling, Arrow II and III). Between 2006 and 2019, a preliminary assessment estimated that the US defence budget appropriations for these programmes amounted to over 4.4 billion US dollars. Along with Israeli financial contributions, these funds have allowed for technology sharing, co-development and coproduction in the missile defence sector.[35] Since 2016, the US has also funded cooperation on anti-tunnel defence activities.[36] Although less direct, some additional forms of US–Israeli scientific and business cooperation have promoted research and products that may be used in a military setting.[37] Moreover, for the past thirty years, Israel has also harboured an emergency US military stockpile (essentially missiles, armoured vehicles and artillery ammunition). Although these goods are US property, the United States may consent to this material being used by Israel in case of a conflict, and it did notably grant Israel access to the stockpile during the July 2006 war on Lebanon and the July 2014 war on Gaza.[38]

---

34 Jeremy M. Sharp, 'U.S. Foreign Aid to Israel', in *CRS Reports to Congress*, No. RL33222 (10 April 2018), pp. 9–10, https://fas.org/sgp/crs/mideast/RL33222.pdf.

35 Ibid, pp. 11–18.

36 Ibid., p. 20.

37 Ibid., pp. 26–8.

38 Ibid., pp. 18–19.

US military assistance in all its forms has certainly facilitated Israel's buildup of a solid domestic defence industry, and 'helped transform [its] armed forces into one of the most technologically sophisticated militaries in the world'. This, in turn, is in line with the repeatedly stated US goal of ensuring that Israel maintains a 'qualitative military edge', that is, a superior military capability in all its forms allowing it to defeat any potential adversary, including more populous states or a coalition of states.[39] Israel's ability to inflict considerable pain in successive wars against the Palestinian population it controls has probably as much to do with Israel's military strength as with the corresponding Palestinian weakness. Yet Israel undoubtedly is the first military power in the Middle East region, not only in conventional terms, and thanks to its strategic alliance with the US, but also given its non-conventional arsenal, in particular its nuclear weapons stockpiles. As mentioned in earlier sections, the successive dismantling of all other non-conventional arsenals and weapons programmes throughout the region has conversely increased the weight of Israeli nuclear weapons by eliminating any form of deterrence.

If we consider the role played by Western states other than the United States, it is not so much characterized by substantial arms sales, as in the case of the Saudi-led coalition in Yemen, as by less obvious forms of partnership and support. These include countries, such as the UK, that sell components to destinations such as Germany, Italy or the United States for incorporation into weaponry then sold to Israel. Although these countries do not officially appear as exporters, they actually contribute to and benefit from sales to Israel.[40] Indirect support to the Israeli military branch also includes, more significantly, EU grants and funds for research. Since Israel joined the European Research Area in 1995, it has been contributing to and benefiting from EU research programmes on equal footing with EU member states. Within the FP7 programme that covered

---

39 Ibid., p. 2.

40 Cahal Milmo, 'Britain Still Arming Israel Despite Fear Weapons Will Be Used Against Gaza', in *The Independent*, 2 July 2015, https://www.independent.co.uk/news/uk/politics/britain-still-arming-israel-despite-fear-weapons-will-be-used-against-gaza-10357621.html.

the 2007–2013 period, Israeli companies from the security and defence sector have benefited from EU grants in quite large proportions: one in five security research contracts within FP7 included an Israeli security partner.[41] Israeli companies from the security and surveillance sector also have benefited from the subsequent EU research programme Horizon 2020: Israel Aerospace Industries, which specializes in unmanned aerial vehicles/drones that it proudly advertises as 'combat proven'; Elbit Systems, a weapons and ammunitions manufacturer; or other companies involved in surveillance, encrypted communication or in the logistics of the occupation, and so on.[42] Overall, numerous firms from the vibrant Israeli military industrial complex have benefited from EU funding and collaboration, simultaneously contributing to Israel's establishment as an experienced partner in the security sector.

Military superiority and the production of insecurity

Similar to what could be observed in the case of Yemen, military support and close cooperation with Israel have been denounced as complicity in the disturbing pattern of very serious human rights violations that Israel has engaged in. Beyond the issue of a now-decades-long occupation used by Israel to confiscate Palestinian resources and deprive Palestinians of their means of economic development and basic subsistence are also the intentional targeting of civilians and civilian infrastructures during each Israeli military intervention in Gaza, the blockade that has been asphyxiating the Strip for a decade, and the purposeful killing or maiming of scores of unarmed protestors during the 'Great March of Return' launched in March 2018.

There is no shortage of reports that have attempted to systematically document and legally assess the forms of abuse. One of the most

41 Ben Hayes, 'How the EU Subsidises Israel's Military-Industrial Complex', in *openDemocracy*, 6 March 2013, https://www.opendemocracy.net/en/how-eu-subsidises-israels-military-industrial-complex. Thanks to Lorenzo Kamel for drawing my attention to Hayes' work.

42 David Cronin, 'EU Funds Israel's War Industry', in *The Electronic Intifada*, 29 March 2018, https://electronicintifada.net/node/23746.

thorough reports to date was that of the UN Fact Finding Mission that investigated violations of international human rights law and international humanitarian law in the context of 2008–9 Operation 'Cast Lead' during which 1,400 Palestinians and 13 Israelis were killed over the course of three weeks. What is commonly referred to as the 'Goldstone Report' concluded that the Israeli armed forces repeatedly committed grave breaches of the Fourth Geneva Convention and war crimes – such as deliberate attacks against the civilian population; destruction of flour mills, chicken farms, sewage treatment plants and housing; use of Palestinian civilians as human shields; and degrading treatment of detained Palestinian civilians.[43] The mission also concluded that 'as a whole', the actions of the Israeli military 'were premised on a deliberate policy of disproportionate force aimed not at the enemy but at the "supporting infrastructure"', and that, '[i]n practice, this appears to have meant the civilian population'.[44]

More recently, the UN Human Rights Council established a commission to investigate the demonstrations held in Gaza between 30 March and 31 December 2018 (widely known as the 'Great March of Return', a movement envisioned by its initiators as a 'fully peaceful march' designed to remind the world of Palestinians' rights under international law, including the right of Palestinian refugees to return to their land, homes and properties[45]) and the response of the Israeli military to these protests. Having investigated all fatalities (over 180) and hundreds of injuries caused by Israeli security forces at the demonstration sites from the end of March until 31 December 2018, the commission 'found reasonable grounds to believe' that, apart from two incidents that occurred respectively on 14 May and on 12 October, 'in all other cases it investigated, the use of live ammunition by Israeli security forces against

---

43 UN Human Rights Council (UNHCR), *Report of the United Nations Fact-finding Mission on the Gaza Conflict* (A/HRC/12/48), 25 September 2009, paras 46, 50–2, 55, 60, https://undocs.org/A/HRC/12/48.

44 Ibid., para. 1886.

45 UNHCR, *Report of the Detailed Findings of the Independent International Commission of Inquiry on the Protests in the Occupied Palestinian Territory* (A/HRC/40/CRP.2), 18 March 2019, para. 200, https://undocs.org/A/HRC/40/CRP.2.

demonstrators was unlawful'.[46] Civilians not directly participating in the hostilities, including medical personnel, paramedics, journalists, children and those with disabilities – who all benefit from a protected status under international humanitarian law – appear to have been intentionally shot on numerous occasions, resulting in death or grave injuries.[47] Underlining that '[u]nless undertaken lawfully in self-defense, intentionally killing a civilian not directly participating in hostilities is a war crime', the commission found that '[s]erious human rights violations were committed which may amount to crimes against humanity'.[48]

Overall the well-documented pattern of serious Israeli breaches of human rights and international humanitarian law in its dealing with Palestinians has fostered a debate about the appropriateness – and lawfulness – of Western support for the Israeli military. EU collaboration with Israeli military and surveillance companies has notably been criticized by numerous civil-society actors. Most prominently, a group of twenty-five renowned lawyers signed a letter in 2017 to call for a halt to the funding of the Israeli Ministry of Public Security through the Law Train project within the EU research and innovation programme Horizon 2020.[49] The grassroots Boycott, Divestment and Sanctions (BDS) movement has also granted particular attention to the role of foreign – notably EU – support to Israeli security companies. Significantly, the 15th Annual Israeli Apartheid Week chose precisely to focus its 2019 edition on Western arms sales and military support to Israel under the

46 Ibid., para. 693.

47 Ibid., paras 512–37.

48 Ibid., Summary, p. 2.

49 Michel Waelbroeck, *Opinion Concerning the Legality of the Participation by the Israeli Ministry of Public Security in a Research Project Financed by the European Union*, 10 April 2017, http://www.aurdip.org/prominent-legal-experts-confirm.html. Endorsed by Richard Falk, Jeff Handmaker, John Dugard, Fabio Marcelli, Pierre Klein, George E. Bisharat, Bill Bowring, Mansoob Murshed, Michael Mansfield, Susan M. Akram, Marco Sassoli, Tom Moerenhout, Araceli Mangas Martín, Geoffrey Bindman, Chantal Meloni, Laurens Jan Brinkhorst, Eric David, Jean Salmon, Paul de Waart, Marcel Brus, François Dubuisson, Michael Bothe, Tareq Shrourou, Alexis Deswaef and Ugo Giannangeli.

theme 'Stop Arming Colonialism'.[50] Calls for an arms embargo on Israel have been made by human rights organizations, such as Amnesty International, and even by the UK's Labour Party in September 2018.[51] In the United States, the most crucial of Israel's partners, there have also been efforts to ensure better legislative control of US aid and arms sales to Israel: a 1952 Mutual Defence Assistance Agreement notably restricts Israel's use of US military equipment to 'defensive purposes', whereas the 'Leahy Law' prohibits assistance to any foreign security force unit when credible information suggests that the unit has engaged in a gross violation of human rights.[52]

Exclusive vs inclusive: Competing understandings of security

These initiatives, largely driven by concerned citizens, have encountered some successes, while still not sufficient to seriously derail the strategic partnership with the US, as well as the trend of ever-growing Israeli integration into EU programmes. But this is not where our analysis should stop. Pursuing our reflection on the connection between Western arms flows, arms control and security in the Middle East region and beyond, it is important to highlight the following point: the voices that challenge the normalization of EU–Israeli relations in the defence and military sector are based upon a certain understanding of security, one that acknowledges Palestinians as being as equally entitled to live in peace and security as their Israeli counterparts. Surely, one may connect this understanding to the notion of human security that was initially coined in the 1990s before becoming a requisite slogan in international circles. Fundamentally, it goes further back to the very idea of equal human rights for all. Most Western states' unconditional support for Israel, including its military sector, on the other hand, is based on a starkly different understanding of

---

50 BDS, *Call Out: 15th Annual Israeli Apartheid Week*, 28 February 2019, https://bdsmovement.net/node/19585.

51 'UK Labour Passes Motion Calling to Ban Arms Sales to Israel', in *Times of Israel*, 25 September 2018, https://www.timesofisrael.com/uk-labour-passes-motion-calling-to-ban-arms-sales-to-israel.

52 Jeremy Sharp, 'U.S. Foreign Aid to Israel', cit., p. 21–2.

security: one focused not only on Israel's right to live unthreatened, but also on its right to use massive military strength and superiority to deter any potential threats (as embodied in the notion of qualitative military edge). This unconditional support thus frees Israel from the need to enter into serious political negotiations or compromise with the Palestinians on the ethnically cleansed territory of whom Israel was established.[53] While the Israeli right to defend itself militarily is repeatedly stressed, Palestinians who engage in military actions against the military apparatus that enables the Israeli occupation are labelled as terrorists, and nothing but a demilitarized Palestinian state on a tiny percentage of the country's initial land could ever be accepted. Astonishingly, this understanding of security is exclusively focused on one side of the conflict, essentially ignoring the other side – millions of men, women and children along with their equal right to and need for security.

Conclusion: Selective

arms flows and arms control, exclusive understandings of security and the production of insecurity

As a whole, Western policies in terms of arms flows to and arms control in the Middle East region have been very selective over the past decades. Selectivity in the transfer of arms, of course, seems less cynical than simultaneous provision of weapons to both sides engaged in a military conflict as some countries did during the Iran–Iraq war in the 1980s, or the Greek–Turkish arms race in the 1990s. Yet the problem, as shown in the two cases analysed, and despite the tenacity of engaged citizens who have been pushing for more responsible practices, is that the Middle Eastern actors that have benefitted from selective Western arms transfers and control processes do not seem to have been elected on the basis of their respect for international norms in general, and human rights in particular.

53 Ilan Pappé, *The Ethnic Cleansing of Palestine*, Oxford, Oneworld Publications, 2006.

What, therefore, is the impact of this selectivity – which is not justified by ethical concerns – on security? It all depends upon the understanding of security that one adopts. If security is understood in exclusive terms as the maintenance of a status quo that benefits a regime to the detriment of its own constituency or of its neighbours, or as the prevalence of one side in a conflict to the detriment of the other, the selective policies described here can indeed be deemed to have substantially increased some actors' security and stability. This, however, is a definition of security that stands at odds, all at once, with the collective, regional, international and human iterations of the concept. Quite evidently, massive military support provided selectively to countries involved in military conflicts, despite reliable evidence that the acquired military superiority is used to engage in unlawful uses of force, and widespread abuse of international humanitarian law or human rights, generates insecurity:

- at the human level, for all individuals directly or indirectly affected by the violations and by the fighting;
- at the national level, for the neighbouring countries under attack, or those fearing such an attack;
- at the regional level, as such situations risk fuelling arms races, which, in turn, further increase the risk of open, military, conflict; and
- at the international and collective levels, as support to countries that blatantly violate international norms weakens the international legal system along with the principle of collective security.

Realizing that Western arms transfers and arms control policies to the Middle East promote insecurity on such large scale, some have been calling for ways to ensure that 'arms sales strengthen, rather than undermine' 'human rights, democratic values, and international norms'.[54] While this may sound like a reasonable goal, the notion that carefully controlled arms transfers can strengthen human rights, democracy and international law needs to be pondered. Not only because of the fierce

54 Jeff Abramson, 'How Congress Can Exert Responsible Oversight . . .', cit.

resistance to efforts to promote a more responsible trade that military-industrial complexes and governments have been opposing, or the repeatedly proven fact that arms exporters actually have little control over the end users of their products.[55] More fundamentally, a vigilant observer of the Middle East and of its relationship with Western countries will have good reasons to doubt that what is required to promote respect for human rights, norms and democracy in the region are additional lethal means, whatever their beneficiaries' claimed values. The same could be said of partial arms control measures that end up strengthening allies with dubious human rights records and undermining the prospect for regional, compromise-based, processes.

55 See, for example, Nima Elbagir et al., 'Sold to an Ally, Lost to an Enemy', in *CNN Exclusive Reports*, February 2019, https://edition.cnn.com/interactive/2019/02/middleeast/yemen-lost-us-arms; or Coralie Pison Hindawi, 'Western Arms Transfers and Arms Control Policies towards the Middle East', cit.

Waleed Hazbun

Chapter 3: Insecurity, Order and Pluralism in the Middle East: An Agenda for a Critical Approach to Security Studies

Since the 2003 US-led invasion of Iraq, the Middle East has been a major area of study by scholars, particularly those focused on international relations (IR) and security studies. Much of this scholarship, however, has been framed around questions that relate to the security interests and policies of the US and its allies. Citing Robert W. Cox, who famously noted that 'theory is always for someone and for some purpose [. . .] [there is] no such thing as theory in itself divorced from a standpoint in time and space',[1] critical security studies scholar Ken Booth contended that security studies as a field has promoted what Cox refers to as 'problem-solving theory'.[2] Such theory accepts the existing power structures of world politics and identifies challenges to them while striving to define the most rational or efficient ways to counter or contain such threats. Building from this observation, this chapter argues that security studies scholarship about the Middle East has been generally framed in relationship to a normative understanding of political order defined in terms of a US-dominated regional order. Threats and insecurity are defined, implicitly or explicitly, in relationship to the US-dominated structures and rules of political order that are understood to provide security.

1 Robert W. Cox, 'Social Forces, States, and World Orders', in Robert O. Keohane (ed.), *Neorealism and Its Critics*, New York, Columbia University Press, 1986, p. 207.

2 Ken Booth, 'Critical Explorations', in Ken Booth (ed.), *Critical Security Studies and World Politics*, Boulder/London, Lynne Rienner, 2005, p. 2.

This chapter argues that to think *critically* about the issue of security in the Middle East requires three main tasks. First, we need to question the dominant normative understandings of regional and global order that shape existing security studies scholarship about the Middle East. This structure of knowledge production is more appropriate for American policy analysis and formation, rather than academic scholarship, be it within the American academia or outside of it. Second, we need to recognize rival understandings of order at the global and regional level, such as those defined by international law, other major powers, or alternative political forces and ideologies in the region. Academic security studies scholarship in the Middle East should seek to recognize how different actors understand and experience insecurity, rather than measure security only in terms of a US-dominated order. Scholars based within institutions outside the United States, especially those in the Arab world, are often better positioned to relate these alterative experiences and understandings of insecurity. And third, security studies scholars should seek to collectively formulate one or more alternative conceptions of political order from which to forge new critical approaches to security studies. In my own work I advocate, in particular, for the notion of a pluralist regional order which seeks to minimize conflict and insecurity without a dominant regional hegemon.

Reading the English-language security studies scholarship published in the US and Europe about the Middle East, even studies of the security challenges faced by Middle East states are largely defined by notions of 'security' framed in reference to US-dominated regional order. Local actors, when recognized to have agency, are viewed in terms of how they sustain such an order – or else represent threats to it – but rarely in terms of their own interests and understandings of insecurity, let alone alternative conceptions of regional order.[3]

As a result, much of the existing security studies scholarship on the Middle East fails to question the hierarchical power relations

---

3 Waleed Hazbun, 'The Geopolitics of Knowledge and the Challenge of Postcolonial Agency. International Relations, US Policy, and the Arab World', in Graham Huggan (ed.), *The Oxford Handbook of Postcolonial Studies*, Oxford, Oxford University Press, 2013, pp. 217–34.

and means of violence deployed to sustain its own understanding of regional order. As a consequence, these studies are also generally blind to the notion that the US has been a major feature of the structure of *insecurity* in the region. That is to say, that regional insecurity is not simply a product of the failure of, or opposition to, US regional policies but is a product of the structure of order the US has sought to impose on the region as well as the policies deployed in the name of supporting that order.[4]

This chapter begins by outlining the geopolitical context of the post-Cold War Middle East in which the US sought to craft a US-dominated regional order. While the US was not able to sustain such a posture beyond a few years in the early 1990s, the notion of a US-dominated regional order became a common baseline framework for the study of international relations and security in the Middle East. The normative expectations of such a framework, however, became increasingly problematic as not only did US dominance over regional order decline in the 2000s, but also the US became a major source of regional insecurity from the view of many actors within the region.

The chapter then highlights the importance of incorporating into security studies scholarship on the Middle East how actors in the region experience insecurity. I draw upon my experience of teaching and conducting research at an institution and with colleagues based in the Arab world to trace the development of my critical perspective on the study of security in the Middle East. The chapter also offers background to the formation of a recent collaborative effort I have been involved in that seeks to foster critical scholarship on the Middle East and US policy by scholars from or working in the Middle East. The working group behind this effort, the so-called 'Beirut Security Collective' (more formally the Working Group on Critical Security Studies in the Arab

4 While many American international relations and security studies scholars opposed the US invasion of Iraq and recognize its disastrous consequences, their analysis remains focused on viewing the region through the lens US policy and interests. See, for example, Barry R. Posen, *Restraint. A New Foundation for U.S. Grand Strategy*, Ithaca/London, Cornell University Press, 2014; Andrew J. Bacevich, *America's War for the Greater Middle East. A Military History*, New York, Random House, 2016.

Region) was initiated and has been funded by the Beirut-based Arab Council for the Social Sciences (ACSS).[5] Drawing on Robert Vitalis's discussion of the rise (and fall) of what he calls the 'Howard School of IR', which challenged the racialized politics of empire that gave birth to American IR in the early twentieth century,[6] this chapter explains why and how these 'offshore' or 'exile' efforts in critical security studies have avoided focusing on US or European security concerns. While much of the existing IR scholarship on the Middle East addresses threats to US, European and Israeli security and interests by actors from the region and is structured around a norm of a Western-dominated security order, in contrast, the work of the Beirut Collective and other Beirut-based IR scholars seeks to promote critical work that focuses on how external intervention and a hierarchical global order define the most salient dynamics that generate insecurity for states and societies in the region.

Finally, I conclude by suggesting an alternative approach for the development of a more global, inclusive and pluralistic scholarly community. The next stage of developing IR scholarship from, about and for the Middle East will require a structural reorganization of existing systems of IR knowledge production. We need to expand and pluralize the scholarly infrastructure with new institutions that better reflect the concerns and experiences of scholars affiliated with the Global South.

3.1 The 'American era' in the Middle East

While security studies developed as a field within the context of the Cold War, most recent security studies scholarship about the Middle East has been defined by a normative expectation of a US-dominated regional order. This understanding of regional geopolitics developed in

5 See ACSS website: *Critical Security Studies in the Arab World*, http://www.theacss.org/pages/wgp-css.

6 Robert Vitalis, *White World Order, Black Power Politics: The Birth of American International Relations*, Ithaca/London, Cornell University Press, 2015.

the early 1990s when the US shifted from a regional strategy defined by 'offshore balancing', calling for only occasional intervention when US interests seemed under threat, to a posture MIT security studies scholar Barry Posen refers to as 'liberal hegemony'.[7] With no global challenger or other major power from which states in the Middle East could seek support, the US quickly came to dominate regional politics and sought to establish a US-dominated regional order.

This effort was shaped by a broader post-Cold War American self-identity as a global hegemon. The early 1990s saw the collapse of communist states and state-controlled economies. The US helped lead the global expansion of efforts to promote neoliberal economic policies, dubbed the 'Washington Consensus'. While the Middle East was not viewed as ready to be immediately assimilated into this liberal international order, the US sought to establish a pro-US security architecture and contain any potential instability the region could pose to the rest of the order.

This effort was made possible by American leadership during the 1990–91 Gulf War when the US mobilized a broad coalition of Arab states against Iraq.[8] In the war's aftermath, the US was able to foster an Arab-Israeli peace process that later included the Oslo Accords between Israel and the Palestinians in 1993 and the signing of the Israel–Jordan peace treaty in 1994. Extending the logic of the Camp David Accords that led to the 1979 Israel–Egypt peace treaty, the US sought to end regional divisions and conflict in order to build a security architecture with an expanding set of pro-US regimes at peace with Israel. The purpose of this strategy was to limit instability as well as the ability of outside powers to gain leverage in the region. At the same time, with an unchallenged military force in the Persian Gulf, the US was able to sustain a policy of 'dual containment' against Iraq and Iran anchored by bases in Turkey, Kuwait, Saudi Arabia, Bahrain and Qatar, and a naval fleet circulating in Gulf and Mediterranean waters.

7 Barry R. Posen, *Restraint*, cit., pp. 5–15.

8 This paragraph draws from Waleed Hazbun, 'A History of Insecurity: From the Arab Uprisings to ISIS', in *Middle East Policy*, Vol. 22, No. 3 (Fall 2015), pp. 55–65.

For a few years in the mid-1990s, the US maintained considerable leverage across the region. American officials played key roles managing day-to-day developments in the peace process and attempting to guide economic reform and foreign investment. Meanwhile, the US was engaging on a regular basis in military and diplomatic containment operations against Iraq and Iran. In the years since, however, this formative era of American engagement in the post-Cold War Middle East is too often remembered as a benchmark for US policy rather than a brief aberration.[9] Too many policymakers as well as scholars seem to have normalized the idea of US dominance and with it the idea of a necessary and benevolent presence in the region seeking to sustain regional order.

By the late 1990s, US control had weakened and its vision for regional order was in decline. Soon the peace process had collapsed and excessive US backing of Israel eroded Arab state support for US policies and mobilized popular dissent across Arab societies. With the outbreak of the Second Intifada in 2000 and Israeli re-invasion of the Palestinian territories in 2002, Palestinians and Israelis became engaged in a low-intensity war. At the same time, neoliberal economic restructuring was being exploited by a narrow elite and failed to bring broad-based prosperity or promote political reform. Meanwhile in the Gulf, the dual containment strategy failed to produce regime change in Iraq and Iran while the US was losing international and regional support for its militarized sanctions and containment strategy.[10] Arab states no longer viewed Iraq as a major threat and Arab societies – increasingly linked by Pan-Arab media such as Al Jazeera – became concerned about the humanitarian costs of the Iraq sanctions regime.

During this era, regime elites in pro-US states became increasingly disconnected from the interests and concerns of their societies. In Jordan and Egypt, civil-society groups mobilized the anti-normalization

---

9 Steven Simon and Jonathan Stevenson, 'The End of Pax Americana: Why Washington's Middle East Pullback Makes Sense', in *Foreign Affairs*, Vol. 94, No. 6 (November/December 2015), pp. 2–10, https://www.foreignaffairs.com/articles/middle-east/end-pax-americana.

10 Marc Lynch, 'The Politics of Consensus in the Gulf', in *Middle East Report*, No. 215 (Summer 2000), pp. 20–3.

movement against their country's peace treaty with Israel and similar groups protested the US-backed sanctions against Iraq. Several states faced increasing societal opposition – often led by Islamist forces – to their regime's dependence on external support from the US that made them beholden to American regional security interests. The American military presence in the Gulf and its militarized containment regime over Iraq provoked domestic opposition and anti-Americanism within key pro-US states such as Jordan, Egypt, Saudi Arabia and the smaller Gulf states. Meanwhile, non-state actors, such as Hamas and Hezbollah (with Iranian backing), evolved as popular, powerful movements challenging US influence and US allies in the region. While the US promoted dominance at the geopolitical level, it was never able to consolidate an order that incorporated the bulk of these societies and eventually faced challenges and mobilized resistance from the bottom up as well as diverging preferences at the state level.

The American invasion of Iraq in 2003 can be understood in part as a product of the George W. Bush administration's unwillingness to accommodate an erosion of US control or a contraction in the American ability to project power in the region. The Iraq war failed, however, to realize the Bush administration's strategic vision for regional transformation and resulted in what many have come to suggest was the end of the 'American era' of dominance over the Middle East.[11] The years since 2003 have witnessed a steady decline in the ability of the US to shape regional politics. The Iraq war was conducted without broad regional support and led to the breakdown of political order and a sectarian civil war in Iraq. Iraq is likely to remain a weak, divided state, influenced by Iran and the anti-American forces of the Sadrist movement. Moreover, the Palestinian–Israeli peace process has remained effectively dead, while the 'two-state solution' is viewed by many as no longer being viable. The breakdown of the peace process led to the

11 Richard N. Haass, 'The New Middle East', in *Foreign Affairs*, Vol. 85, No. 6 (November/December 2006), pp. 2–11. See also Stephen M. Walt, 'The End of the American Era', in *The National Interest*, No. 116 (November/December 2011), pp. 6–16, https://nationalinterest.org/files/digital-edition/1319494178/116DigitalEdition.pdf.

repolarization of regional politics along an Arab-Israeli axis, with US support for Israel eroding Arab support for US policies and mobilizing popular dissent in Egypt and Jordan which had in turn, with US backing, signed peace agreements with Israel. These trends were starkly illustrated during the 2006 war between Hezbollah and Israel. By the late phase of the Bush administration, US allies in the region had become threatened by instability and Islamist forces while regional states, such as Iran, and outside powers, such as Russia, China and the European Union, looked to play an increasingly important role in the region.

While the era of the Arab uprisings is often viewed in terms of domestic political struggles, one of its major underappreciated causes is the widespread view in the Arab world that the terms of the US-dominated regional order, and at the global level the US-backed liberal international order, are unjust and that much insecurity in the Arab world is *caused* by the actions of external powers and pro-US regimes like Israel's. Moreover, the Middle East sits in a very awkward position in relation to the liberal international order. The Middle East contains regions of vital security and economic interest to the US and other Western powers. The Arab states, however, have remained outside the community of states that practice its collective and cooperative governance. At the same time, the Middle East has also been a deeply penetrated space, repeatedly suffering from great power intervention and from numerous external efforts to divide and order the region, such as the British and French mandate system after World War I.

American IR scholars such as G. John Ikenberry who celebrate the idea of a US-backed liberal international order argue that global US hegemony serves the interests of other states since 'for most countries, the U.S.-led order is a negotiated system wherein the United States has sought participation by other states on terms that are mutually agreeable'.[12] Ikenberry has gone on to argue that 'the rise of the non-Western powers and the growth of economic and security interdependence are creating new constituencies and pressures for the liberal international order'.[13]

12 G. John Ikenberry, 'Illusions of Empire: Defining the New American Order', in *Foreign Affairs*, Vol. 83, No. 2 (March/April 2004), p. 146.

13 G. John Ikenberry, 'America's Challenge: The Rise of China and the Future of Liberal International Order', in *New America Foundation*, 12 July 2011, p. 2.

He suggests that states like China have an interest in the maintenance of such a rule-based order because it can best protect its own interests and global influence.

As Robert Vitalis points out, Ikenberry's vision of the liberal international order is dismissive of the relevance of past colonial experiences and what Ikenberry refers to as the 'crude imperial policies [of the US], most notably in Latin America and the Middle East'.[14] And to the degree that other non-Western countries have become integrated into the liberal international order, it is in terms and within institutions already established by the North Atlantic states. The incorporation of non-Western states into a system of global order may not be sustainable without structural change in the rules and institutions of that order.[15]

The 2011 NATO-led intervention in Libya highlights these tensions as the Arab League originally sought to back a narrow UN mandate for a no-fly zone, but the US pushed to promote a more extensive military intervention leading to regime change, which was supported by only some Arab states and opposed by most African states.[16] More broadly, in the Middle East, the US has often worked to suppress, or to deploy very selectively, international institutions and international law as mechanisms for governing its own behaviour and that of allied states in the region. For example, America's key ally Israel is frequently shielded

---

14 G. John Ikenberry, 'Illusions of Empire', cit., p. 146, quoted in Robert Vitalis, 'Theory Wars of Choice. Hidden Casualties in the "Debate" Between Hegemony and Empire', in Charles-Philippe David and David Grondin (eds), *Hegemony or Empire? The Redefinition of US Power under George W. Bush*, Aldershot, Ashgate, 2006, p. 30.

15 See Waleed Hazbun, 'The Geopolitics of Knowledge and the Challenge of Postcolonial Agency', cit.

16 Siba N. Grovogui, 'Looking Beyond Spring for the Season: An African Perspective on the World Order after the Arab Revolt', in *Globalizations*, Vol. 8, No. 5 (2011), pp. 567–72; Jeff Bachman, 'Libya: A UN Resolution and NATO's Failure to Protect', in Karim Makdisi and Vijay Prashad (eds), *Land of Blue Helmets. The United Nations and the Arab World*, Berkeley, University of California Press, 2016, pp. 212–30.

from sanction by the actions of the Security Council.[17] Meanwhile, the Arab Gulf states remain critical US allies but have long failed to embrace international norms regarding human rights, labour standards, freedom of expression and democracy.[18]

The Arab uprisings, unfortunately, have failed to transform or liberalize the political systems in the region, and in many cases due to an authoritarian counter-revolution resulted in a more repressive political and intellectual atmosphere. At the same time, however, the era of the uprisings led to a greater awareness in the region and beyond of a proliferation of alternative voices and a mobilization of popular social opinion that seeks to redefine understandings of 'national security' away from a US-dominated regional architecture and towards concerns with human security, dignity and participatory government. While scholars such as Bahgat Korany, now at the American University in Cairo, had long sought to broaden the agenda of security studies in the Arab world to include issues of human security and development,[19] these issues often were quickly securitized within mainstream security studies scholarship and framed in terms of challenges to a US-dominated global order.[20] With the relative decline of US regional leverage, a broader trend has been the increasing assertiveness of regional 'middle powers' such as

---

17 Karim Makdisi and Vijay Prashad, 'Introduction', in Karim Makdisi and Vijay Prashad (eds), *Land of Blue Helmets. The United Nations and the Arab World*, Berkeley, University of California Press, 2016, pp. 1–4.

18 Kristian Coates Ulrichsen, 'Rebalancing Global Governance: Gulf States' Perspectives on the Governance of Globalisation', in *Global Policy*, Vol. 2, No. 1 (January 2011), pp. 65–74.

19 See Bahgat Korany, 'Strategic Studies and the Third World: A Critical Evaluation', in *International Social Science Journal*, Vol. 38, No. 4 (1986), pp. 547–62; Bahgat Korany, Paul Noble and Rex Brynen (eds), *The Many Faces of National Security in the Arab World*, London, Palgrave Macmillan, 1993; United Nations Development Programme (UNDP), *Arab Human Development Report 2009. Challenges to Human Security in the Arab Countries*, New York, UNDP, 2009, http://www.arab-hdr.org/Reports/2009/2009.aspx.

20 Mark Duffield, *Global Governance and the New Wars. The Merging of Development and Security*, London/New York, Zed Books, 2001.

Iran, Turkey, Qatar and Saudi Arabia.[21] Each of these states has sought to project its influence and articulate its own vision for regional order. As a consequence, in recent years media outlets, think tanks, and to some degree academics based in or supported by these states, offer a new range of perspectives on regional security issues. The development of a critical approach, however, needs to be built from the region 'bottom up' rather than produced to serve the particular interests and geopolitical visions of rival regional states.[22]

3.2 Experience, 'exile' and knowledge production in Beirut[23]

As David Lake recognises, 'Our life experiences shape our intuitions, which in turn guide our theoretical suppositions'.[24] Exposure to alternative perspectives does not simply provide additional data, but more critically, it also enables pathways for the production of different forms of knowledge. My own motivation for the development of a critical approach to security studies in the Middle East developed in 2007 when I took a leave of absence from my position at the Johns Hopkins University in Baltimore, USA, to spend a year teaching at the American University of Beirut (AUB). I arrived in the wake of the devastating 2006 war between

---

21 Waleed Hazbun, 'Regional Powers and the Production of Insecurity in the Middle East', in *MENARA Working Papers*, No. 11 (September 2018), http://www.menaraproject.eu/?p=1261.

22 Karim Makdisi as cited in Eliza Friederichs, 'The Middle East: Thinking About and Beyond Security and Stability', in *Documenti IAI*, No. 19|06 (March 2019), https://www.iai.it/en/node/10168.

23 This section and the section 'Contextualizing "insecurity"' below draw on Waleed Hazbun, Karim Makdisi and Coralie Pison Hindawi, 'Writing about Insecurity and Global Politics in Beirut', in *MENA Politics Newsletter*, Vol. 2, No. 1 (Spring 2019), pp. 11–14, https://wp.me/paLmeW-1L.

24 David A. Lake, 'White Man's IR: An Intellectual Confession', in *Perspectives on Politics*, Vol. 14, No. 4 (December 2016), p. 1115.

Israel and the Lebanese Hezbollah movement.[25] Beyond Lebanon and Israel, the war in Iraq had regional implications that included a violent insurgency and refugee crisis that spread across borders and the growing power and influence of Iran that generated insecurity fears across many pro-US regimes.

In addition to our engagement with diverse non-American students, the experience of myself and my colleagues at AUB was defined by our complex relationships to North American political science, our collaborations with scholars based in Europe and our commitment to build ties across the Global South. Working at an English-language, American-style university in the Arab world leads us to resemble what Edward Said has called 'exiles', in that we are familiar with multiple contexts and perspectives, and 'this plurality of vision gives rise to an awareness of simultaneous dimensions, an awareness that – to borrow a phrase from music, is *contrapuntal*'.[26]

Working with my Beirut-based colleagues, I benefited from the collectively cultivated contrapuntal insights we developed across multiple dimensions, including academic disciplines, theoretical approaches, national contexts, and languages. Our work was defined by living between, on the one hand, the close affinity of IR scholarship with American strategic interests and, on the other hand, our experience of living in a community and region that is often suspicious about, if not actively opposed to, US interests and policy. For many in the region, crossing a range of political perspectives, the US has long been viewed as a major source of regional insecurity and instability. While many IR debates within North America include 'critical' perspectives, these approaches are generally critical in the sense that they offer alternative ways to understand US interests, discourses and policies. In contrast, our research and teaching has sought to closely follow how Arab political

---

25 I write about this experience in 'War Stories. Letters from Lebanon', in *The Baltimore Sun*, 18 February 2007. I would relocate to AUB in 2010 and wrote about how my students viewed the Arab uprisings in 'From Lebanon, with Pessimism and Hope', in *Opinionator*, 3 March 2011, https://nyti.ms/eJ7vsg.

26 Edward W. Said, *Reflections on Exile and Other Essays*, Cambridge, Harvard University Press, 2000, p. 186 (emphasis in original).

elites, scholars and activists, as well as communities across the broader society, differently understand the sources of insecurity their states and societies face.[27]

Viewed through the lens of these experiences, one can detect how most of IR scholarship an 'American' educational institution might be expected to teach privileges US-defined forms of regional and global order. In contrast, faced with teaching international politics to a heterogeneous collection of Lebanese, Arab, European and American students we have sought to formulate alternative ways to understand regional politics and theorize the dynamics of insecurity that our students witness and experience.[28]

Freed from the expectations of North American academia and policy relevance, our scholarship has been directly shaped by experiences of living in Beirut. Collectively, together with our students, we have felt the regional consequences of the 2003 US invasion of Iraq, experienced the impact of the devastating 2006 war between Israel and Lebanon, witnessed the spill-overs from the war in Syria and occupation of Palestine, and closely followed the ongoing conflicts in Libya and Yemen. Our location has obliged us to think and teach about civil war, refugees, transnational jihadism, sectarianism, occupation and violence not merely as de-contextualized security issues, but also as complex social realities with their attendant contradictions and disputes anchored in contested histories.

---

27 Other examples of such work have tended to be produced by scholars in the region. See Bahgat Korany and Ali E. Hillal Dessouki (eds), *The Foreign Policies of Arab States. The Challenge of Globalization*, Cairo, American University in Cairo Press, 2008; and Mehran Kamrava, *Troubled Waters. Insecurity in the Persian Gulf*, Ithaca/London, Cornell University Press, 2018.

28 For example, teaching 'Introduction to International Politics' at AUB, Coralie Pison Hindawi sought to cultivate 'the students' ability to engage with the major questions and challenges they witnessed in international politics (from their location and experiences in Beirut)'. See Waleed Hazbun and Morten Valbjørn, 'The Making of IR in the Middle East: Critical Perspectives on Scholarship and Teaching in the Region', in *MENA Newsletter*, No. 5 (Fall 2018), p. 8, https://wp.me/paLmeW-X.

3.3 Contextualizing 'insecurity'

Informed by both these personal experiences and postcolonial critiques of IR, one can observe that the problem of 'security' is usually posed as a question of how to promote a Western-dominated order while somehow ignoring what can be palpably felt from locations such as Beirut: the hierarchical power relations and means of violence deployed to sustain such an order. Local actors, when they are recognized to have agency, are viewed in terms of how they sustain such an order – or else represent threats to it. They are rarely understood in terms of their own interests and understandings of insecurity.[29] Lacking agreed parameters for a regional security order, and with many states fragmented between political forces with rival security interests, the development of security studies within the Arab region generally lacks common norms and expectations to identify sources of insecurity. The alternative approach we seek to develop follows Pinar Bilgin's call for closely examining the 'insecurities experienced by various state and non-state actors in the Arab world, as well as the military, economic and societal dimensions of insecurity'.[30]

A critical contribution of such scholarship is its effort to explore how these local and regional conceptions of insecurity are often at odds with those embedded and enforced by the 'international community'. Much of the research by me and my former colleagues in Beirut draws on local readings and counter-discourses/narratives to explore the limits of Western-dominated institutions and security regimes such as over arms control,[31] the UN and

29 Waleed Hazbun, 'The Politics of Insecurity in the Arab World: A View from Beirut', in *PS: Political Science & Politics*, Vol. 50, No. 3 (July 2017), pp. 656–9, https://doi.org/10.1017/S1049096517000336.

30 Pinar Bilgin, 'Inquiring into Others' Conceptions of the International and Security', in *PS: Political Science & Politics*, Vol. 50, No. 3 (July 2017), p. 654, https://doi.org/10.1017/S1049096517000324.

31 Coralie Pison Hindawi, 'Iraq. Twenty Years in the Shadow of Chapter VII', in Karim Makdisi and Vijay Prashad (eds), *Land of Blue Helmets. The United Nations and the Arab World*, Berkeley, University of California Press, 2016, pp. 194–211; Karim

peacekeeping,[32] or the shifting role of the US in the region following the Arab uprisings.[33]

A central feature of our contrapuntal approach is to excavate and explore rival understandings of insecurity and the contexts that sustain them. For example, Karim Makdisi has sought to highlight how the US 'global war on terror' after 2001 reconfigured the US-dominated 'international community's' view of the requirements for peace and security in countries such as Lebanon.[34] For instance, most of the vast IR and security studies scholarship and policy debates addressing the 2006 Israel–Lebanon war works squarely within the US–Israeli parameters defined by the US 'war on terror'. This scholarship tends to offer little acknowledgement of the rival understandings of diverse actors in Lebanon and their agency in disrupting, shaping or adapting to larger forces at play around them. In contrast, Makdisi suggests that efforts to craft a UN Security Council resolution to bring an end to the 2006 war had to negotiate between rival narratives that, in turn, were shaped by developments on the ground. Such narratives included those within Lebanon and Israel as well as those of Qatar (that represented the Arab bloc in the Security Council during this period) and regional rivals including Syria and Iran, on the one hand, and Saudi Arabia on the other.

These efforts to make the study of global politics and security more inclusive and pluralistic reflect the challenging contradictions within the global system. The notion of 'human security', developed as a critical

---

Makdisi and Coralie Pison Hindawi, 'The Syrian Chemical Weapons Disarmament Process in Context: Narratives of Coercion, Consent, and Everything in Between', in *Third World Quarterly*, Vol. 38, No. 8 (2017), pp. 1691–709.

32 Karim Makdisi and Vijay Prashad (eds), *Land of Blue Helmets. The United Nations and the Arab World*, Berkeley, University of California Press, 2016.

33 Waleed Hazbun, 'Beyond the American Era in the Middle East: An Evolving Landscape of Turbulence', in Rasmus Alenius Boserup et al. (eds), *New Conflict Dynamics. Between Regional Autonomy and Intervention in the Middle East and North Africa*, Copenhagen, Danish Institute for International Studies, pp. 31–41, https://www.diis.dk/en/node/7186.

34 Karim Makdisi, 'Constructing Security Council Resolution 1701 for Lebanon in the Shadow of the "War on Terror"', in *International Peacekeeping*, Vol. 18, No. 1 (2011), pp. 4–20.

approach for rethinking security, and concepts such as the Responsibility to Protect (R2P) have come to enjoy considerable support from scholars and political elites in Western states, often invoked to justify foreign intervention in the Middle East and elsewhere. In contrast, we seek to explore the significance of such concepts and doctrines for peoples who have, in frequent instances, suffered insecurity from the failures of their own states and from a too narrowly defined 'international community' embodied in the United Nations.[35]

The effort to explore and address these rival understandings is not a call for the privileging of a particular geopolitical position or subjectivity. Rather, it offers a challenge to scholars of IR and security studies to broaden the scope of their research and understanding by engaging with both diverse understandings of insecurity and scholarship from the region.

3.4 The construction of security in the Middle East

In my own research project developed while in Beirut, I began to focus on identifying the sources of insecurity for different communities in the Arab region and exploring the role US interventions have played in generating insecurity.[36] One of my main concerns has been to try to map the heterogeneous nature of the security environment in the region composed of diverse state, non-state and transnational actors who

---

35 Coralie Pison Hindawi, 'What If R2P Was – Truly – Everyone's Business? Exploring the Individual Responsibility to Protect', in *Alternatives*, Vol. 41, No. 1 (February 2016), pp. 29–48.

36 See Waleed Hazbun, 'US Policy and the Geopolitics of Insecurity in the Arab World', in *Geopolitics*, Vol. 15, No. 2 (April 2010), pp. 239–62; Waleed Hazbun, 'A History of Insecurity: From the Arab Uprisings to ISIS', cit. My work has focused on the 'Arab region'. This region includes many non-Arab communities, such as the Amazigh in Morocco and Kurds in Iraq and elsewhere, whose experiences of insecurity are important to understand and address in any effort to forge a pluralist approach to regional order.

serve as both agents of security and insecurity and how these actors are embedded in transnational security relationships. Across the Middle East, societal actors often understand the sources of insecurity they face in ways that differ from those of state elites and political regimes. This disjunction is in large part due to the way the region became integrated into global political and economic structures and the resulting patterns of state-building. Middle East regimes have tended to gain security directly from external powers or else collect the needed resources from external or rentier sources (like oil receipts or foreign aid). To the degree that Arab states fail to serve the security interests of their societies, they lose their ability to function as the primary political affiliation for their citizens. These dynamic, rather than primordial, identities or the artificial boundaries of states promote the proliferation of sub-state and transnational identities that cause the security interests of societies to diverge from those of state elites.

As Steve Niva has explored, across the region, since at least the late nineteenth century, there have existed powerful discourses of regional insecurity about the threat posed by external, Western forces to the region.[37] As part of this understanding, the nation-states created by European powers embedded in regional structures hierarchical relationships in which local state elite were dependent on external powers for their security. As a result, throughout the 1950s and 1960s, conflicts between regime and societal understandings of insecurity were defined by the rise of radical-populist Arab nationalism, which sought to challenge the role of Western powers in Arab regional politics. The mobilization of Arab nationalist forces compelled some states to follow Arabist policies even when they challenged the regime's own interests and that of their external patrons. By the 1970s, the consolidation of state power and the suppression of dissenting social forces resulted in foreign policies more reflective of regime preferences, often tied to the security interests of

37 Steve Niva, 'Contested Sovereignties and Postcolonial Insecurities in the Middle East', in Jutta Weldes et al. (eds), *Cultures of Insecurity. States, Communities, and the Production of Danger*, Minneapolis/London, University of Minnesota Press, 1999, pp. 147–71. This paragraph draws from Waleed Hazbun, 'The Politics of Insecurity in the Arab World', cit., p. 656.

external powers. However, new disjunctures between societal groups and regimes about the understanding of insecurity arose by the 1990s. Throughout the 1990s, the dominant regional and global position of the United States and its effort to build a US-centred security architecture for the Middle East led to the framing of a generation of security studies scholarship on the Middle East around the framework of US hegemony in the region. Geopolitics and security were understood in terms of actions that either supported or opposed US-defined order, ignoring alterative conceptions. Security studies scholarship was only framed in 'problem-solving' terms, addressing a series of issues understood as threat to the US-defined order.

The original insight that sparked the development of a project in critical security studies following the 2003 US invasion of Iraq was the observation, too often unnoticed, that American efforts to intervene in the Middle East in the name of American security interests had the effect of generating insecurity for populations across the Arab world.[38] While US-based scholars quickly noticed the instability and violence that followed the invasion, these consequences were generally framed as a product of poor planning, faulty execution, bad intelligence or else a misguided policy shaped by 'oil interest' or pressure from the Israel lobby. Meanwhile, with the rise of civil war, sectarian violence and transnational jihadism, new questions emerged about how to understand the sources of conflict within the Arab world. This context established a frame for security studies defined by problem-solving questions such as 'How to establish stability in Iraq?' My efforts to suggest that the US had created a problem that was 'not solvable' was not considered a valuable research agenda within American security studies or IR scholarship during the post-invasion era.

In contrast, relocating to Beirut established a new context for research and teaching. Colleagues, students and research centres across

---

38 See Waleed Hazbun, 'American Security and Arab Self-Determination', in *Jordan Times*, 27 October 2003. While the destabilizing impact of US interventions in the Middle East did not go unnoticed in US-based scholarship, such understandings tended to be found in the work of critical scholarship in history, geography and Middle East Studies rather than security studies and international relations.

the Middle East and Europe welcomed efforts to understand how US interventions in the Middle East generated forms of insecurity for Arab societies and why these interventions persisted when they seemed to fail to make America more secure.

At the same time, without an overriding concern for how to re-establish a US-dominated order in the region, I was able to observe and consider alternative structures and mechanisms for political order and security. Drawing from both the challenge to suggest an alternative grand strategy for the US in the Middle East[39] and my own effort to make sense of the politics of security in Lebanon,[40] I have sought to study the dynamics of 'pluralist, multipolar' systems of security at the region and domestic levels. Such systems seek to accommodate diverse, heterogeneous actors that have rival and often conflicting understandings of the sources of insecurity. In such contexts, I suggest that the possibilities for 'order' are best understood as forms of pluralism, without a dominant hegemon but consisting of a 'constantly shifting, unbalanced system'.[41] While not a model to idealise, what I observed within the context of Lebanon was a dynamic I referred to as an 'assemblage of conflicting state and non-state actors that constantly negotiate among rival understandings of insecurity'.[42] In such as system, 'no one party is able to attain hegemony and eliminate its rivals' as actors 'negotiate among rival understandings and produce shared – albeit highly contingent – understandings of how to address security threats'.[43] Within such an order, 'tensions among rival understandings of security are constantly defused but possibly never eliminated'.[44]

---

39 Waleed Hazbun, 'US Policy and the Geopolitics of Insecurity in the Arab World', cit., pp. 256–9.

40 Waleed Hazbun, 'Assembling Security in a "Weak State": The Contentious Politics of Plural Governance in Lebanon since 2005', in *Third World Quarterly*, Vol. 37, No. 6 (2016), pp. 1053–70.

41 Waleed Hazbun, 'US Policy and the Geopolitics of Insecurity in the Arab World', cit., p. 257.

42 Waleed Hazbun, 'The Politics of Insecurity in the Arab World', cit., p. 657.

43 Ibid.

44 Ibid., p. 658.

3.5 In the wake of US hegemony: Turbulence or pluralism?

While many states and political elites across the Middle East in the 1990s had little choice but to work within the possibilities of a US-defined order,[45] the regional consequences of the 2003 invasion of Iraq and the rise of Iranian regional influence fragmented political order in Arab states. These conflicts helped drive the shift from the era of Arab uprisings into the subsequent slide into civil war in several states and the rise of the 'new Arab wars'.[46] In the process, regional politics of the Middle East has transformed from a system organized around and against a US-managed security architecture into a multipolar system lacking norms, institutions or balancing mechanisms to constrain conflict and the use of force. This shift is not a result of the retreat of the US or a consequence of a so-called 'power vacuum', but a product of repeated US efforts to order the region through coercive force within the context of the emerging multipolar system at the global level.[47]

The relative decline of US regional leverage, US policies that violate the norms of the putative order it claims to sustain and the growing debate about rethinking what US interests are and should be in the Middle East have made the notion of a US-backed regional order less and less feasible, opening the door to the current confusions and incoherence of US policy. And without the US structuring the region's alliances, rival regional powers have increasingly taken their own initiative – and in their own way, like the US, they have rejected strategies that might foster a

---

45 Ibrahim A. Karawan, 'Arab Dilemmas in the 1990s: Breaking Taboos and Searching for Signposts', in *Middle East Journal*, Vol. 48, No. 3 (Summer 1994), pp. 433–54.

46 Marc Lynch, *The New Arab Wars. Uprisings and Anarchy in the Middle East*, New York, PublicAffairs, 2016.

47 This claim is developed in Waleed Hazbun, 'In America's Wake: Turbulence and Insecurity in the Middle East', in POMEPS, 'Shifting Global Politics and the Middle East', in *POMEPS Studies*, No. 34 (March 2019), p. 14-17, https://pomeps.org/?p=10700.

pluralist order in which actors negotiate fragile, contingent agreements among rival understandings of insecurity.

As a result, the Middle East regional system has become shaped by how rival states across the region's multiple geopolitical divides each seek to influence and control state and non-state actors, with the result being a turbulent regional system in which state interests are often hard to discern and shift in complex ways. While Iran, Turkey and Qatar have all sought to promote new, but differing, norms for regional politics, seeking to develop an order based around their own interests, Saudi Arabia and the UAE have advanced a revisionist agenda built from a growing capacity and willingness to project power and intervene militarily across the region.[48] These efforts by multiple regional and global powers to assert their narrow strategic interests in the context of the post-uprisings Arab world have led to increased disarray in the region, including the fragmentation of Syria, Yemen and Libya and massive humanitarian crises.

With a Middle East regional system fragmented between political forces with rival security interests, the development of security studies within the Arab world lacks a self-defined normative order to collectively identify sources of insecurity. Rival normative frameworks are being offered by rival powers and in such a multipolar system, media outlets, think tanks and to some degree academics operating within or with support from rival powers have come to offer a new range of conflicting perspectives on regional security issues. In contrast, in my own work I have sought to suggest the notion of a pluralist regional order which seeks to minimise conflict and insecurity without a dominant regional hegemon.

48 Waleed Hazbun, 'Regional Powers and the Production of Insecurity in the Middle East', cit.

3.6 Towards a 'Beirut School' of critical security studies

It was framed by these concerns that I began working within a transnational collective of scholars, backed by the Beirut-based Arab Council for the Social Sciences, to help build an infrastructure to sustain IR knowledge production by and for scholars based in or connected to the region.[49] My goal has been to go beyond the development of my own critical approach to security studies defined by a normative understanding of pluralism within a regional political order. I am also interested in fostering pluralism within the global structure of knowledge production which could lead to openings for a diverse range of perspectives and theories.

The collective motivation for the development of what we have tentatively referred to as a 'Beirut School' of critical security studies is not to attempt to speak from the margins or a subaltern periphery. Rather, we are seeking to pluralize IR scholarship, inspired by the work of Edward Said and more broadly postcolonial approaches, refusing to define security relationships in terms of a 'self' we identify with against the threat of an unknown 'other'. This approach allows our scholarship to speak from and about the region to the global community of IR scholarship with its diverse perspectives and interpretative communities.

We take inspiration in part from the spread outside of North America of theory-driven alternative schools of critical security studies, such as the Aberystwyth, Paris and Copenhagen schools.[50] While we adopt some theoretical tools from these critical approaches, the Beirut School is more rooted in the effort to develop a postcolonial approach to security studies.[51]

---

49 Samer Abboud et al., 'Towards a Beirut School of Critical Security Studies', in *Critical Studies on Security,* Vol. 6, No. 3 (2018), pp. 273–95; Waleed Hazbun, 'The Politics of Insecurity in the Arab World', cit.

50 See C.A.S.E. Collective, 'Critical Approaches to Security in Europe: A Networked Manifesto', in *Security Dialogue*, Vol. 37, No. 4 (2006), pp. 443–87.

51 See, for example, Tarak Barkawi and Mark Laffey, 'The Postcolonial Moment in Security Studies', in *Review of International Studies*, Vol. 32, No. 2 (April 2006), pp. 329–52.

Functionally, the Beirut Security Collective consists of a growing group of scholars from, who work in or have ties to the Arab region who through a series of meetings and workshops have produced what we call a manifesto, 'Towards a Beirut School of critical security studies', recently published in the journal *Critical Studies on Security*.[52] The collectively written text maps out our ongoing efforts to work through critical approaches to the study of security and global politics with a focus on the Middle East and North Africa, engaging both experiences and voices of scholars from and working in the region. In it we affirm and extend the contributions that postcolonial international relations and critical approaches to security have made to scholarship on the region, and to our own work. We also reflect on our commitment to decolonial pedagogy, and how our collective experiences organizing a bi-lingual Beirut-based summer school on critical security studies for graduate students and junior scholars living and working in the region have shaped the project. The manifesto concludes with a series of individual reflections by each author about their own work to highlight the plurality of approaches to the project.

A useful comparison is to consider the function of what Vitalis identifies as the 'Howard School of International Relations'.[53] In the first half of the twentieth century, the field of international relations developed in the United States was preoccupied by the question of how to upgrade the institutions of colonial rule to serve the post-World War I international order.[54] Vitalis identifies a group of African-American scholars based at the historically black Howard University in Washington DC as representing the most important centre of opposition to the project of 'white' IR as they highlighted the role of racism in sustaining imperialism. Not blinded by notions of American exceptionalism, Howard School scholars could identify how the post-World War II global order built by the US reproduced the structures of empire in the North's relationships with the Global South.

52 Samer Abboud et al., 'Towards a Beirut School of Critical Security Studies', cit.

53 This paragraph draws from Samer Abboud et al., 'Towards a Beirut School of Critical Security Studies', cit., p. 286.

54 Robert Vitalis, *White World Order, Black Power Politics*, cit., p. 12.

What is particularly useful about the Howard School example, as depicted by Vitalis, is that what connects this loosely defined 'school' was not a particular theory or collective understanding of their own racial identity, but rather a (marginalized) institutional position in relationship to the dynamics of power, funding and prestige that came to define mainstream, (what Vitalis insists we view as) 'white', IR. Based within a historically black institution within a highly racially segregated higher education system, even though they often published essays about IR in mainstream academic and popular journals, for the most part the Howard School remained a network of scholars who worked within a separate, underfunded, institutional infrastructure and whose work would eventually disappear from the field of IR with little trace (until recently). Only recently has there been an effort to recover, rebuild and expand this American approach to IR. It comes at a time where there are more efforts across the globe to critically engage the (racially defined) hierarchy that orders international politics.

3.7 Building a global infrastructure for knowledge production

While the Howard School faded due to its exclusion and lack of resources, the goal of the Beirut School is to promote similarly critical perspectives, but in order sustain them, we also need to build an institutional infrastructure for security studies knowledge production in and connected to the region. The challenge of producing knowledge from and for the Global South is outlined by Arlene Tickner's centre-periphery model for understanding the global division of labour in IR knowledge production.[55] Southern locations, she notes, tend to serve as sites of 'data', while theory production occurs mainly within institutions located in the

55 Arlene B. Tickner, 'Core, Periphery and (Neo)Imperialist International Relations', in *European Journal of International Relations*, Vol. 19, No. 3 (2013), pp. 627–46.

North. Tickner offers a compelling explanation for this dynamic, shaped by patterns and practices that reproduce power differentials within the field. These differentials are reflected by the North–South distribution of prestigious, influential academic journals and PhD-granting institutions. At the same time, IR in the Global South is often driven by national interests and policies at the state level (and thus of little 'theory' value to the core discipline), or else scholars from the South seek to 'fit in' the core discipline by framing their scholarship in terms of the theories and concerns that dominate Northern scholarship.

To a large degree the mission at the heart of the 'Critical Security Studies in the Arab World' project is to generate regional nodes for knowledge production that could help build an alternative institutional infrastructure for security studies knowledge production across the Global South. Given this support and autonomy, scholars located in different geo-cultures are more likely to produce work that cannot all be measured within the same or a single template.

This effort to build an institutional infrastructure for security studies knowledge production should eventually include a range of diverse nodes, such as in Beirut, Cairo, Tunis, Doha and elsewhere. These locations should each seek to offer publishing outlets, training programmes, funding sources, mentoring from established senior scholars and institutional support from local universities and research centres. These scholarly communities need to be engaged with but also autonomous from the academic hierarchy of security studies centred in North America and Europe.

Our efforts to develop knowledge production centres across the Arab world should eventually join other nodes from across the Global South. Such an effort at the same time can cultivate allies within the existing academic institutions, such as the ACSS and the Global South Caucus of the International Studies Association. The result might, following Theodor Adorno, be referred to as a constellation, denoting a 'juxtaposed, rather than integrated cluster of changing elements that resist reduction to a common denominator, essential core, or generative first principle'.[56]

56 Cited in Daniel J. Levine, *Recovering International Relations. The Promise of Sustainable Critique*, Oxford, Oxford University Press, 2012, p. 101.

Taken together, these efforts might not result in a coherent approach or a distinct theory of security, but they nevertheless aspire to engage in global debates bringing in new perspectives and voices in the long-overdue project of making the study of global politics more *global*. Doing so can contribute to the effort to envision a more pluralist global order and with it more pluralistic understandings of security and insecurity.

Elijah J. Magnier

Chapter 4: Beyond Security and Stability

Terrorism could be defined as deliberate behaviour, premeditated acts carried out by individuals, groups or states using threats and violence[1] with the intention of causing terror and death. But since there is no single definition of terrorism, its causes and motivations, so the problem cries out for multi-dimensional solutions: these of necessity have both military and socio-political aspects, focusing on community policing,[2] but above all paying attention to the root causes of terrorism and its global expansion. Terrorism can be triggered by democratic states as they instigate their foreign policies. Their military interventions overseas, over-militarization, targeted killing and excessive use of fire power create armed conflict, destruction and the violation of basic human rights.

Terrorism is currently a primary global issue, threatening many societies around the world but mainly, though not exclusively, implicating Muslim countries.[3] It is not limited to societies in conflict: societies apparently at peace can produce individual home-grown terrorists, who offer their expertise[4] in support of a

1 Martha Crenshaw, 'The Causes of Terrorism', in *Comparative Politics*, Vol. 13, No. 4 (July 1981), p. 380.

2 Gayle Fisher-Stewart, *Community Policing Explained: A Guide for Local Governments*, Washington, US Department of Justice, Office of Community Oriented Policing Services, July 2007, p. 2, https://cops.usdoj.gov/pdf/vets-to-cops/cp_explained.pdf.

3 'Some 87 percent of all attacks occurred in just 10 countries'. Ivan Briscoe and Bibi van Ginkel, 'The Nexus between Development and Security: Searching for Common Ground in Countering Terrorism', in *ICCT Policy Briefs*, March 2013, p. 2, http://dx.doi.org/10.19165/2013.2.01.

4 Hanna Rogan, 'Al-Qaeda's Online Media Strategies: From Reuter to Irhabi 007', in *FFI-Rapport*, No. 2007/02729 (1 December 2007), p. 81, https://www.ffi.no/no/Rapporter/07-02729.pdf.

cause[5] they believe in. But war can be considered its main trigger, amplifying destruction, anger and inevitably the desire for revenge.

Moreover, wars in the name of regime change are creating poverty and displacing populations in many Muslim countries, generating a major flow of migrants who then represent additional terrorism risk factors[6] dangerously close to the heart of European society.[7]

Perpetrators of religious terrorism do not all necessarily begin as ideologues or religious fanatics.[8] Lone wolves and in particular grassroots jihadists,[9] who may have access to lethal means, adopt terrorism in order to avenge family members, fight for a cause, gain recognition, attract attention[10] or even just boost their adrenaline levels.[11] Terrorism is not a new phenomenon: it did not start with 9/11 but has its roots in the French Revolution. In the eighteenth century, Maximilien de Robespierre said: 'Terror is nothing other than justice, prompt, severe, inflexible; it is therefore an emanation of virtue; it is not so much a special principle as it is a consequence of the general principle of democracy applied to our country's most urgent needs'.

---

5 Alex P. Schmid, 'Prevention of Terrorism: Towards a Multi-Pronged Approach', in Tore Bjørgo (ed.), *Root Causes of Terrorism. Myths, Reality and Ways Forward*, London/New York, Routledge, 2005, p. 227.

6 Anthony Faiola and Souad Mekhennet, 'Tracing the Path of Four Terrorists Sent to Europe by the Islamic State', in *The Washington Post*, 22 April 2016, http://wapo.st/1Sf1uma.

7 Brian Michael Jenkins, *The Implications of the Paris Terrorist Attack for American Strategy in Syria and Homeland Security*, Testimony presented before the Senate Homeland Security and Governmental Affairs Committee, 19 November 2015, p. 2, https://doi.org/10.7249/CT445.

8 Elijah J. Magnier, 'Lone Wolf: Radicalisation and De-Radicalisation, How Internet Changes the Life of Young Europeans', in *Al-Ray*, 10 May 2016, https://wp.me/p47Jgd-hp.

9 Scott Stewart, *Understanding Grassroots Terrorism*, Stratfor Threat Lens, 2016, http://cdn2.hubspot.net/hubfs/515194/B2B_Content/Protective_Intelligence/Understanding_Grassroots_Terrorism_STRATFOR_042016.pdf

10 Martha Crenshaw, 'The Causes of Terrorism', cit., p. 386.

11 Elijah J. Magnier, 'Lone Wolf', cit.

Since the US announced its 'Global War on Terror',[12] terrorist attacks have proliferated,[13] taking different shapes[14] and becoming more sophisticated, intelligent and lethal, targeting extensive territories,[15] and hitting various individual cities without warning.

Terrorist groups have been recruiting online via the internet, adapting and using the latest western communication[16] technologies and propaganda tools. Their publicity has attracted the attention of the mainstream media to the point where an implicit and unholy partnership has been established: in certain conflicts every piece of material or propaganda spread by terrorist groups has then been adopted and distributed worldwide by the media. In addition, there are journalists, academics and researchers who have become activists, themselves working as advocates for regime change (notably in Syria).[17]

The world view presented by the mass media replaces the reality on the ground, to the point where terrorists and mainstream media clearly espouse the same objectives: overthrowing regimes in the Middle East. It has become acceptable to support jihadists to overthrow the Syrian

12 White House, *Address to a Joint Session of Congress and the American People*, Washington, 20 September 2001, https://georgewbush-whitehouse.archives.gov/news/releases/2001/09/20010920-8.html.

13 Michael Jensen, Gary LaFree and Erin Miller, 'Global Terrorism Data Show That the Reach of Terrorism is Expanding', in *Monkey Cage*, 15 August 2014, https://wapo.st/1nXe3io.

14 Bruce Hoffman, 'Terrorism Trends and Prospects', in Ian O. Lesser et al., *Countering the New Terrorism*, Santa Monica, RAND, 1999, pp. 8–10, https://www.rand.org/pubs/monograph_reports/MR989.html.

15 Ian Johnston, 'The Rise of ISIS: Terror Group Now Control an Area the Size of Britain, Expert Claims', in *The Independent*, 3 September 2014, https://www.independent.co.uk/news/world/middle-east/the-rise-of-isis-terror-group-now-controls-an-area-the-size-of-britain-expert-claims-9710198.html.

16 Michael Steinbach, 'How Technology Has Transformed the Terrorist Threat Fifteen Years After 9/11', in *Stein Counterterrorism Lecture Series*, 21 September 2016, https://washin.st/2V6XIUz.

17 Greg Simons, 'News and Syria: Creating Key Media Moments in the Conflict', in *Cogent Social Sciences*, Vol. 2, No. 1 (11 April 2016), p. 2, https://doi.org/10.1080/23311886.2016.1170583.

government, even at the cost of creating a failed state and a jihadists' haven in the Levant.

This kind of manipulation, particularly during the wars in Syria and Iraq, attracted the two superpower countries on the ground, where they confronted each other, changing the game into a race for dominance between the United States and Russia. Little room was left for the local populations to decide their own fate, and certainly not peacefully.

The Middle East became a battlefield for global hegemony on a global scale, while many European countries took sides in order to align themselves with the interests of the United States. The peoples of the Middle East, however, are looking for partners and not for an external powers who make no secret of their objective to dominate them.

Europe is the closest continent to the Middle East and has a long tradition of commerce and political contact with this neighbouring region. Following recent wars in the Middle East, the old continent is well placed to play a constructive role in rebuilding what was destroyed (not only destroyed infrastructure, but also the broken trust of the hearts and minds of a now sceptical population) and aim for a robust and durable relationship.

The deepest challenge for the future is to look closely at the legitimacy and effectiveness of counter-terrorism measures and overseas intervention in the Middle East, to avoid the repetition of mistakes so that a more adequate answer may be offered to the problem of terrorism.

4.1 Blowback from over-militarization and foreign military interventions

'Any measures taken by Member States to prevent and combat terrorism must comply fully with the Charter of the United Nations [...] and must be consistent with their obligations under international law, in particular international human rights law.'[18]

---

18 UN General Assembly, *Plan of Action to Prevent Violent Extremism* (A/70/674), 24 December 2015, para. 5, https://undocs.org/en/A/70/674.

John Horgan, a terrorism researcher, has argued that terrorism is, in fact, a socio-psychological phenomenon.[19] This makes it tempting to hunt for a specific profile of the aberrant-sick-terrorist who lives among ordinary people. However, Horgan also believes that the search for the terrorist personality is doomed to failure because causes for this phenomenon can be multiple and dissimilar.

The causes of terrorism are multiple. They include: poverty, social exclusion, political injustice, religious zealotry,[20] discrimination, criminality, grievances and family history. Often psychopathology is also involved.[21] The lack of the rule of law (in a country, state or area) may also strongly contribute to the development of terrorism.

Moreover, terrorism can be triggered by democratic states' foreign policies, where their military intervention overseas actually creates armed conflict, destruction, violation of basic human rights[22] and itself promotes the rise of terrorist groups and their supporters.

Today, terrorism has reached a critical level of menace to the world. In the early 2000s, the numbers involved in violent extremist groups (al-Qaeda and its different franchises and other religious non-state actors)[23] were numbered in the hundreds or a few thousand. Today, there are tens of thousands of people joining non-state actors, and these are increasingly becoming better equipped and financed.[24] These

---

19 John Horgan, *The Psychology of Terrorism*, 2nd edition, London/New York, Routledge, 2014.

20 Amy Zalman, 'Top Major Causes and Motivations of Terrorism', in *ThoughtCo*, updated 22 December 2018, https://www.thoughtco.com/the-causes-of-terrorism-3209053.

21 Martha Crenshaw, 'The Causes of Terrorism', cit., p. 380.

22 George R. Mastroianni, 'Looking Back: Understanding Abu Ghraib', in *Parameters*, Vol. 43, No. 2 (Summer 2013), pp. 53–65, https://ssi.armywarcollege.edu/pubs/parameters/issues/Summer_2013/6_Mastroianni_Article.pdf.

23 Seth G. Jones, *A Persistent Threat. The Evolution of al Qa'ida and Other Salafi Jihadists*, Santa Monica, RAND, 2014, https://www.rand.org/pubs/research_reports/RR637.html

24 Daniel Byman and Jennifer Williams, 'ISIS vs. Al Qaeda: Jihadism's Global Civil War', in *The National Interest*, 24 February 2015, https://nationalinterest.org/node/16309.

groups are metamorphosing into more violent bodies, adapting to their new environment and accumulating precious warfare and governance experience to increase their longevity and attract more recruits to grow larger and give potential to the threat to societies.

Terrorism is causing death, fear[25] and insecurity to individuals and families in different societies across the world. There is an urgent need to address the root causes of this phenomenon, with its devastating and destructive effects and to reduce its consequences and powerful reach. States in particular fear the threat and practice of terrorism and they formulate policies to contain it and protect citizens from it.[26] These policies authorize a range of counter-terrorism methods at home and a wide range of overseas military responses.

To combat terrorism, governments implement militarization responses. Military-response campaigns, including targeted killing, use of drones, airstrikes, the deployment and collection of intelligence capabilities and raids by special operations forces – all these are considered by many states to be the counter- terrorism means necessary to use to achieve results. This assumption is more than doubtful.

The policy of over-militarization, when used to overturn governments while causing the deaths of hundreds of thousands of innocent civilians[27] (part of the 'collateral damage' of some military campaigns)[28] leads, as a by-product, to an increase in terrorism. The effects of these military

25 M. L. R. Smith, 'Review Article. William of Ockham, Where Are You When We Need You? Reviewing Modern Terrorism Studies', in *Journal of Contemporary History*, Vol. 44, No. 2 (April 2009), pp. 319–34; quoted by Vian Bakir, *Torture, Intelligence and Sousveillance in the War on Terror. Agenda-Building Struggles*, London/New York, Routledge, 2013, p. 1.

26 Christopher Andrew, Richard J. Aldrich and Wesley Wark, *Secret Intelligence. A Reader*, London/New York, Routledge, 2009.

27 Neta C. Crawford, 'Human Cost of the Post 9/11 Wars: Lethality and the Need for Transparency', in *Costs of War Papers*, November 2018, https://watson.brown.edu/costsofwar/papers/2018/human-cost-post-911-wars-lethality-and-need-transparency.

28 Josie Ensor, 'Coalition Air Strikes "Kill More Than 200 People" in Mosul', in *The Telegraph*, 23 March 2017, https://www.telegraph.co.uk/news/2017/03/23/coalition-air-strikes-kill-100-civilians-one-building-mosul.

options are therefore debatable and controversial, particularly as they cause so many non-combatant civilian deaths.

Military responses include the use of airstrikes and drones as these replies are considered a low-risk and effective option in US counter-terrorism policy, and they meet with Congress's approval.[29] These are the most violent and coercive tactics, designed and executed to kill specific targets, not bring them to justice. The effectiveness and 'collateral damage' of these tactics make them more than controversial. These effects are laundered by designating them the 'consequences of war',[30] with no respect for human lives.

President Ronald Regan approved operation El Dorado Canyon against the Libyan leader Muammar Gaddafi, killing Gaddafi's daughter.[31] The use of drones and airstrike killings has registered many successful hits against key individuals: the killing of Taliban leader Mullah Akhtar Mansour;[32] the killing of Abu Mus'ab al-Zarqawi in Iraq;[33] many al-Qaeda in the Arab Peninsula (AQAP); and leaders in Yemen (Anwar al-Awlaki,[34] Nasir al-Wuhayshi[35]) to mention a few examples. These practices send a strong message to terrorists, forcing them to hide and instilling fear[36] but they fail to halt the election of other leaders to replace those killed

---

29 Richard F. Grimmett, 'Authorization for Use of Military Force in Response to the 9/11 Attacks (P.L. 107-40): Legislative History', in *CRS Reports for Congress*, No. RS22357 (16 January 2007), https://fas.org/sgp/crs/natsec/RS22357.pdf.

30 Gabriella Blum and Philip B. Heymann, *Laws, Outlaws, and Terrorists. Lessons from the War on Terrorism*, Cambridge/London, MIT Press, 2010, p. 148.

31 Gregory L. Trebon, 'Libyan State Sponsored Terrorism – What Did Operation El Dorado Canyon Accomplish?', in *DTIC Student Reports*, No. 88-2600 (April 1988), p. 28, https://apps.dtic.mil/docs/citations/ADA194854.

32 Peter Bergen and David Sterman, 'Will President Trump Restart the Drone War in Pakistan?', in CNN, 21 January 2017, http://cnn.it/2kcJyLh.

33 Alan Dershowitz, '"Targeted Killing" of Abu Musab al-Zarqawi', in *The Huffington Post*, 25 May 2011, https://www.huffingtonpost.com/alan-dershowitz/targeted-killing-of-abu-m_b_22520.html.

34 Charlie Savage, 'Court Releases Large Parts of Memo Approving Killing of American in Yemen', in *The New York Times*, 23 June 2014, https://nyti.ms/1qEI6Sh.

35 Greg Miller and Hugh Naylor, 'Al-Qaeda Leader in Yemen Is Said to Be Killed in U.S. Drone Strike', in *The Washington Post*, 16 June 2015, http://wapo.st/1LbASzA.

36 Jason Burke, 'Bin Laden Letters Reveal Al-Qaida's Fears of Drone Strikes and Infiltration', in *The Guardian*, 1 March 2016, https://gu.com/p/4h78a.

and they do not necessarily alter the activity and effectiveness of the organizations they belong to.[37] All these methods have forced terrorist groups to develop counter-measures and evolve their own defensive procedures. Not only that, family members (for example Hamza, son of Osama Bin Laden) of those killed or affected by foreign intervention have joined terrorist groups which then become more numerous than ever.

In Pakistan alone, from 2004 to 2018, an estimated 430 drone attacks were confirmed, resulting in between 2,515 and 4,026 killed, including between 424 and 969 civilians (including hundreds of children) and, between 1,162 and 1,749 were wounded, according to the Bureau of Investigative Journalism data base.[38] In 2013, US Senator Lindsey Graham said drone strikes killed 4,700 people.[39] The hawkish South Carolina senator declined to offer further details on where and when these strikes took place, nor would he state how many innocent people were killed during these attacks. In 2016, the US dropped 1,337 bombs on Afghanistan, a 40 per cent rise on 2015,[40] and over 24,287 bombs were dropped on Iraq and Syria,[41] killing hundreds of al-Qaeda (AQ) members and al-Qaeda in the Indian Subcontinent (AQIS) operatives and Emirs,[42] but also many more civilians. In Afghanistan, US drones killed 1,147 people while targeting 41 specific terrorist targets.[43] The use of the drone

37 Alastair Jamieson, 'New AQAP Leader Qassim Al-Rimi Is Key Terrorist Recruiter', in *NBC News*, 16 June 2015, https://www.nbcnews.com/news/amp/ncna376141.

38 The Bureau of Investigative Journalism website: *Drone Strikes in Pakistan*, https://www.thebureauinvestigates.com/projects/drone-war/pakistan.

39 Spencer Ackerman, 'Senator Lists the Death Toll from U.S. Drones at 4,700 People', in *WIRED*, 21 February 2013, https://www.wired.com/2013/02/graham-drones.

40 Jessica Purkiss and Jack Serle, 'Obama Covert Drone War in Numbers: Ten Times More Strikes Than Bush', in *The Bureau of Investigative Journalism*, 17 January 2017, https://www.thebureauinvestigates.com/stories/2017-01-17/obamas-covert-drone-war-in-numbers-ten-times-more-strikes-than-bush.

41 Micah Zenko and Jennifer Wilson, 'How Many Bombs Did the United States Drop in 2016?', in *CFR Blog*, 5 January 2017, https://on.cfr.org/2AdwJse.

42 US Department of Defense, *Press Briefing by General Nicholson in the Pentagon Briefing Room*, 2 December 2016, https://dod.defense.gov/News/Transcripts/Transcript-View/Article/1019029.

43 Spencer Ackerman, '41 Men Targeted but 1,147 People Killed: US Drone Strikes – The Facts on the Ground', in *The Guardian*, 24 November 2014, https://

is much criticized for killing thousands of innocent civilians, and for setting a dangerous precedent that even more irresponsible governments will abuse.[44] The wars in Afghanistan and Iraq are good examples of over-militarization, subsequently exploited by ISIS.[45]

These doctrines, which face legitimate legal challenges and limits, sometimes achieve effective results but they simultaneously produce counterproductive by-products (such as torture, killing of civilians, violation of human rights and regime change). They underestimate the response ability of populations acting by themselves against repressive ruling systems.

Terrorists use the Western failure to be consistent in applying its own promoted democratic values and laws as an efficient recruitment tool. Overseas interventions deny agency to the local population and create more death and destruction, and the military responses push the boundaries of legal limits, and the many attacks carried out overseas are open to challenge. Such responses necessitate the application and development of transparency, accountability and a continuous review and evaluation of the West's foreign policy and the disastrous results of its military interventions.

The right to self-defence, targeted killing and political assassinations[46] are terms bandied about to designate counter-terrorism options that have indeed been part of the favoured choices, notably of the US establishment.[47]

---

gu.com/p/43t2q. See also the Bureau of Investigative Journalism website: *Drone Strikes in Afghanistan*, https://www.thebureauinvestigates.com/projects/drone-war/afghanistan.

44 Daniel L. Byman, 'Why Drones Work: The Case for Washington's Weapon of Choice', in *Brookings Articles*, 17 June 2013, http://brook.gs/2bWjfGp.

45 Susan G. Chesser, 'Afghanistan Casualties: Military Forces and Civilians', in *CRS Reports for Congress*, No. R41084 (6 December 2012), https://fas.org/sgp/crs/natsec/R41084.pdf.

46 Executive Order 11905 of 18 February 1976, banning political assassination. The word 'political' was removed by President Carter (Executive Order 12036), quoted by Adam R. Pearlman, *Legality of Lethality: Paradigm Choice and Targeted Killing in Counter Terrorism Operations*, 23 March 2010, p. 3, https://dx.doi.org/10.2139/ssrn.1583985.

47 Jameel Jaffer, 'How the US Justifies Drone Strikes: Targeted Killing, Secrecy and the Law', in *The Guardian*, 15 November 2016, https://gu.com/p/5bbfm.

The US paradigm employs the undefined word 'assassination' which may indicate a decision-maker's choice to leave the door open to his own interpretation[48] to justify the killing,[49] even of non-combatants.[50]

Democratic states[51] and other Middle Eastern countries[52] have embraced assassination as an intentional form of targeted killing, a designated weapon to be used against their enemies around the globe without the consensus of other sovereign states even if these were considered allies or friends.[53] Often, many civilian lives have been lost,[54] constituting not only a violation of human rights and overriding the sovereignty of other states, but also laying the groundwork for the birth

48 Michael N. Schmitt, 'Pre-emptive Strategies in International Law', in *Michigan Journal of International Law*, Vol. 24, No. 2 (2003), https://repository.law.umich.edu/mjil/vol24/iss2/1.

49 Adam R. Pearlman, *Legality of Lethality*, cit., p. 4.

50 CIA was behind the car bomb attack on March 1985 aiming at Sheikh Mohammed Hussein Fadlallah. See Bob Woodward, *Veil. The Secret Wars of the CIA, 1981–1987*, New York, Simon and Schuster, 1987, quoted by Stephen Engelberg, 'Casey Reported Behind '85 Lebanon Bombing', in *The New York Times*, 27 September 1987, https://nyti.ms/2UMq5I1. Also quoted by Nathan Thrall, 'How the Regan Administration Taught Iran the Wrong Lessons', in *Middle East Review of International Affairs*, Vol. 11, No. 2 (June 2007), p. 17.

51 'Osama Bin Laden was intentionally targeted and killed in a raid that took place without Pakistani knowledge, consent, or cooperation, on Pakistani soil'. See Stephen M. Pezzi, 'The Legality of Killing Osama bin Laden', in *Harvard Law School Student Articles*, 16 May 2011, http://harvardnsj.org/2011/05/the-legality-of-killing-osama-bin-laden.

52 'Yassin was to become a focal point in the campaign of the Khammas against Israel [. . .]. He became the target of successive operations designed to eliminate him and was finally killed in 2003. His elimination was viewed as a feather in the cap of the Israeli Security Agency and the Israeli Air Force'. Efraim Halevy, *Man in the Shadows. Inside the Middle East Crisis with a Man Who Led the Mossad*, New York, St. Martin's Press, 2006, p. 177.

53 'If we have actionable intelligence about high-valued terrorist targets and President Musharraf will not act, we will'. Barack Obama, *The War We Need to Win*, Speech at the Wilson Center, Washington, 1 August 2017, https://www.americanrhetoric.com/speeches/barackobamawilsoncenter.htm.

54 Kenneth Anderson, 'Targeted Killing in U.S. Counterterrorism Strategy and Law', in *Brookings Counterterrorism and American Statutory Law Working Papers*, 11 May 2009, p. 2, http://brook.gs/2bGjRCY.

of additional terrorists. UN officials go even further, pointing out the obvious but neglected observation that states themselves can also be guilty of terrorism[55] and should be held accountable.

Historically, targeted killing has been a rare[56] option adopted by certain states in fighting terrorism[57] and generally considered unacceptable.[58] In 1976, U.S. President Gerald R. Ford signed an executive order 11905 banning American Intelligence forces from engaging in assassination[59]. Moreover, until just before 9/11, the concept itself of reverting to targeting-killing was seen by the CIA director George Tenet as a "terrible mistake".[60] Defence Secretary Dick Cheney considered that

---

55 The UN Secretary-General argued that: 'The report of the High-Level Panel offers us a way to end these arguments. We do not need to argue whether States can be guilty of terrorism, because deliberate use of armed force by States against civilians is already clearly prohibited under international law'. See 'UN Secretary-General's Keynote Address to the Closing Plenary of the International Summit on Democracy, Terrorism and Security [...]', Madrid, 10 March 2015, https://www.un.org/sg/en/node/189119; Javier Rupérez, 'The United Nations in the Fight Against Terrorism', Lecture to the 132nd International Senior Seminar/Statement by the CTED Executive Director, Tokyo, 26–28 February 2006, p. 7, https://www.un.org/sc/ctc/wp-content/uploads/2017/01/2006_01_26_cted_lecture.pdf.

56 'In the past assassination targets included Egyptian intelligence officers involved in orchestrating infiltrations into Israel in the 1950s'. Asaf Zussman and Noam Zussman, 'Targeted Killings: Evaluating the Effectiveness of a Counterterrorism Policy', in *Bank of Israel Research Department Discussion Papers*, No. 2005.02 (January 2005), p. 2, https://www.boi.org.il/deptdata/mehkar/papers/dp0502e.htm.

57 Gary LaFree, Laura Dugan and Erin Miller, *Putting Terrorism in Context. Lessons from the Global Terrorism Database*, London/New York, Routledge, 2015, p. 12.

58 Paul Burke, *Military and Security Responses to Terrorism*, 2018, Module Booklet Part 1, 6. Topic 1, video: 'Legality 1, Decapitation – USAF General sacked for suggesting it as a tactic in 1990'.

59 President Gerald R. Ford's Executive order 11905: United States Foreign Intelligence Activities, February 1976. https://fas.org/irp/offdocs/eo11905.htm

60 Paul Burke, *op. cit.*, p. 11: 'The Director of the CIA, just one week before the 11 September attacks, said it would be a "terrible mistake" [...] to employ such a weapon' (Daniel Benjamin and Steven Simon, *The Age of Sacred Terror*, New York, Random House, 2002). Former US Defense Secretary Dick Cheney considered a poor judgment – by General Michael J. Dugan, the US Air Force Chief of Staff and sacked him – by Dugan to consider targeting foreign opponents.

targeting specific foreign individuals a "violation of Executive Order 12333[61] which specifically prohibits assassinations".[62]

However, following that significant and large-scale terrorist attack (9/11), assassination was widely embraced by various countries[63] and over time its use is growing in intensity, despite its mixed and controversial effects. Certain analysts believe that the assassination of a terrorist-classified leader or commander reduces or alters the organization's capability,[64] creating a positive capability gap.[65]

Light was shed on Israel's complex targeted killing operations[66] during the ongoing struggle against Palestinians and the Lebanese Hezbollah. Air strikes were claimed to be effective in Bosnia,[67] but were quite ineffective against Hezbollah in Lebanon.[68] During 2006, the Israeli war against Hezbollah in Lebanon did not undermine the structure or the power of the organization, nor did it allow Israel to win the war.[69] Once

61 Executive Order 12333, United States Intelligence Activities, IC Legal Reeference Book, federal Register Vol. 40, N. 235 (December 8, 1981). https://www.dni.gov/index.php/ic-legal-reference-book/executive-order-12333

62 John M. Broder, Air Force Chief Fired by Cheney: Military: gen. Dugan used 'poor judgment' in discussing possible Iraq targets, the defense secretary says. The General talked of attacking Hussein and his family, in Los Angeles Times, 18 September 1990. https://www.latimes.com/archives/la-xpm-1990-09-18-mn-585-story.html

63 Steven R. David, 'Israel's Policy of Targeted Killing', in *Ethics & International Affairs*, Vol. 17, No.1 (March 2003), p. 111, https://www.law.upenn.edu/institutes/cerl/conferences/targetedkilling/papers/DavidIsraelPolicy.pdf

64 Paul Burke, *Military and Security Responses to Terrorism*, cit., p. 4.

65 Ibid., p. 10.

66 'Israel has killed at least eighty-six Palestinians [in this manner] and [killed] another forty Palestinian bystanders'. Yael Stein, 'Any Name Illegal and Immoral', in *Ethics & International Affairs*, Vol. 17, No. 1 (March 2003), p. 127, quoted by Seumas Miller, 'The Ethics of Assassination and Targeted Killing', in *Jahrbuch für Recht und Ethik / Annual Review of Law and Ethics*, Vol. 19 (2011), p. 315.

67 Ivo H. Daalder, 'Decision to Intervene: How the War in Bosnia Ended', in *Brookings Articles*, 1 December 1998, http://brook.gs/2bWOlwf.

68 Amos Harel and Avi Issacharoff, *34 Days. Israel, Hezbollah, and the War in Lebanon*, New York, Palgrave Macmillan, 2008.

69 Gilbert Achcar and Michel Warschawski, *The 33-Day War. Israel's War on Hezbollah in Lebanon and its Aftermath*, London, Saqi Books, 2007.

again, more civilians than militants were reported to have been killed. Despite the availability of precise guided bombs, air strikes using smart weapons may not always reduce the killing of non-combatants:[70] the bombing of the UN compound in South Lebanon was a grave mistake, killing only civilians who had reached the United Nations base to escape the war.[71]

The actual effectiveness of these assassinations is controversial and unproven: the assassination of Hezbollah Secretary General Sayyed Abbas Mussawi[72] created room for another, even more charismatic and skilful, leader.[73] The result is that almost three decades later, Hezbollah has succeeded in becoming one of the most powerful armies in the Middle East. It has the capability to become a regional rather than domestic force and make a complete integration with a large part of the population. As a consequence, nowadays Hezbollah has three members in the new Cabinet but enjoys the support of seventeen out of thirty ministers and seventy-three out of 128 members of the parliament. The Israeli intervention in Lebanon changed radically the country's political course and the political-power dynamic and governance.

Moreover, even the very complicated and successful assassination[74] of Osama Bin Laden failed[75] to weaken that organization. Today believers

---

70 Paul Burke, *Military and Security Responses to Terrorism*, cit., Module Booklet Part 2, slide 3, 'Are airstrikes more "humane"? "Smart weapons reduce the risk of killing non-combatants"'.

71 W. Michael Reisman, 'The Lessons of Qana', in *Yale Journal of International Law*, Vol. 22, No. 5 (1977), pp. 381–99, https://digitalcommons.law.yale.edu/fss_papers/970.

72 Lisa M. Brennen, *Hezbollah Psychological Warfare against Israel*, Thesis, Naval Postgraduate School, March 2009, p. 17, http://hdl.handle.net/10945/4839.

73 Lina Khatib, 'Hizbullah's Image Management Strategy', in *CPD Perspectives on Public Diplomacy*, No. 1 (January 2012), p. 16, https://www.uscpublicdiplomacy.org/resources/hizbullahs_image_management_strategy.

74 APV Rogers and Dominic McGoldrick, 'Assassination and Targeted Killing – The Killing of Osama Bin Laden', in *International and Comparative Law Quarterly*, Vol. 60, No. 3 (July 2011), pp. 778–88.

75 Yara Bayoumy, Noah Browning and Mohammed Ghobari, 'How Saudi Arabia's War in Yemen Has Made al Qaeda Stronger – and Richer', in *Reuters Investigates*, 8 April 2016, https://www.reuters.com/investigates/special-report/yemen-aqap.

in al-Qaeda ideology are stronger than ever in Yemen[76] (AQAP) and very powerful in Syria,[77] operating under various names (Al-Nusra aka Fateh al-Sham aka Hay'at Tahrir al-Sham and Hurras El-Deen), giving birth to another even more fanatical organization, the 'Islamic State' (ISIS).[78] Indeed, ISIS occupied a third of Iraq and half of Syria before it was territorially defeated. This 'terrorism surge' is causing a hydra effect,[79] impoverishing the Middle East and leaving behind traumatized families, refugees and death.

4.2 Legitimacy and effectiveness of counter-terrorism measures

In 2004, the European Council established a Counter-Terrorism Coordinator (CTC) to combat terrorism, respond to its threat and monitor the implementation of the EU Counter-Terrorism Strategy. In December 2011, the CTC report 'did not substantially consider the implications of the EU's counter-terrorism strategy for fundamental rights and democratic control [. . .]. This may be attributable to the fact that the CTC's mandate does not include any obligation to assess the legitimacy and effectiveness [of] EU counter-terrorism measures'.[80]

---

76 Glen Carey, 'Al-Qaeda in Yemen Seen Stronger Than Ever as War Wears On', in *Bloomberg*, 2 February 2017.

77 Colin P. Clarke, 'Al Nusra Is Stronger Than Ever', in *The RAND Blog*, 2 November 2016, https://www.rand.org/blog/2016/11/al-nusra-is-stronger-than-ever.html.

78 Cole Bunzel, 'From Paper State to Caliphate: The Ideology of the Islamic State', in *The Brookings Project on U.S. Relations with the Islamic World Analysis Papers*, No. 19 (March 2015), http://brook.gs/2bjRKoa.

79 Gabriella Blum and Philip B. Heymann, *Laws, Outlaws, and Terrorists*, cit. p. 165.

80 Ben Hayes and Chris Jones, 'Report on How the EU Assesses the Impact, Legitimacy and Effectiveness of Its Counterterrorism Laws', in *SECILE Assessment Reports*, No. D2.3 (2013), p. 25. http://www.statewatch.org/news/2013/dec/secile-how-does-the-EU-assess-its-counter-terrorism-law.pdf.

It took over fourteen years of combatting terrorism for the world powers to gain momentum and unite in their fight against terror-financing and illegal trade. It was only in December 2015 that the United Nations Security Council adopted,[81] unanimously, a resolution to curb ISIS's estimated 1 billion dollars yearly funding[82] from stolen oil in Iraq and Syria, selling of antiques and the imposition of taxes on the several millions living under its control.

Following the Paris attack[83] that killed 129 people in November 2015, the European Commission said that the next year it would expand its legislation to include sanctions on foreign fighters, on facilitating travel for Jihad, or receiving training to carry out an attack.

Grassroots terrorists with warfare experience are more likely to execute successful attacks than those lacking this characteristic. In the first years of war in Iraq and Syria, most Western fighters encountered no legal obstacles when they left home to fight with ISIS. They crossed through Turkey, a NATO member, without being stopped. For years there was no arrangement with Turkey to close the border. No international legislation was drawn up to stop the influx of foreign fighters.

Moreover, the West and its Middle Eastern allies provided military support to Salafist Jihadists fighting with designated terrorist organizations. European fighters were indoctrinated with ideological teaching and given military training before joining the front. So far few of these have returned home. However, it would only require a few hundred out of the thousands concerned to damage Western societies with suicide attacks, if they were so inclined.

'We feel vulnerable in many different places where we used to feel safe – in cafes or at concerts, at sporting events, at home or at work. The killers are not just those coming in from abroad, but they are already

---

81 'Islamic State: UN Resolution Aims to Curb Funding', in *BBC News*, 18 December 2015, https://www.bbc.com/news/world-middle-east-35120441.

82 'Islamic State Monthly Revenue Totals $80 million, IHS Says', in *HIS Newsroom*, 7 December 2015, https://news.ihsmarkit.com/node/20470.

83 CNN Library, 2015 Paris Terror Attacks Fast Facts, 19 December 2018, https://edition.cnn.com/2015/12/08/europe/2015-paris-terror-attacks-fast-facts/index.html

here, some even born here.'[84] Terrorism is not confined to the Middle East; it has managed to invade many European homes and is living in western societies.

The Paris attack shows that terrorists do indeed live among us, in the continent. Retaliation against ISIS as a reaction to the Paris attack may not lead to its destruction. It is a tactical response that will not protect civilians in Europe or the United States. To reduce terrorism, it is essential to address root causes related to Western military intervention in Middle Eastern affairs.

Western society is facing fear and confusion resulting from the failure to anticipate and prevent terrorist attacks and provide protection. The EU political record is far from inspiring, not least in its response to the most recent of major terrorist challenges.[85]

Europe is crying out for further understanding of where ISIS ideology and hate teaching are being promoted in Western societies,[86] with particular attention to specific mosques and Islamic centres. Reza Safa estimates that:

> since 1973, the Saudi government has spent an unbelievable $87bn to promote Wahhabism in the United States, Africa, Southeast Asia and Europe. According to official Saudi information, Saudi funds have been used to build and maintain over 1,500 mosques, 202 colleges, 210 Islamic Centers wholly or partly financed by Saudi Arabia, and almost 2,000 schools for educating Muslim children in non-Islamic countries in Europe, North and South America, Australia and Asia.[87]

---

84 Jessica Stern, 'How Terror Hardens Us', in *The New York Times*, 5 December 2015, https://nyti.ms/1XK2mUb.

85 Richard English, *Terrorism. How To Respond*, Oxford, Oxford University Press, 2009, p. 119.

86 Nina Shea, 'This Is a Saudi Textbook (After the Intolerance Was Removed)', in *The Washington Post*, 21 May 2006, https://www.washingtonpost.com/archive/opinions/2006/05/21/this-is-a-saudi-textbook-after-the-intolerance-was-removed/d3c982c6-dff0-40af-988a-6654d987d71d.

87 Mark Silverberg, The Wahhabi Invasion of America, in *Citizen Warrior*, November 2007, http://www.citizenwarrior.com/2007/11/wahhabi-invasion-of-america.html. See also Reza F. Safa, *Inside Islam. Exposing and Reaching the World of Islam*, Lake Mary, Frontline, 1996, p. 52.

Wahhabism is the extreme religious doctrine adopted by al-Qaeda and its more violent metamorphosed version, ISIS.

Before invading Afghanistan, President George W. Bush said 'the enemy of America [. . .] is a radical network of terrorists, and every government that supports them. Our war on terror [. . .] will not end until every terrorist group of global reach has been found, stopped and defeated'.[88] Al-Qaeda and ISIS ideology is one and the same. They share the same teaching promoted in the mosques financed by Saudi Arabia which, in theory, should therefore be Europe and America's first priority to stand firm against its expansion. Yet, this same ideology is tolerated in all mosques built by these oil-rich Middle Eastern countries throughout the world, and in particular on the European continent.

Foreign military intervention fuels terrorist actions. Terrorist organizations take advantage of the West's contradictory policies. On the 20 September 2001, Bush said the Taliban makes 'no distinction among military and civilians' and accused the group of 'sponsoring and sheltering and supplying terrorists'.[89] Yet, under President Donald Trump, the government in Afghanistan controlled territory containing only 63.5 percent of the country's population[90]. The US establishment is actually engaged in dialogue with the Taliban to secure a smooth withdrawal of US forces from the country[91].

Moreover, US allies such as Qatar and Saudi Arabia provided (2011–17) modern weapons, training and financial support to terrorist organizations and terrorist-linked groups in Syria, complemented by Turkey's medical services, oil sales (from Syria and Iraq) and military supplies.

Experts in counter-terrorism suggest the need to maintain strong credibility in counter-terrorism arguments. Alas, Iraq's usage of chemical

---

88 White House, *Address to a Joint Session of Congress and the American People*, cit.

89 Ibid.

90 David Zucchino, U.S. Military Stops Counting How Much of Afghanistan Is Controlled by Taliban, The New York Times, 1 May 2019, https://www.nytimes.com/2019/05/01/world/asia/us-afghanistan-territory-taliban.html

91 SIGAR, Special Inspector General For Afghanistan Reconstruction, 43d Quarterly Reports, https://www.sigar.mil/quarterlyreports/index.aspx?SSR=6, p.112 https://www.sigar.mil/pdf/quarterlyreports/2019-04-30qr-section3-governance.pdf

weapons – against the Iranians and the Iraqi Kurds, killing 45,000 since 1984[92] – went unpunished or even mentioned for almost two decades when the country was considered the West's ally. Nineteen years later, the US declared war on Iraq on the basis of its alleged possession of weapons of mass destruction, an allegation that was later disproved.

United States sanctions have had devastating consequences in Iraq, causing the death of hundreds of thousands of children.[93] For the US, in U.S. Secretary of State Madeline Albrights' words, it was 'worth it'. Years later, when the US army occupied Iraq, it again caused the death of additional hundreds of thousands of civilians.[94] Many Iraqis were put in jail without trail; some US jails in Iraq were identified as 'Jihadi universities'.[95] US Major General Douglas Stone, a prison commander in Iraq, said about the Mujahedeen: 'If you were looking to build an army, prison is the perfect place to do it. We gave them health care, dental care, fed them, and most importantly, we kept them from getting killed in combat.'[96]

The war on Iraq was not decided overnight: retired 4-star US Army General Wesley Clark, Supreme Allied Commander of NATO during the 1999 war on Yugoslavia, explained that the US forces were planning to 'take out seven countries in five years, starting with Iraq, and then Syria, Lebanon, Libya, Somalia, Sudan and, finishing off, Iran', because the US has 'a good military' and 'can take down governments'. He confirmed that he was told no WMD in Iraq or links to al-Qaeda had been found.[97]

---

92 Seth Carus, 'Chemical Weapons in the Middle East', in *The Washington Institute Policy Focus*, No. 9 (December 1988), p. 4, https://washin.st/2VhciIY.

93 Sheldon Richman, 'Iraqi Sanctions: Were They Worth It?', in *Global Policy Forum*, January 2004, https://www.globalpolicy.org/component/content/article/41952.html.

94 Kerry Sheridan, 'Iraq Death Toll Reaches 500,000 Since Start of U.S.-Led Invasion, New Study Says', in *Huffington Post*, 15 October 2013, https://www.huffpost.com/entry/iraq-death-toll_n_4102855.

95 US Major General Douglas Stone, quoted in Alissa J. Rubin, 'U.S. Military Reforms Its Prisons in Iraq', in *The New York Times*, 1 June 2008, https://nyti.ms/2GzXVr5.

96 Michael Weiss and Hassan Hassan, *ISIS: Inside the Army of Terror*, 2nd edition, New York, Regan Arts, 2016, p. 85.

97 Amy Goodman, 'Gen. Wesley Clark Weighs Presidential Bid: "I Think About It Every Day"', in *Democracy Now!*, 2 March 2007, https://www.democracynow.org/2007/3/2/gen_wesley_clark_weighs_presidential_bid.

On the other hand, President Obama said he was at war with al-Qaeda and its terrorist affiliates who support attacks against the United States, its allies and partners.[98] But for six months, the US took part in a military campaign and air bombardment against Yemen, not against al-Qaeda. This terrorist group in the Arabian Peninsula became stronger than ever, controlling cities, more territories and a direct access to the sea. In Syria, the US trained and armed hundreds of Syrian rebels who joined, with their US weapons, al-Qaeda and its allies.

To date neither ISIS nor al-Qaeda have pursued the destruction of the United States of America, but they have made public appeals for the withdrawal of US troops from the Middle East. ISIS encourages 'lone wolves', like the San Bernardino attack,[99] after the US coalition bombarded its stronghold in Syria. It should have left the task to the Syrian and Iraqi governments who are well positioned and the most concerned about fighting these terrorists on their respective territories. If defeat of the terrorist groups was the priority, the US and their European partners would have been better off supporting the central government in each country to fight their own domestic war.

A robust counter-argument to offer to the Muslim community for validation in Europe is to recognize the wrongdoing and ill-conceived policies carried out by the United States and allies in the Middle East, and their killing of innocent people, to counter the terrorists' rhetoric that uses the West's denial of it in its recruiting propaganda. It is equally important to stand against Western public figures that define Muslims as 'rabid dogs'[100] or propose that Muslims carry a special form of ID.[101]

---

98 Toby Harnden, 'Barack Obama Declares the "War on Terror" Is Over', in *The Telegraph*, 27 May 2010, https://www.telegraph.co.uk/news/worldnews/barackobama/7772598/Barack-Obama-declares-the-War-on-Terror-is-over.html.

99 Homeland Security Committee, *Homeland Security Means Keeping Assault Weapons Off Our Streets*, 22 September 2016, https://homeland.house.gov/node/10783.

100 Alana Wise and Erin McPike, 'Republican Ben Carson Compares Syrian Refugees to "Rabid Dogs"', in *Reuters*, 20 November 2015, http://reut.rs/1Ojvd9K.

101 Alan Yuhas, 'Trump Won't Rule Out Special ID for Muslim Americans Noting Their Religion', in *The Guardian*, 20 November 2015, https://gu.com/p/4ecd3.

Fortunately, such demands are generally being rejected,[102] but this rejection needs to be amplified.

On the other hand, it is important that the public see images of ISIS defeated in its last strongholds in Iraq and Syria. Publicizing the testimony of ISIS militants and their humiliated families who walked hours across the desert to reach safety away from the Caliphate would be an effective counter-terrorism tactic. These militants can be heard denying responsibility for their deeds or expressing on camera how they were misguided and disappointed by their fate during the last years of ISIS rule.

4.3 Lessons learned from history

Terrorist behaviour clearly indicates they are pursuing something more important than life itself. They justify their acts in the name of divine authority and consider Muslims, non-Muslims and anyone who doesn't share the same ideology or who won't adopt their cause or accept their authority as an enemy. Therefore, combatting terrorism cannot be limited to physically hunting down individuals or groups. It is vital also to find proper counter-arguments to nullify the philosophy of hate[103] and undermine the specific online propaganda, able to worm its way into the minds of idle (and idealistic) youths.

The US and the West are facing terrorist organizations that have developed lethal tactics, striking at the heart of Western culture and capitalism.[104] In the twentieth century, the US has for the most part been

---

102 US Attorney General Loretta Lynch, quoted in Jonah Hicap, 'U.S. Attorney General Vows to Take Action Against "Anti-Muslim Rhetoric" That "Edges Toward Violence"', in *Christian Today*, 6 December 2015, https://www.christiantoday.com/article/u-s-attorney-general-vows-to-take-action-against-anti-muslim-rhetoric-that-edges-toward-violence/72654.htm.

103 Scott Shane, 'Saudis and Extremism: "Both the Arsonists and the Firefighters"', in *The New York Times*, 25 August 2016, https://nyti.ms/2bC0ln5.

104 Leon Trotsky, *The History of the Russian Revolution*, New York, Simon and Schuster, 1932, https://www.marxists.org/archive/trotsky/1930/hrr.

at war, though never on its own territory. Terrorist organizations have lately sought to respond to the US and Europe's presence, intervention and occupation of parts of Middle Eastern countries by striking them on their home ground and where they are present in the Middle East.

Using the latest communication technology, terrorists no longer need to travel, as they can recruit online and adhere to horizontal network organizations whose ideas and ideology recognize no borders. Furthermore, terrorists justify their strikes and fuel their propaganda by criticizing US foreign policies and intervention in the Middle East that are denying agency to the local population and creating more death, poverty and regime change.

Terrorists draw examples from over-militarized actions, overseas military bases, troop interventions, abusive drone strikes and killing of civilians in Yemen, Afghanistan, Syria, Iraq and Palestine to justify their cause of Jihad.

To what extent are Western decision-makers aware of the consequences of their foreign policies? Has the right international legislation and measures been adopted domestically and overseas to limit foreign intervention, thus effectively crippling or reducing the reasons and means for terrorism to recruit and expand?

It is important to emphasise that Middle Eastern wars are not sectarian conflicts between Sunni and Shia although they have been advertised as such. There were sectarian aspects to the war in Iraq, but sectarianism was not the primary reason behind this century's Middle Eastern wars. The largest number of victims of religious terrorist groups are Muslims in the first place and other minorities in the second place.

Terrorism doesn't have a religion. The New Zealand attack is one example of many of how terrorism can strike anywhere and anyone. The world is not facing a war between Islam and the West but between the agents of Western foreign intervention and those rejecting the US hegemony of the world. What the West calls terrorist attacks are often responses to the unfairness of US policy regarding Palestine and other victims of US acts of war meant to re-shape the region and create a New Middle East. If the West doesn't change its foreign policy and its manipulation of the destiny of other countries, we will indeed have to live with more and more terrorism.

When the US, with the support of some European countries, decides to intervene in the Middle East, all rules are ignored. The US imposes the rules of the jungle. Western forces use pretexts and unfounded justifications to land in the Middle East to occupy it. Many countries allowed their nationals to travel to Syria, when it became the most-favoured destination for those willing to join the jihad to topple President Bashar al-Assad – under the watchful eye of the US forces in Iraq who had full knowledge of ISIS plans for expansion.

ISIS became a colossal, wealthy group with 8 million inhabitants living under its black banner, to the point that it was not easy to remove its occupation of the large territory it was based on. That gave Russia, a superpower, the opportunity to intervene in Syria. With the presence of two superpowers, Russia and the US, the situation reached an unprecedented and a significantly dangerous level of friction where the two forces were walking on the edge of an abyss.

Moreover, thousands of US and coalition soldiers took up positions in north-east Syria without the permission of the central government, with the aim of helping to change the regime and without any alternative plan. The only anti-government rulers on the ground in Syria were ISIS and al-Qaeda. Today, with the defeat of ISIS, al-Qaeda remains the most powerful group among all the anti-government forces.

Governmental experts can proficiently dismantle extremists' mindsets and support counter-terrorists' arguments by promoting Muslims, mainly in mosques and Islamic centres, who wish to dispute and dismantle extremist ideas. Muslim communities are the most affected by terrorism and are the most motivated to fight ISIS; this group killed on an annual basis more people in Lebanon, Syria, Egypt, Libya, Nigeria and Iraq than all the victims of the US 9/11, London 7/7 and Paris attacks[105] put together. It is therefore necessary to invest in the Muslim communities that can identify and dismantle radical discourses

105 Ben Farmer, 'Who is Salah Abdeslam and Who Were the Paris Terrorists? Everything We Know About the Isil Attackers', in *The Telegraph*, 18 March 2016, https://www.telegraph.co.uk/news/worldnews/europe/france/11996120/Paris-attack-what-we-know-about-the-suspects.html.

that encourage Hijra (migration) to join ISIS or any terrorist group that can mushroom in the future.

Western intervention in the Middle East has created much damage, contributing to the radicalization of people and killing hundreds of thousands of innocents during the 'war on terror'. The United States has lost credibility in the region by the strengthening of terrorist groups, particularly in Yemen[106] and in Syria in order to support its allies' policy in the Middle East.

Accordingly, a radical change of strategy in the West's counter-terrorism approach is required. Superpower countries are allowing an insecure environment to expand in the Middle East, hence contributing to the creation of a perfect safe haven for terrorist groups. Non-state religious organizations proliferate in societies at war or marked by social insecurity, poverty and failure. There are many countries with a basic lack of security,[107] like Syria, Iraq, Somalia, Libya, Yemen, and more other states where terrorists are prominent due to lack of central-government control over the whole country. These countries live today in civil and political insecurity, which is fertile ground for the proliferation of terrorism.

The Middle East has become the domain for a struggle of dominance between the two superpowers, the USA and Russia. There is no place and little benefit for Europe to stand in the middle of the struggle or to take either side. The USA is not – geographically – as close to Europe as is the Middle East and its problems can easily spill over into the nearby continent. Therefore, it is time for the liberal countries of Europe to rethink their strategy and to adopt an independent approach in order to create a constructive foothold in the Middle Eastern region.

Liberal countries cannot allow themselves to match terrorist violations of human rights by violating them themselves: military

---

106 Elijah J. Magnier, The rich Al-Qaeda Is Winning The "Hearts and Minds" in Yemen, Introducing New Names, 4 March 2016. https://ejmagnier.com/2016/03/04/the-rich-al-qaeda-is-winning-the-hearts-and-the-minds-in-yemen-introducing-new-names/

107 Abu Bakr Naji, *The Management of Savagery. The Most Critical Stage Through Which the Umma Will Pass*, translated by William McCants, 23 May 2006, https://www.aldorar.net/2015/07/book-idart-twhsh-abu-bakr-naji-.html.

methods which take the lives of innocent people are theoretically and democratically undesirable, not just for reasons of principle, but because of their horrendous political consequences in these countries and the overturning of positive mainstream values and principles.

Moreover, counter-terrorism will not be best served by liberal democratic countries using military responses to change regimes; the pattern of military escalation is part of the problem. It may be best were the governments of countries where terrorists are operating be appropriately empowered to join the effort to cripple and degrade these organizations. Teamwork must not be limited to global unilateral methods; it is essential in local situations. There must be a joint effort to face this global threat, cut its financing, produce an effective counter-narrative, bring terrorists to justice and finally contain terrorism by constructing robust, literate societies with governments that can assure them basic infrastructure and protect basic human rights.

Arshin Adib-Moghaddam[1]

Chapter 5: Contra-Identity: Psycho-Nationalism after the 'Middle East'

5.1 'The Middle East' and its discontents

The Middle East is an invention. It was the US American naval officer Alfred T. Mahan who popularized the term, designating this area in West Asia and North Africa in an article published in the British *National Review* in 1902. The geographical delimitation catered to the strategic interest of the British Empire and thus focused upon Aden, India and the Persian Gulf area. Thereafter, the term 'Middle East' was used by the *Times* of London where part of Mahan's article was published. Subsequently, a *Times* correspondent by the name of Valentine Chirol published a series of articles focusing on the 'Middle Eastern Question', centring around India as the so-called 'crown jewel' of the British Empire. With shifting colonial and 'strategic interests', the delineation of the 'Middle East' changed as well: at the time when Winston Churchill was British Colonial Minister of Britain, the term referred to Bosporus and the borders of India, and when imperial interests shifted towards Egypt after the Second World War, Egypt itself was considered to be the centre of this 'Middle East'. Therefore, the imagined borders of this 'non-region' changed in accordance with the interests of external powers,

1 I would like to thank Professor Lorenzo Kamel for his helpful comments about this chapter.

that is Great Britain and, after the Second World War until very recently, the United States.[2]

Although the etymology of the term can be traced back even to antiquity when Roman historians referred to this so-called 'Middle East', the current map of the region largely emerged out of the break-up of imperial structures, that is, the Ottoman Empire and the Qajar Empire in Persia.[3] The two pivotal nodal points that have been repeatedly referred to in analyses of the map we are dealing with and which remains largely unaltered until today are firstly the 'Sykes–Picot zeitgeist' at the beginning of the twentieth century – the imperial 'lines in the sand' drawn by European strategists which effectively divided the Arab provinces of the Ottoman Empire outside of the Arabian peninsula into areas of future British and French control or influence and partitioned the whole of Syria and Iraq and a large part of southern Turkey. France's area corresponded to the future states of Syria and Lebanon and Britain's area to Iraq and Transjordan. France achieved direct control of the Mediterranean coastal regions and Britain gained the provinces of Basra and Baghdad in today's Iraq. In accordance with these rather arbitrary delineations, which are easily recognisable by the straight 'pseudo-borderlines' between newly constituted entities such as Syria, Iraq or Jordan, the new 'Middle East' was engineered.

The second event of historical importance is, of course, the Balfour Declaration of 1917 which refers to a letter from the United Kingdom's Foreign Secretary Arthur James Balfour to Baron Rothschild, a leader of the British-Jewish community, for transmission to the Zionist Federation of Great Britain and Ireland. The letter was incorporated into the peace treaty with the Ottoman Empire and gave impetus to the creation of the state of Israel within the British mandate in Palestine. The analytical bottom line of the previous paragraphs is that the contemporary regional system, so Eurocentrically termed 'the Middle East', came about within a

---

2 Arshin Adib-Moghaddam, *A Metahistory of the Clash of Civilisations. Us and Them Beyond Orientalism*, London, Hurst, 2011, p. 5.

3 For a deeper analysis of the term 'Middle East' see Lorenzo Kamel, *The Middle East from Empire to Sealed Identities*, Edinburgh, Edinburgh University Press, 2019, pp. 31–3.

period of imperial hegemony which necessitated the invention of nation-state boundaries and their corresponding identities in a way that had never occurred before in that area of the world. This region was ordered for hundreds of years in accordance with confessional sovereignties and legitimacy steeped in religious thought systems: Sunni Islam in the Ottoman Empire, Shia Islam in Iran, at least since the Safavid Dynasty which was established in 1501. In the absence of organic nation-state structures, 'national identity' became a violently contested issue, as nationalism is always also dependent on the definition of self and other (foreign policy becomes central exactly because it regulates the relationship between the internal boundary and the external, the realm beyond the self).

The arbitrary creation of this 'Middle East' constituted by imperial interest, rather than strategic viability, gave impetus to a 'post-colonial' identity dilemma which haunts the region until today. Apart from the cases of Israel, Iran and Turkey where there was a better scope to delineate 'the nation', national identity was a scarce resource exactly because the Arab states that emerged out of the Ottoman Empire did not exist in this shape and form at any time in human history. Being Jordanian, Iraqi or Syrian had to be engineered and different types of 'psycho-nationalisms' were created to that end.[4]

This post-colonial identity dilemma manifests itself in the repeated challenge to – and erosion of – state sovereignties for instance by transnational ideologies: pan-Arabism at the time of Nasser especially in the late 1950s and 1960s or pan-Islamism throughout the period after the ending of the caliphate in 1921. Some of the crisis occurring in the region today, the implosion of Syria, the confessional and ethnic strife in Iraq or the Kurdish question for Turkey, can be explained by this apparent inadequacy of the 'nation-state' as we know it to institutionalize a national identity that is flexible enough to accommodate the widest constituencies in support of the legitimacy of the state. Psycho-nationalisms carried forward by the military strata of society, which had the easiest recourse to weapons and to the budget of the state, were quite natural answers to the

4 Arshin Adib-Moghaddam, *Psycho-nationalism. Global Thought, Iranian Imaginations*, Cambridge, Cambridge University Press, 2018.

governance dilemma that was compounded if not constituted by the lack of an organically growing bureaucracy and institutional infrastructure that could carry the meaning of the nation in the first place. The Ba'thist states in Syria and Iraq or the deep state in Egypt are typical examples for a form of militarized governance that sheds its light onto the region until today.

5.2 Psycho-nationalism explained

I have argued that in the absence of institutional and administrative structures to govern, the post-colonial states of the Arab world, even after nominal independence in the 1950s, experimented with radical forms of nationalism that were ideological and not pluralistic. All governments use a range of national narratives imbued with emotional vigour and tantalizing myths. The point is that in the familial language of (psycho-)nationalism, in the Arab world and elsewhere, the nation is routinely represented almost like an irresistible muse, a siren song with distinctly emotional undertones. 'God bless America', 'Roma o morte' as Italian psycho-nationalists proclaimed or Gamal Abdel Nasser's repeated references to the greatness of the Arab nation – the target of such phrases is our state of mind and our emotions. My term psycho-nationalism derives from such psychological manipulation. Government, the media, social networking sites such as Twitter and Facebook, even popular culture in the form of soap operas and music have emerged as the primary carriers of the symbols of this emotive discourse. The target of these subtle yet indelible forms of political manipulation is our mind and our emotional habitat.

At the same time, the state hovers over a complex system in which psycho-nationalist narratives are moulded and implemented. Hence it claims the *Gewaltmonopol*, which was famously defined by the German sociologist Max Weber as the monopoly of the legitimate use of physical force within a given territory. So if 'romantic' persuasion is not enough, if the siren song of the nation fails to entice, the nation-state can be enforced through violence, brute if necessary. You can be beaten into submission. There are important differences in the ways in which state violence is implemented against assertive dissenters, but governments routinely crush opposition in the name of the nation and in West Asia and North Africa such state violence has repeatedly been particularly endemic. In most countries of the 'West', this systematic power of the state is professionally and meticulously applied through the intense machinery of laws, norms and regulations. If these strategies are not enough to deter a revolt, the state in Europe and North America as well uses violence through its security forces, police, the military, and so on. This latter form of state power is rather more prevalent in West Asia and North Africa as indicated, but it lingers behind the liberal facade of the state all over the world.

While the Italian philosopher Giorgio Agamben does not depart from a firmly Eurocentric universe, his analysis of the 'state of exception' is a viable tool to conceptualize this violence of state sovereignty.[5] The state allows itself to suppress. Thus, our lives are determined by this nation-state, whether we like it or not. From provisions for housing, university fees and food to war and peace, the nation-state continues to be a major factor in the lives of its citizens all over the world. In many ways the nation-state is more consequential in our lives than our parents. It 'stalks' us all the way to our living rooms, regulating everything from TV programmes and mortgage applications to schooling issues. Indeed, with the rapid advancement of artificial intelligence, this type of human management is even more effective and pervasive, resembling an automated form of techno-politics. If this regulatory bio-power, which always also includes surveillance of the body and the mind, is not checked properly by civil society it threatens to turn into a form of arbitrary techno-tyranny.

Therefore, this chapter takes seriously the power of the nation-state and modes of resistance to it. I will attempt to dislocate some of the debates on nationalism by investigating several 'sites' where 'psycho-nationalist' dynamics appear. I will keep a close eye on 'new', avant-garde disciplines

---

5 See further Giorgio Agamben, *State of Exception*, Chicago, University of Chicago Press, 2005.

such as global thought, global history and comparative philosophies, and my evidence is primarily discussed in terms of concepts and political ideas, what I have called 'psycho-nationalism' in particular, and not so much in terms of empirical case studies which go beyond the confines of this analysis.[6]

Nationalist thinking in Turkey, Israel, Iran and the Arab world has been controversially discussed from various angles. Generally speaking, mainstream social science research in Europe and North America tends to locate the emergence of 'modern' nationalism in the so-called 'West'. In a rather less Eurocentric study of this issue, it is observed that the 'West' saw nationalism as the 'quintessential expression of inclusive tolerance. And this image was then often reinforced by a distinction between the West's "civic" nationalism and illiberal "ethnic" nationalism'.[7] In typical 'Orientalist', the non-Western world was juxtaposed to this self-image in a strict binary: 'As the central organizing principle of modern politics, nationalism was thus dichotomized between a noble Western invention and an ignoble non-Western imitation'.[8] In this way, nationalism was claimed as a particularly 'Western' invention and stripped off its global genealogy.

While there is overlap due to the intense dialectic between the global 'East' and the so-called 'West' during the colonial period which created common Euro-Asian spaces, it is principally erroneous to reduce the emergence of nationalism to European ideas. The concept of an organized community is central to the canons of eastern philosophy and its *belles lettres*. The Muslim philosopher Ibn Khaldun (d. 1406), for instance, redefined '*asabiyya*' (social solidarity) from its pre-Islamic origin and Quranic legacy, in the first systematic sociological conceptualization of a polity, in his famous *Muqaddimah* (Introduction to history), as early as in 1377 AD. Ibn Khaldun followed the line of classical philosophers of the Muslim enlightenment, such as Ibn Arabi, Abu Nasr Farabi,

---

6 This subsection draws from Arshin Adib-Moghaddam, *Psycho-nationalism*, cit., pp. 26–34.

7 Anthony W. Marx, *Faith in Nation. Exclusionary Origins of Nationalism*, Oxford, Oxford University Press, 2003, p. vii.

8 Ibid., p. viii.

Omar Khayyam, Razi, Ibn Sina (Avicenna) and Ibn Rushd (Averroes). Comparable to their ideas, he was a distinctly original and cosmopolitan thinker for his period who took full advantage of the scholarly currents at this intellectually rich juncture of global history. Despite rather sloppy references to 'negroes' whom Ibn Khaldun deemed emotional and excitable and outdated links between environmental factors and levels of civilization that would be deemed racist in our current understanding, the core of Khaldun's theories offers an inclusive conceptualization of a social community based on research (however inadequate), rather than ideology or some aggressive imperial impulse. Khaldun was no Ernest Renan, who lent his limited knowledge about the region to French imperial strategists due to his conviction that the Orient had to be civilized. This rather less 'ideological' approach of Khaldun comes out in his depiction of the non-Arab 'other', in this case the 'Persians':

> Thus, the founders of grammar were Sîbawayh and, after him, al-Fârisî and az-Zajjâj. All of them were of non-Arab (Persian) descent. [...] They invented the rules of (grammar) [...]. Most of the [great jurists] were Persians [...]. Only the Persians engaged in the task of preserving knowledge and writing systematic scholarly works. Thus, the truth of the following statement by the prophet becomes apparent: 'If scholarship hung suspended in the highest parts of heaven, the Persians would attain it.' [...] The intellectual sciences were then the special preserve of non-Arabs [the Persians], left alone by the Arabs, who did not cultivate them. This situation continued in the cities as long as the Persians and Persian countries, the 'Irâq, Khurâsân and Transoxania, retained their sedentary culture.[9]

According to Khaldun, *asabiyya* (social solidarity) is an important factor in the cyclical rise and fall of civilizations and empires. From his perspective, good governance enhances the social solidarity of the community. Ideally, this socially constructed, politically administered consciousness would strengthen the community against external aggression and internal subversion. Here, Ibn Khaldun reveals himself as a theorist of state power and sovereignty. The more the state is able to foster this sense of tribal community and kinship, the more likely it is to survive the vicissitudes of history, which is a pre-requisite for legitimated

9 Ibn Khaldun, *The Muqaddimah: An Introduction to History, Vol. 1*, translated by Franz Rosenthal, Princeton, Princeton University Press, 1989, pp. 429–30.

rule. In a clear re-conceptualization of Aristotle's notion of *koinonia* (community), Khaldun emphasises the importance of social organization (or *ijtima*) for this dialectical interaction between state and society which appreciates the impact of the demos. Human social organization (*al-ijtima al-insani*) would be moulded by this ideal state in order to bring out the inherently civilized (*madani*) nature of the citizenry. Khaldun wrote during a period of internal division of the Muslim empire partially caused by external threats, which explains his emphasis on sovereignty and legitimacy. Whilst he had a clear interest in re-inscribing the authority of the state as a prophylaxis to internal divisions, he emphasised that no state can exist without fostering social cohesion amongst its citizenry. Hence, Khaldun shared this preoccupation about the social construction and maintenance of a community with European theorists of modernity, such as Emile Durkheim and Ernest Gellner:

> Both Ibn Khaldun and Ernest Gellner have developed persuasive theoretical models that challenge such views and place group solidarity at the heart of long-term social change. Moreover, their work demonstrates how difficult it is to generate and maintain cohesive networks of individuals over longer periods of time, and how changed social conditions profoundly affect patterns of group solidarity: while for Ibn Khaldun the opulent urban lifestyles inevitably corrode social cohesion built in the shared ascetic living of tribal warriors, for Gellner modernity forges a new form of solidarity built around the promise of continuous economic growth, moral equality and cultural homogeneity among citizens inhabiting their own nation-state.[10]

Even Ibn Khaldun's largely sober, contra-identitarian and research-led inquiries about world history were abused as tropes in psycho-nationalist narratives. This was not intended by this philosopher, of course. As discussed above, Ibn Khaldun was a complex thinker, whose concepts were nuanced and balanced. He did not have a dichotomous notion of self and other, or an aggressive manifesto for political action or racist identities. Racism, defined as a systematic designation of the other as 'sub-human' and hence worthy of being systematically subjugated and if necessary exterminated, did not develop as a biopolitical perversity in

---

10 Siniša Malešević, 'Where Does Group Solidarity Come From? Gellner and Ibn Khaldun Revisited', in *Thesis Eleven*, Vol. 129, No. 1, p. 97.

the Muslim world, exactly because the Quranic syntax never lent itself to a race-based ideology.

And yet, even Ibn Khaldun became a major reference point in the discourse of Arab psycho-nationalists, in particular at the beginning of the twentieth century when Arab (psycho-) nationalism was sponsored by British and French imperial strategists as a means to weaken the Ottoman Empire – the Lawrence of Arabia effect if you like.[11] For instance, in the voluminous writings of Sati Al-Husri (1882–1962), the Ottoman-Syrian nationalists whose ideas became a pillar of Ba'thist ideology, Ibn Khaldun appears as a purveyor of Arab nationalism. Al-Husri borrowed generously from the German romanticists, von Ranke and Fichte, in his reinvention of Khaldun as an Arab nationalist. In typically psycho-nationalist fashion, he reinterpreted *asabiyya* as a spiritual bond among the members of a nation which is defined in terms of language and a shared memory or historical consciousness. According to this view, there is a metaphysical kinship between society and the nation.

In al-Husri (and Michel Aflaq), we find all the ingredients characteristic of psycho-nationalism that I have indicated with admittedly abstract brush strokes so far: the nation is represented as the protective mother that Arabs need to honour and sacrifice for; love for the nation entices the individual to unite and fight for a better, utopian tomorrow; nationalism motivates 'just' struggles and revolts; politics is configured as an arena of blood, sacrifice and honour; passion is presented as a potent psycho-cognitive force with an ideological edge.[12] This amounts to the deification of the in-group which always also incubates the discrimination of 'others' who are deemed or designated, in this case, 'non-Arab'. In the words of al-Husri: 'We must remember that the nationalist idea enjoys a *self-motivating power*; it is a *driving impulse* to action and to struggle. When it *enters the mind* and dominates the soul, it is one of the *motive*

11 See further Nurullah Ardıç, 'Genealogy or *Asabiyya?* Ibn Khaldun between Arab Nationalism and the Ottoman Caliphate', in *Journal of Near Eastern Studies*, Vol. 71, No. 2 (October 2012), pp. 315–24.

12 See further Bassam Tibi, *Arab Nationalism. Between Islam and the Nation-State*, 3rd edition, Basingstoke/London, Macmillan, 1997.

ideas [...] which *awaken* the people and inspire them to sacrifice'.[13] The psychological elements are obvious here and they are far removed from anything Ibn Khaldun had to say about politics in general and *asabiyya* in particular. Al-Husri is clearly constructing a psychologized narrative – an ideological straight-jacket, designed with anthropomorphic language, which is geared to create an anatomy of his idea of an Arab super-state. In a final ideological stroke which links his psycho-nationalism to the idea of a nation-state, al-Husri says: 'When the language became the heart and spirit of the nation, then the people who spoke one language possessed one heart and a common spirit and therefore formed a nation. It then became necessary that they create one state'.[14] Ibn-Khaldun would have smiled at such a hysterical and anti-philosophical definition of a nation. As a philosopher his ideas lacked ideological venom.

If Ibn Khaldun is one of the forerunners of the idea of community, then Ferdowsi must be recognized as one of the icons of the eastern *belles lettres*. A supremely gifted poet, Ferdowsi finished the millennial book of kings in 1010 AD. Unfortunately, there is a real lack of studies in comparative political theory that would juxtapose thinkers in Iran and the Arab/Muslim world, which in itself is an obvious effect of and the rationale behind psycho-nationalist division strategies. But like Ibn Khaldun, Ferdowsi was concerned with society, politics, community, the rise and fall of empires, and so on. While this ambition was similar, the approach of Ferdowsi was different. Ibn Khaldun spoke as a social scientist; Ferdowsi used the language of romance characteristic of a Persian literati. Accordingly, the *Shahnameh* charts the history of Persia from pre-Islamic kingdoms to the Muslim conquest in the seventh century AD. From the perspective of European Orientalists, this emphasis on Iran's pre-Islamic heritage and his interest in using Persian (Farsi) as

---

13 Quoted in William L. Cleveland, *The Making of an Arab Nationalist. Ottomanism and Arabism in the Life and Thought of Sati' Al-Husri*, Princeton, Princeton University Press, 1971, p. 105, emphasis added.

14 Ibid., p. 105.

a literary medium was indicative of Ferdowsi's aversion to Arabs and Islam in general.[15]

Orientalist themes played a major role in turning the *Shahnameh* into a psycho-nationalist trope for Iran's nascent dynasties in the nineteenth and twentieth century. Furthermore, Persian-language journals such as *Kaveh* and *Iranshahr*, which were published in Berlin by a group of influential Iranian intellectuals with a nationalist conviction, presented Ferdowsi as an icon of a unique and distinctive Iranian national identity. At that time and certainly also today, exile compounded the search for authenticity, identity and other fertile ingredients for a psycho-nationalist reading of the nation. In particular Hassan Taqizadeh (1878–1969), the veteran activist of Iran's Constitutional Revolt who edited *Kaveh* between 1916–22, superimposed western Orientalism onto the legacy of Ferdowsi. Highly influenced in his reading of Ferdowsi by Theodor Höldeke's (1836–1930) *Das Iranische Nationalepos* (the Iranian national epic), Taqizadeh famously proclaimed that Iranians had to embrace everything European wholeheartedly.[16] It was this Europeanized Seyyed, in Iran's intellectual history, a lecturer at SOAS, University of London among other prominent institutions, who was instrumental in inventing the *shahnameh* as a source of Iranian national identity.[17] In true psycho-nationalist parlance, Taqizadeh argued that Ferdowsi was the one who 'spun Iranian history and the national story into a perfectly structured narrative, and by establishing this narrative he has created one of the causes of glory for the Iranian nation and has preserved the national story down until today'.[18] The invention of history is obvious here. Taqizadeh

---

15 See further Alireza Asgharzadeh, *Iran and the Challenge of Diversity. Islamic Fundamentalism, Aryanist Racism, and Democratic Struggles*, New York, Palgrave Macmillan, 2007.

16 See further Hamid Dabashi, *Post-Orientalism. Knowledge and Power in a Time of Terror*, London, Transaction Publishers, 2009.

17 See further Afshin Marashi, *Nationalizing Iran. Culture, Power, and the State, 1870–1940*, Seattle, University of Washington Press, 2008, p. 123–5.

18 Quoted in Afshin Marashi, 'The Nation's Poet: Ferdowsi and the Iranian National Imagination', in Touraj Atabaki (ed.), *Iran in the 20th Century. Historiography and Political Culture*, London, I.B. Tauris, 2009, p. 99. See also *Kaveh* (in Persian), new edition, No. 10 (3 October 1921), p. 12, http://digitale-sammlungen.ulb.uni-bonn.de/ulbbnioa/periodical/structure/3080123.

uses a distinctly emotive and modern language in order to present the *shahnameh* as a source of a purified national pride and consciousness. In this way, he is a psycho-nationalist par excellence and he should be read and understood in conjunction with Fichte, Herder, Mazzini, von-Ranke and others.[19]

Psycho-nationalism is always also intertwined with a political economy of truth making (or history writing). Undoubtedly, Ferdowsi was not indifferent to the politics of his day, not least because his livelihood was dependent on the patronage of the Ghaznavid court. As he concedes in the *shahnameh* itself: when the poet comes to the Shah, 'he cannot choose but sit before the throne'. Comparable to the tracts of Ibn Khaldun, there is a lot in the *shahnameh* about the conduct in politics, community relations, humanity, governance and identity centuries before scholars and poets in Western and Central Europe experimented with similar tropes. Yet it is central to my argument that the psycho-nationalist interpretations were superimposed. Neither Ibn Khaldun nor Ferdowsi advocated worshipping the state and the nation. The hysterical emphasis on romance and love with reference to national sentiments is a typically modern project. A global reading of such historical junctures demonstrates that eastern modernities produced their own pioneers of such psycho-nationalism. Iran is simply one example amongst many and Arab countries produced equally deceptive psycho-nationalist 'heroes'.[20]

Moreover, in Ferdowsi, the 'other' does not emerge as ultimately alien, discomforting and fundamentally different, as psycho-nationalists would have it. The *shahnameh* displays literary genius written in a cosmopolitan mode, rather typical for intellectuality in Iran which has had a very pronounced connection to global matters. The idea that the book presents a manifesto of purely Iranian origin, undiluted by the vicissitudes of history, and an ideological manifesto against everything non-Iranian, is a modern fallacy trumpeted primarily for political reasons.

---

19 Taqizadeh mingled with the 'Orientalists' of his day including A. J. Arberry and Walter Bruno Henning. He went on to chair several organizations in 'Iranian Studies'.

20 See further Jack Goody, *Renaissances. The One or the Many?*, Cambridge, Cambridge University Press, 2010.

It is true that Ferdowsi glorified what he imagined to be Iranian culture, but the *shahnameh* is rather more of a cultural festival than an ideological phalanx pointed against the non-Iranian world. As Dick Davies rightly points out in his extensive research about this subject: Ferdowsi also introduced what he considered to be non-Iranians who are portrayed in a positive light, such as women from all over Asia, in particular Sindokht, Rudabeh, Manizheh and Farigis. The only central female character who is portrayed in a negative light is Soudabeh, who is represented as the ultimate 'femme fatale' who tries to lie and cheat her way to her step-son Siyavash in order to seduce him. You and I may not deem this a great offence, but in accordance with the patriarchal reading of society characteristic of his period, Ferdowsi must have thought those rather bad character traits. The husband of Soudabeh, the King of Persia Kaykavoos, on the other side, is repeatedly portrayed as incompetent and reckless. In fact, all heroes of the *shahnameh* have a mixed lineage and are far from purely 'Iranian' or 'Aryan': the mother of the main protagonist, Rostam, is part Indian and part of demonic descent, and the mothers of the princes Siyavash and Esfandiyar come from Central Asia and Rum (the Christian West) respectively.

Divested of psycho-nationalist ideology, then, the *shahnameh* displays literal hybridity and aesthetic synergy rather than purity and difference. It narrates 'a society that embodies constant internal contradictions and conflicts; that has an extremely porous rather than simply oppositional relationship with surrounding cultures'.[21] The *shahnameh* shows social life in its heterogeneous manifestations. 'If there is a unity to be found in these tales it is a unity of diversity, of *dis*unity [...], rather than of a single geographic area, or of a single bloodline, or of a single tribe [...], or of a single religious tradition'.[22] Persian culture, Hamid Dabashi recently wrote, is imbued with global thought and world culture.[23] Conversely,

21 Dick Davies, 'Iran and Aniran: The Shaping of a Legend', in Abbas Amanat and Farzin Vejdani (eds), *Iran Facing Others. Identity Boundaries in a Historical Perspective*, New York, Palgrave Macmillan, 2012, pp. 46–7.

22 Ibid., p. 47.

23 See further Hamid Dabashi, *The World of Persian Literary Humanism*, Cambridge, Harvard University Press, 2012.

prominent doyens of 'Iranian Studies' such as Ehsan Yarshater are wrong to assume that 'Iranian identity is clearly asserted in the inscriptions of Darius the Great (522–486 B.C.), who as an Aryan and a Persian was fully conscious of his racial affiliation and proud of his national identity'.[24] It is problematic, typical and retroactive to assume that language carries identity, that Persian can ever be 'the chief carrier of the Persian world view and Persian cultures'.[25] Indeed, I would go one step further and add that imagining an 'original' Iran has been the cardinal sin of contemporary Iranian history. As we will continue to find out, several depictions of Iran (or 'Irans') have been invented in accordance with political currents. There is no original identity to Iran. Originality is the standard parody that psycho-nationalists routinely display, in Iran and elsewhere.

So the myths of a particularly Iranian or Persian identity were created within a historical context that was geared to psycho-nationalist currents, as demonstrated. Several studies have shown how in the twentieth century the *shahnameh* was re-invented as a source for Iran's psycho-nationalist project, which was intimately linked to imagining a nation ruled by a monarch represented by the Pahlavi dynasty. The *shahnameh* as a psycho-nationalist trope was meant to function for the Pahlavi monarchs in at least two ways: first, it was thought to be functional in linking their legitimacy to the emperors of pre-Islamic Persia, and second to emphasise Iran's difference to the 'Semitic' Arabs. From this perspective, Islam was deemed 'other' to Iran's 'true' identity which was invented as Aryan, closer to Europe, even France as the Shah argued in 1963 in an article for *Life* magazine. Hence, a *shahnameh* 'industry' emerged in Iran in the 1920s and 1930s, institutionalized in educational curricula in Iranian schools after the first Pahlavi monarch assumed power in 1925. Subsequently, building on ideas developed by Taqizadeh in the aforementioned Berlin-based journals *Kaveh* and *Iranshahr*, Reza Shah sponsored the newly established Society for National Monuments

---

24 Ehsan Yarshater, 'Persian Identity in Historical Perspective', in *Iranian Studies*, Vol. 26, Nos 1–2 (1993), p. 141.

25 Ibid., p. 142.

(*anjoman-e asar-e melli*) to build a mausoleum for Ferdowsi in Tus, located in north-eastern Iran.[26] The architecture of the mausoleum reflects its political utility: it was built in the Achaemenidian style perfectly in tune with the penchant of the Pahlavi dynasty for pre-Islamic Persian empires. Uniformity in discourse facilitated uniformity in culture, which subdued the mosaic, multicultural beauty of architectural designs in Iran. Furthermore, the *farvahar*, a Zoroastrian symbol central to the empire of Cyrus, satisfied the political quest to disassociate Iranian history and identity from Islam. Not entirely unlike the swastika which has been a prominent symbol in Hindu, Buddhist and Jainist religious folklore for millennia and which was then abused by the Nazis in Germany as a symbol for racial purity, the *farvahar* too travelled a long way from its neo-Assyrian habitat to Pahlavi Iran, where it was used as an emblem for Aryan/Persian purity.

5.3 Psycho-nationalism and conflict

The problem with the ideological underpinnings of psycho-nationalism is obvious: indulging in the glory of 'our' race or culture almost always entails the suppression of equal status for the race or culture that is represented as its *other*. West Asia and North Africa are no exception. Iranian and Arab identity politics thwarted, perverted and dismembered communitarian thinking for long periods in the twentieth century and the same applies to other forms of psycho-nationalism in Turkey and Israel. Today, some of the insidious legacies of psycho-nationalistic thinking are being resurrected throughout the region, certainly in the hysterical narratives of the Saudi Crown Prince Mohammad bin Salman who likened Iran to a Nazi state, to the detriment of symbiotic relations among the peoples of the region.

---

26 See further Afshin Marashi, 'The Nation's Poet', cit., pp. 93–111.

In Iran itself, psycho-nationalism was subdued as a part of the internationalism and emancipative message behind the revolution in 1979 which was hijacked and turned into a new discourse of hegemony constructed around a hybrid Shia-Persianized Islam that proclaimed a new form of ideological hysteria. And so psycho-nationalism survived and it is being actively resurrected as an expedient shortcut to gain the support of the resurgent bourgeoisie of Iranian society. Chauvinism against Arabs continues to guide the thinking of some Iranian commentators, especially in the Diaspora. The latent powers of deeply internalized ideological constructs, it seems, do not disappear upon the demise of states based on them. 'Persianism' nurtured by the Pahlavis has outlived, in a modified form, the emancipative and internationalist momentum triggered by the revolution in 1979.

These antecedents of Iranian psycho-nationalism can be traced back to the writings of late-nineteenth-century figures such as Mirza Fath Ali Akhunzadeh and Mirza Aqa Khan Kermani[27] and even before as I have argued elsewhere.[28] Demonstrating affinity with Orientalist views of the supremacy of the 'Indo-European peoples' and the mediocrity of the 'Semitic race', Iranian psycho-nationalist discourse idealized pre-Islamic Persian empires, whilst negating the 'Islamization' of Persia by Muslim forces. As I have argued above: Iranian psycho-nationalism had its heyday during the Pahlavi dynasty. The Shah's decadent celebration of 2,500 years of Iranian empire in Persepolis in 1971 and his decision to abandon the Islamic solar *hegra* calendar in favour of an imperial one exemplify this adherence to the idea of 'Persianism' and its anti-Islamic connotations.

By virtue of its psycho-nationalist ideology, Pahlavi Iran needed the 'Arab other' to essentialize the Iranian self. Distinguishing the 'Iranian-Aryan' in-group from the 'Arab-Semitic' out-group, political psychologists would point out, was achieved by emphasiing the

---

27 Arshin Adib-Moghaddam, 'Reflections on Arab and Iranian Ultra-Nationalism', in *MR Online*, 20 November 2006, https://mronline.org/2006/11/20/reflections-on-arab-and-iranian-ultra-nationalism.

28 Arshin Adib-Moghaddam, *Psycho-nationalism*, cit.

superiority of the pre-Islamic Iranian heritage and undervaluing the Muslim identity of the majority of Iranians. That failure to forge an inclusive identity was anathema to communitarian relations with Iran's neighbours. No wonder then that some Arab governments perceived the Shah's aggressive military build-up under the patronage of the United States, claims to Bahrain that were dropped only after a plebiscite in the sheikhdom voted against unification with Iran, and the seizure of half of the Abu Musa island from Sharjah and the Greater and Lesser Tunbs from Rais al-Khaimah in 1971 as part of a grand strategy to 'Iranianise' the area. This might not have been the Shah's ambition, but his adherence to a chauvinistic rhetoric gave all the wrong signals. Ultimately, it widened the gulf between the peoples of the region and inhibited the institutionalization of a functioning regional security architecture – a necessary endeavour that has not been implemented to this day.

The development of psycho-nationalism as a part of state conduct in the Iranian context was comparable, albeit not identical, to the ideological evolution of Arab psycho-nationalism. Whilst the Iranian variant during the Pahlavi era showed closed affinity with French notions of Indo-European supremacy most forcefully elucidated by Ernest Renan, the branch of Arab psycho-nationalism developed by al-Husri and institutionalized in the Ba'th (rebirth) party by Michel Aflaq was closer to the tradition of German romanticism. Following Johann G. von Herder's idea of a *Kulturnation*, that is, a cultural community transcending the confine of the state (the idea later developed by Johann Gottlieb Fichte), al-Husri, as we have established in the previous section, advocated the view that the 'Arab *umma*' was a cultural nation held together by a common national language and shared common folklore.

So, like Pahlavian psycho-nationalism, which developed insidiously racist narratives during periods of crisis, the Arab variant too gave birth to its own abominations. Nowhere was the process of psycho-nationalistic radicalization of Arabism more pronounced than in Saddam Hussein's Iraq where anti-Iranianism (next to anti-imperialism and anti-Semitism) became a central ideological pillar of the Ba'thist state. Pamphlets such as Khairallah Talfah's *Three Whom God Should Not Have Created: Persians,*

Jews and Flies, books such as *Ta'rikh al-hiqd al-Farsi 'ala al-'Arab* (The History of Persian Hatred of the Arabs), serials entitled *Judhur al-'ada al-Farsi li-l-umma al-'Arabiyya* (The Roots of Persian Hostility toward the Arab Nation) and proverbs such as *Ma hann a'jami 'ala 'Arabi* (An *ajam*, or Persian, will not have mercy on an Arab) repeatedly depicted Iranians as cruel and merciless, the ultimate bearers of *shu'ubyya* possessed by a 'destructive Persian mentality' (*aqliyya takhribiyya*). The myth was created that hatred towards Arabs was an integral part of the Persian character and that this racial attribute had not changed since the days of the Islamization of the Sassanian empire in the seventh century AD. No wonder then that Saddam Hussein ordered the establishment of the 'Arab Gulf Office' in 1977. By disseminating maps designating the Gulf as *Khaliji Basra* (the Gulf of Basra) or *al Khalij al-'Arabi* (the Arab Gulf), Saddam Hussein claimed a prominent role in the region, appealing to (Iraqi-centric) Arab nationalist sentiments with anti-Iranian precepts. Some of these racist sentiments towards Iranians continue to be easily discerned, especially in the pamphlets of terror movements such as ISIS or al-Qaeda.

The phenomenon of psycho-nationalist discourse in Iran and Iraq sketched here is an example of the invention of nations and nation-states examined by Ernest Gellner and Eric Hobsbawm among others. (Psycho-)nationalism was a means to mobilize the support of the populace and a symbol of legitimacy for the authoritarian regimes in power. In order to manufacture salient state identities, differences were accentuated and commonalities underplayed, hardening the invented self–other dichotomy between the peoples of the region, Iranians and Arabs, as well as Turks, Kurds and/or Israelis. At the peril of abstraction we can say that in all contexts, psycho-nationalism has served political ends that proved to be anathema to regional cohesion and harmony. For Iranian psycho-nationalists, representation of the 'Arab other' was perverted in order to herald Iran's distinctiveness and the country's 'natural' affinity with the 'West'. Arab psycho-nationalism, on the other hand, was invoked as a political strategy to exclude Iran from the arena of inter-Arab politics. The politics of identity, then, created a regional system imbued with insecurity and recurrent conflict.

5.4 After psycho-nationalism: Therapies for the future

In the lived reality of the peoples of the region and beyond, national narratives are never immutable; they are impure, creolized phenomena, porous and polluted spaces that are open to interpretive manipulation. In order to govern that reality, psycho-nationalisms are socially engineered to simulate uniformity and positive distinction from the 'other'. In this sense, psycho-nationalism is a border-creating device; it is meant to create 'iron walls' staffed by intolerant gatekeepers (for example, the planned wall between the United States and Mexico and the separation wall between Israel and the West Bank). In its traditional manifestation, psycho-nationalism provokes distinctly fascist politics. In Apartheid South Africa and in Israel among the right wing, it has informed policies of separation and oppression. And in continental Europe today, it is challenging the idea of the European Union in the name of an anti-immigration agenda – borders are re-staffed, barbed wire rolled out and fences are being put up. The resurgence of the politics of identity spearheaded by Geert Wilders and Marine Le Pen is a strong contemporary indicator of the dangers of psycho-nationalism. The so-called 'Left' is trapped in ideological controversy that merely proclaims a counter-identity, admittedly more optimistic, but without a great leap towards a politics of radical federal democracy that empowers citizens and communities rather than the central state.

And yet, as I have tried to demonstrate in *On the Arab Revolts and the Iranian Revolution*, any effort to separate the 'self' from the 'other' creates a very particular form of interdependence, a 'disjunctive synthesis' that does not yield neatly delineated identities.[29] Thus, representations of 'self' and 'other' are entirely interdependent even when they are geared towards antagonistic politics. The deeply dialectical history of this region and its hybrid ethnic and cultural make-up provides many historical examples for this reality. It is exactly because of this ancient hybridity that psycho-nationalism, even if in its most horrific manifestation, never

29 Arshin Adib-Moghaddam, *On the Arab Revolts and the Iranian Revolution. Power and Resistance Today*, London, Bloomsbury, 2013.

really subdued a common regional spirit and humanity amongst the majority of the people living in West Asia and North Africa. Iranians may have parodied seemingly divergent identities with their significant others – Arabs, Europeans, Americans – aimed at setting themselves apart as a separate and authentic 'nation', but their performative acts achieved the opposite. By allocating to the other side a prominent discursive presence, the interdependence between the national narratives suggesting 'an Iran' are now entirely dependent on the ideational territory presumed to be beyond those imagined confines. In other words, Iran's significant 'others' are now subsumed in the meaning of Iran. The same applies to the 'Arab' space which is entirely interspersed by its significant others: Turks, Iranians, even Israelis. Moreover, this creolized space is lived on a daily basis throughout the region in cosmopolitan centres such as Beirut, Doha, Dubai, Tehran or Istanbul. The lived reality in the region is a constant therapeutic antidote to the psycho-nationalism of the state, and within the right historical context it could be a panacea to the crisis of governance throughout the region. The Arab revolts, despite their limited success in terms of 'good governance' to date, were a beginning to that end.

It is true, as Asef Bayat argues, that daily 'anti-order' practices and activities such as setting up 'illegal' street businesses in main squares, squatting in public parks and tourist hubs or challenging moral sensitiveness through provocative dress, have always been part and parcel of public life in the region and beyond.[30] But these 'non-movements' are decisively morphed into a political upheaval during revolts exactly because the anarchic, daily actions that questioned public order are suddenly coordinated and enriched with political symbols and imagery that promise a better future for the people. Under the pressure of such an event, daily routines that rupture public order transform into active detachment from the demands of the state: the street vendor marches to the public square to demonstrate; the squatters set up camps with the help of organized student movements; and housewives sabotage infrastructure as a part of a grand strategy to overcome the oppression of society.

30 See further Asef Bayat, *Life as Politics: How Ordinary People Change the Middle East*, Stanford, Stanford University Press, 2010, p. 77 ff.

In other words, daily dissent transmutes into a revolt with transversal capability that challenges both established norms within society (horizontal movement) and the truth conditions held up by the state and the normative order of the international system (vertical movement). The revolts in Tunisia and Egypt which heralded the 'Arab Spring', despite the subsequent disappointments, were exactly multi-dimensional in this sense. As the Lebanese political theorist Ali Harb correctly argues in an important book published in Beirut: these uprisings comprised civil, political, economic, technical and ethical realms and engendered an irresistible momentum that was both Arab and global.[31]

Second, until Tunisia and Egypt erupted, the dominant narrative was that Arab and Muslim societies are beset by radicalism and that al-Qaeda is a viable political force. In the twenty-first century, the fight against 'Muslim radicalism' (or what Bernard Lewis infamously called 'Muslim rage') has seen huge resources allocated to the wars in Iraq and Afghanistan; to the regime-change strategy in Iran, Lebanon and Gaza; and to huge military budgets and many national-security papers.[32] With the Arab revolts, a deep transformation exposed the failures and follies of this approach. The uprisings in the Arab world and beyond were a key agent of this process of renewal. Perhaps for the first time since the violent rupture of colonialism, the range of discourses signifying the meaning of resistance in the region were geared towards universal aspirations for freedom and democracy. Today then, 'Arab' and 'Muslim' societies are equipping themselves with a political language that could institutionalize those norms systematically and for the long run. These are the antidotes to psycho-nationalism that continue to permeate the civil societies in the region. They proved to be exemplary for other resistance movements in Europe and North America, such as the Occupy Wall Street Movement and the anti-austerity demonstrations throughout

---

31 See further Ali Harb, *Soft Power Revolutions in the Arab World. The Deconstruction of Dictatorships and Fundamentalisms* (in Arabic), Beirut, Al Dar Al Arabiya Liloloum Publishers, 2011.

32 Who would doubt that a weakened Saddam Hussein would have been swept away by the Arab revolt without the death of hundreds of thousands of Iraqis and the displacement of millions?

Europe which were modelled after the methods of political organization in Tunisia and Egypt.

As a way of summarizing my argument: in today's ideational tapestry in West Asia and elsewhere, there is quite literally no intellectual and geographic space that imagined communities such as Jews, Turks, Iranians, Palestinians, Arabs, Christians, Muslims, Copts, Kurds might claim for themselves in total independence from the neighbour even if psycho-nationalism simulates such divisions. In the nomadic, intimately interconnected and interdependent spaces of West Asia and North Africa, the neighbour is immanent to the self; waging war against her is always also an act of self-mutilation. This is particularly apparent in the Israeli–Palestinian dialectic, but it is equally apparent in the failed efforts to delineate Arab, Turks and Iranians, beyond matters of citizenship. The twenty-first-century reality is that peace cannot be safeguarded on a national or 'civilizational' basis, and that the rational option is to make a viable neighbour policy a priority. What is needed is more intellectual engagement, cultural diplomacy and scholarly exchanges that bring out the truth about the obvious commonalities of the peoples of this region. The global security threats that we are facing, in particular the scourge of global terror in the name of religion or race, require a strategy that moves beyond notions of territoriality and psycho-nationalist cohesion and embraces as far as possible a contra-identarian and humanistic approach to human affairs. To these ends, emphasizing and then moving beyond the linkages between 'us' and 'them' rather than any supposed opposition is not only vital to combat globalized forms of terrorism, but also essential to finally start thinking about a security architecture in West Asia and North Africa. Both a new generation with a global mindset and members of minorities expressing ideas from outside the mainstream are well placed to contribute to this process. In many ways they are proof that for a long time, and without realizing it, we have been living in the end times of the 'West' and the 'East', the Orient and the Occident or the myths of national 'origin' invented by angry and hysterical ideologues all over the world. It's time to cast psycho-nationalisms aside, all the better to live at peace with who we truly are, which is a reflection of our neighbours.

Abdullah Al-Arian

Chapter 6: Islamists and the Arab Counter-Revolutions

In one of his first interviews with a Western media outlet since assuming the presidency of Egypt, Abdel Fattah al-Sisi, the field marshal who overthrew Egypt's first ever democratically elected president, warned *Time* magazine that the crisis of militant extremism as posed by the Islamic State of Iraq and Syria (ISIS) represented a threat to the Arab region at large. Speaking in 2014, Sisi justified the Egyptian military's violent intervention in the country's nascent post-authoritarian transition as a force for stability, boasting, 'If we hadn't saved Egypt, there would have been a major problem created'.[1] Noting that although many Egyptians had expressed misgivings about the resurgent authoritarianism that followed the 3 July 2013 coup, a *New York Times* journalist later reported that 'A catchphrase has become popular here: "At least we are not Syria or Iraq".'[2]

As Western policymakers and commentators continue to grapple with the question of regional insecurity in the Middle East over the course of the past decade, a narrative has taken form that maintains that the popular uprisings launched in late 2010 paved the way for widespread insecurity whose sole remedy was a return to authoritarianism. According to this analysis, the uprisings were deemed to have unearthed a number of longstanding divisions within Arab societies, with destructive consequences for individual states and the region at large. Divisions across social class, religious practice, sectarian identification, regional affiliation and national identity all emerged as perceptible fault lines in

1 Bryan Walsh, 'After the Revolution: Sitting Down with Egyptian President Abdul Fattah al-Sisi', in *Time*, 24 September 2014, http://time.com/3426794.

2 David D. Kirkpatrick, 'As Egyptians Grasp for Stability, Sisi Fortifies His Presidency', in *The New York Times*, 7 October 2014, https://nyti.ms/1xnbDAB.

the challenges to a deep-seated political order. Of those, the challenge of political Islam as an agent for possible systemic change appeared to activate the fiercest response on the part of counter-revolutionary forces, often leading to an escalation of political conflict. The conceptualization of a so-called 'Islamist winter' that succeeded the Arab Spring revolutions shifted the discourse from framing the conflict as one between popular forces for freedom and democratization and those of repression and authoritarianism, to one between religious fanaticism and the forces of stability.[3]

This chapter seeks to problematize the question of regional insecurity, electing to explore it through the prism of the conflict between the forces of political Islam and those of the Arab counter-revolutions. While Islamist movements were by no means the sole or even primary actors in the initial launch of popular mobilizations, as the most organized force of political opposition and the focal point of the subsequent counter-revolutionary wave, they offer a particularly useful lens through which to question some of the basic assumptions surrounding the causes of regional insecurity. The sections that follow dissect this conflict largely through deconstructing some faulty binaries that commentators have employed in their discussions of recent developments. The most salient of these are the 'religion vs secularism', 'stability vs instability' and 'violence vs non-violence' binaries that appear to colour nearly every discussion surrounding contemporary political events in the Arab region. Ultimately, this chapter contends that discussions around regional instability that make use of these frames are fundamentally flawed and tend to reflect the hegemonic discourses advanced by local authoritarian rulers, regional powers and their international backers.

---

3 For examples of discussions of the 'Islamist winter', see Feisal G. Mohamed, 'Has the Islamist Winter Killed the Arab Spring?', in *Dissent Magazine*, 6 December 2011, https://www.dissentmagazine.org/?p=24256. See also Michael J. Totten, David Shenker and Hussain Abdul-Hussain, 'Arab Spring or Islamist Winter? Three Views', in *World Affairs*, Vol. 174, No. 5 (January/February 2012), pp. 23–42; and James Phillips, 'The Arab Spring Descends into Islamist Winter: Implications for U.S. Policy', in *Heritage Foundation Backgrounders*, 20 December 2012, https://www.heritage.org/node/12035.

6.1 Countering revolutions

In order to address this question properly, it is first worthwhile to posit a few preliminary observations related to the conceptualization of the various actors and the phenomenon being studied. In examining the role of Islamist movements in the political developments of the last decade, this study refers to movements advocating for an Islamically oriented political order within the framework of the existing nation-state structures. This primarily includes organizations such as the Muslim Brotherhood, founded in Egypt during the first half of the twentieth century and which then expanded to other parts of the Arab region in the years since. Although the Muslim Brotherhood's various chapters have maintained some links over the course of the movement's development, its branches are independent actors operating within a decidedly national context. In that regard, it is worth emphasising that the Egyptian Muslim Brotherhood developed quite uniquely from the Syrian, Libyan, Tunisian and Yemeni branches of the organization. Moreover, the emergence of a strong Salafi trend across various contexts in the Arab region since the 1970s has added a further layer of diversity and pluralization of Islamist activism, which became increasingly apparent in the immediate political contestation that resulted from the fall of authoritarian rulers since early 2011.

Beginning in the late 1990s, some scholars referred to the political evolution of these movements in the context of 'post-Islamism'. As Asef Bayat defined it, post-Islamism 'represents an endeavour to fuse religiosity and rights, faith and freedom, Islam and liberty. It is an attempt to turn the underlying principles of Islamism on its head by emphasizing rights instead of duties, plurality in place of a singular authoritative voice, historicity rather than fixed scriptures, and the future instead of the past'.[4] Regardless of the choice of label, the qualitative shift exhibited by these movements over time became most perceptible in the wake of the political openings offered by the prospects for a post-authoritarian

---

4 Asef Bayat, 'What Is Post-Islamism?', in *ISIM Review*, No. 16 (Autumn 2005), p. 5, http://hdl.handle.net/1887/17030.

transition to democratic forms of governance. At the height of the Arab uprisings, Islamist political parties put forward pluralistic platforms meant to embed them within existing political structures rather than the establishment of new ones. In that respect, these groups were hardly the revolutionary forces they were quite often made out to be. As Bayat later noted, the mobilization of Islamists during the Arab uprisings was more aptly described as 'refo-lutions', due to their preference for reforming existing institutions.[5] Meanwhile, trends that manifested as militant movements seeking to overthrow the prevailing political order, such as al-Qaeda and the Islamic State, exist on the opposite end of the ideological spectrum of Islamism, and therefore operate as external factors in the competition between forces for political change and those striving to maintain the status quo.

The counter-revolutionary wave that formed in response to the events of the Arab uprising referred initially to elements within existing regimes that demonstrated considerable resilience against the popular mobilizations.[6] In what was frequently labelled as 'the deep state', entrenched institutions, particularly intelligence and security agencies, utilized their wealth of power and experience to counteract any fundamental changes to the reigning political order.[7] Over time, however, descriptions of the counter-revolution incorporated the role of regional powers, such as the governments of Saudi Arabia and the United Arab Emirates, along with their local proxies in countries such as Egypt, Yemen and Libya, who aimed to preserve as many elements of the authoritarian status quo as possible.[8] Provided that these figures and institutions enlisted in the broader agenda for the region, they received significant logistical, diplomatic and financial support from

5 Asef Bayat, 'Paradoxes of Arab Refo-lutions', in Bassam Haddad, Rosie Bsheer and Ziad Abu-Rish (eds), *The Dawn of the Arab Uprisings. End of an Old Order?*, New York, Pluto Press, 2012, pp. 28–32.

6 Hussein Agha and Robert Malley, 'The Arab Counterrevolution', in *The New York Review of Books*, 29 September 2011.

7 Jean-Pierre Filiu, *From Deep State to Islamic State. The Arab Counterrevolution and Its Jihadi Legacy*, London, Hurst, 2015.

8 David Hearst, 'July 3: The End of One Revolution and the Start of Another', in *Middle East Eye*, 6 July 2017, https://www.middleeasteye.net/node/64551.

these governments in the service of upending the possibilities for a post-authoritarian transition. Quite often, forces such as those of Field Marshal Khalifa Haftar in Libya or President Abdrabbuh Mansur Hadi in Yemen, along with Sisi in Egypt, set their sights on Islamist groups as their primary target in attempting to return the country to a state of repressive authoritarianism, receiving generous backing from Gulf regimes in the process. By painting all Islamist actors as terrorist, then proceeding to conflate them with the broader revolutionary movements, these counter-revolutionary forces managed to pursue their larger goal of not only eradicating the Islamist opposition, but also of silencing all expressions for structural change.

6.2 Approaching the Arab uprisings

Another point of contention that has inhibited proper analysis of the issue at hand relates to the question of periodization. The conventional wisdom among many scholars and commentators writing in the current moment appears to classify this as a 'post-Arab Spring' era.[9] However, a historical view that accounts for the ways in which events unfold over longer stretches of time would caution against moving on from the events of the Arab uprisings. Although they have witnessed a series of different phases, the developments that began with the popular mobilizations have not ended. Whatever one may want to conclude about the supposed end of the brief era of mass mobilization (at times quite a bloody end at that) it does not serve our analysis to classify the current moment as an entirely new era. In fact, most of the current developments unfolding in the region, from the renewed authoritarianism in Egypt, and the combination of civil and proxy wars in Libya, Syria and Yemen, to the

---

9 See, for example, Marc Lynch, 'After the Arab Spring: How the Media Trashed the Transitions', in *Journal of Democracy*, Vol. 26, No. 4 (October 2015), pp. 90–9, https://www.journalofdemocracy.org/wp-content/uploads/2015/10/Lynch-26-4.pdf.

rise of a new mode of political authority in Saudi Arabia, are all the direct outcomes of the uprisings and continue to be informed by their most salient features. As Alain Gabon has noted, the particularly violent response by despotic rulers 'which surpasses everything we saw before 2011, gives the measure of their fragility'.[10]

Taking the long view, then, would allow us not only to contextualize these contemporary developments more deeply, but also allows for the possibility that mass mobilization as an expression of popular will has by no means ended in light of the resurgent forces of authoritarianism. Hence, what we have witnessed unfolding in Jordan, Sudan and Algeria during the last two years in terms of mass protests cannot be separated from these broader developments. Nor can we dismiss the continued mobilization of populations in traditional sites of protest that have endured an authoritarian resurgence such as Egypt, though as Gabon points out, that mobilization occurs "on a smaller scale and in localized, less spectacular, and in different forms'.[11]

Beyond the question of periodization, there also exists a need for greater conceptual clarity in studying the Arab uprisings. In their initial days, the uprisings were treated as a common phenomenon and conceptualized as a single unit of analysis. The 'Arab Spring' as a whole became an object of study, one that rose and fell as a single unit, without much care for the vast differences across various national contexts. The commonalities were usually emphasised at the expense of the differences. Even when the events were broken down on the basis of the roles of certain actors (for instance, the military, intelligence services, oligarch class, Islamist movements, workers, revolutionary youth, and so on), there was a tendency to try and bridge the divisions across all Arab states experiencing these developments, rather than locate the inherent differences among them. It was only in the later years of these events, as we began to witness radically different outcomes in places like Egypt, Syria, Tunisia, Libya, Bahrain and Yemen, that we began to see a disaggregation of the Arab Spring as no longer being a cohesive,

10 Alain Gabon, 'Eight Years On, the Arab Spring is Far from Over', in *Middle East Eye*, 17 December 2018, https://www.middleeasteye.net/node/74940.

11 Ibid.

solitary unit of analysis, but a disparate set of political, military and socioeconomic conflicts unique to their particular national contexts.

While I would tend to argue in favour of this more critical approach, as I have utilized it in my research on the divergence of various Islamist movements emerging from the Muslim Brotherhood's school of thought across a variety of cases within the Arab uprisings, I would nevertheless concede that there is some utility in taking a broader approach, especially when viewed through the lens of regional competition and consolidation, particularly among elements of the counter-revolution. Therefore, the discussion that follows cautiously takes the regional approach, one that looks at the broader sets of developments, while nevertheless accounting for the crucial differences that exist within and among the various cases within the phenomenon of the Arab uprisings.

6.3 Islam vs secularism

The mischaracterizations prevalent in the overarching narratives regarding regional insecurity stem in large part from a number of false binaries that have come to dictate how the Arab uprisings are perceived and discussed. The first of these is the 'religious vs secular' myth. This narrative suggests that in the events that unfolded during the early stages of the uprisings, the forces of religious opposition, led primarily by Islamist parties, were at odds with other civil-society groups, represented in part by revolutionary youth movements along with liberal and leftist forces.[12] While there were certainly differences between them, it would be mistaken to characterize them as religious vs. secular in nature. These

---

12 See, for example, Stephen M. Walt, 'Arab Secularism and its Discontents', in *Foreign Policy*, 1 July 2012. See also Daniel Steinvorth, 'Islamist vs. Secularists: The Post-Revolution Struggle for the Arab Soul', in *Der Spiegel*, 4 December 2012, https://spon.de/adOEW; Michael Hoffman and Amaney Jamal, 'Religion in the Arab Spring: Between Two Competing Narratives', in *Journal of Politics*, Vol. 76, No. 3 (May 2014), pp. 593–606.

were quite often differences in strategy regarding the nature of the post-authoritarian transitions.

In Egypt, for instance, the Muslim Brotherhood's Freedom and Justice Party (FJP) recognized the advantage it maintained in the nascent electoral system, and had no truly revolutionary impulses of which to speak. Unsurprisingly, the group's leadership favoured a reformist approach on the question of whether the post-Mubarak transition should immediately move to parliamentary and presidential elections overseen by the ruling military council, or take on the task of rewriting the constitution before settling on the political leadership of the transition period. Even once the Muslim Brotherhood found itself with a parliamentary majority and the presidency, the ensuing disputes were hardly over the vision of the role of Islam in the state, though that was certainly the way the media and the opposition characterized it.[13] For all of the talk that the FJP's constitution put forward by President Mohamed Morsi was to curtail religious freedoms and impose Islamic rule, there was actually very little in that document that departed from the traditional conceptions of the role of Shari'a as a source of legislation that go back to the Sadat era. To that end, the Coptic Church and a number of civil-society groups signalled their approval of earlier iterations of the Morsi constitution before those relationships broke down over other, more immediate political differences regarding the path forward. Specifically, as a political opposition coalesced around the objective of toppling the Morsi government, there was little incentive to remain invested in a process that required mutual compromise and accommodation, particularly on the part of parties that did not enjoy an electoral mandate.

In the case of Tunisia, the leadership of the Ennahda Party decided that, as a nation that possessed a common Islamic identity and frame of reference, there was no need for the constitution to explicitly invoke the Shari'a at all. Perhaps learning the lessons of the Muslim Brotherhood in Egypt, Ennahda was further willing to share power with the opposition as part of a unity government, rather than govern on the basis of its electoral

13 Peter Beaumont, 'Mohamed Morsi Signs Egypt's New Constitution into Law', in *The Guardian*, 26 December 2012, https://gu.com/p/3cm3a.

mandate. Even when divisions emerged, these primarily concerned the posture of the transition, balancing the demands of the revolutionaries for structural change with the fears of antagonizing traditional political and economic elites, rather than reflecting serious disagreements over the role of Islam in the nascent Tunisian political system. Finally, to dispel all doubts, at its party conference in spring 2016, Ennahda's leadership redefined the party's mission as firmly rooted in upholding a civil state, not unlike the Christian Democrats of Europe.[14]

In the case of some of the sites of violent political contestation, including Syria and Yemen, a number of scholars have recently attempted to counterbalance the overwhelming perception that sectarian religious identity is at the root of these contemporary conflicts. Writing on Syria, one scholar challenged the contention that the Assad regime represented a secular bulwark against religious fanaticism, writing that, 'While it is undeniable that the Syrian protesters mobilized religious references from the beginning of the uprising, they did it within the discursive limits of a religious nationalism that was elaborated and fostered by Bashar al-Assad's government itself.'[15]

In fact, when one examines the larger picture, the instrumentalization of religion is by no means the domain of Islamist groups alone. The narrative of a religious–secular binary was instituted in part to sow divisions within the ranks of the uprisings, while also paving the way for the introduction of Islamic alternatives. As the editors of a recently published text on the subject put it, 'While it is true that religious identities are more salient in the politics of the Middle East today than they were in previous periods, it is also true that these identities have been politicized by state actors in pursuit of political gain.'[16] Examples abound

---

14 Fabio Merone, 'Politicians or Preachers? What Ennahda's Transformation Means for Tunisia', in *Carnegie Articles*, 31 January 2019, https://carnegie-mec.org/publications/?fa=78253.

15 Paulo Gabriel Hilu Pinto, 'The Shattered Nation: The Sectarianization of the Syrian Conflict', in Nader Hashemi and Danny Postel (eds), *Sectarianization. Mapping the New Politics of the Middle East*, New York, Oxford University Press, 2017, p. 124.

16 Nader Hashemi and Danny Postel, 'Introduction: The Sectarianization Thesis', in Nader Hashemi and Danny Postel (eds), *Sectarianization. Mapping the New Politics of the Middle East*, New York, Oxford University Press, 2017, p. 20.

of states utilizing religious discourses in attempting to marginalize and repress the Islamist opposition. Since 2015, Egypt's authoritarian ruler has embarked on a project to affirm a single legitimate interpretation of the Islamic tradition. Enlisting the support of Azhari elites, the nation's premiere religious officials, Sisi has offered himself as a leading promoter of a 'moderate' Islam, and aggressively enforced his interpretation in regular religious observances such as the Friday sermons. At one point Sisi was even hailed across the Western press and by Western political leaders as Islam's 'Martin Luther'.[17]

Similarly, the government of the United Arab Emirates, which has been on an aggressive security campaign against all forces of opposition, especially those from the Muslim Brotherhood's school of thought, has attempted to offer an alternative form of quietist Islam that is freed of all political ambitions and compliant with the UAE agenda for the region. This has manifested itself in a number of ways. The UAE's ambassador to Russia published *Letters to a Young Muslim*, ostensibly yet another plea for moderation, but which reads more clearly as a call for a quietist interpretation of religion that would not seek to challenge the status quo. There has also been the establishment of various institutional bodies such as the so-called 'Forum for Promoting Peace in Muslim Societies', endorsed by a number of influential scholars around the world, as well as the UAE's Orwellian-sounding 'Ministry of Tolerance'.[18] In February 2019, the country hosted a papal visit in an effort to boost the UAE's profile as a leader of interfaith tolerance and peace in the Muslim world, in total contrast to its aggressively violent efforts to root out popular movements and mass mobilizations across the Arab region.[19]

---

17 Michele Dunne and Katie Bentivoglio, 'Is Sisi Islam's Martin Luther?', in *Diwan*, 16 January 2015, https://carnegie-mec.org/diwan/57738.

18 Walaa Quisay and Thomas Parker, 'On the Theology of Obedience: An Analysis of Shaykh Bin Bayyah and Shaykh Hamza Yusuf's Political Thought', in *Jadaliyya*, 14 January 2019, http://www.jadaliyya.com/Details/38295.

19 Graeme Wood, 'The Vatican and the Gulf Have a Common Enemy', in *The Atlantic*, 6 February 2019, https://www.theatlantic.com/article/582088.

Finally, the Saudi kingdom has also engaged in the instrumentalization of Islamic doctrines, stoking the flames of sectarian divisions, building on its rivalry with Iran and extending its influence to sites of religious and sectarian pluralism across the region, from Iraq, Syria and Lebanon to Yemen and Bahrain. During his well-publicized tour of the United States in 2018, Crown Prince Mohammad bin Salman repeatedly echoed a carefully crafted narrative that Saudi Arabia only ventured into promoting its particularly intolerant brand of Islam following the events of 1979, in a misguided effort to combat the Iranian Revolution.[20] Presenting himself as the enlightened reformer determined to restore the kingdom to its liberal ways, Bin Salman relied on this narrative as a means of shrouding his country's otherwise destructive policies that have attempted to crush attempts at the establishment of more representative rule throughout the region and the formation of an Islamic alternative not derived from Saudi royals.

Historically, there have been numerous efforts by Arab regimes to instrumentalize Islam to legitimize themselves, but the most recent attempts cannot be divorced from the challenges posed by the Arab uprisings. From the standpoint of the Saudi ruling family, for instance, it could abide neither the possibility of Arab populations seeking self-government through a transition to democracy, nor the emergence of an Islamic political project build on an entirely different foundation as that put forward by parties like Ennahda and the FJP, which sought democratic legitimacy for their Islamist platforms, not monarchical authority as in the case of Saudi Arabia. Even in cases where the Saudi state supposedly supported some form of regime change, as in Libya and Syria, it became quite clear early on in those upheavals that whatever would come to replace the Gaddafi and Assad regimes would be no more than another authoritarian regime, except one that was more dependably allied with Saudi aims in the region.

---

20 Spencer Ackerman, 'Trump's Publisher Pal Puts Saudi Propaganda Magazine in U.S. Supermarkets', in *Daily Beast*, 26 March 2018, https://www.thedailybeast.com/trumps-publisher-pal-puts-saudi-propaganda-magazine-in-us-supermarkets.

6.4 Stability vs instability

This elicits another false binary, that of 'stability vs instability', in which the forces behind the Arab uprisings are to be associated with instability, while the counter-revolutionary wave that followed was to be characterized as a stabilizing force for a region that was not quite ready for democracy or representative rule of any kind. With their final words as despotic rulers, Zine el-Abidine Ben Ali, Ali Abdullah Saleh, Hosni Mubarak and Muammar Gaddafi all warned that their removal would simply usher in a state of chaos, disarray and violence. Their erstwhile sponsors, specifically in Saudi Arabia and the UAE along with their allies in the US and Israel, appeared determined to prove these ominous predictions to be correct. As I have previously documented, the impossible false choice confronting millions of Arab citizens has been one between tyranny and terror.[21]

In fact, there remains a strong need to counteract these narratives of instability and insecurity as directly parallel to mass mobilizations and post-authoritarian transitions. Taking Egypt as an example, the 3 July 2013 coup that brought Sisi to power on the heels of mass protests against Morsi legitimized itself by essentially declaring the revolution a failure and pledging to restore security and economic prosperity in return for abandoning all hopes for representative rule. The Sisi era has failed miserably on both of those counts. In addition to the instances of brutal state violence such as that which occurred during the Rabaa Massacre of August 2013, the long-standing Sinai insurgency has escalated drastically during Sisi's rule. Despite the scorched earth policy they have adopted, Egyptian security forces have proven incapable of neutralizing the insurgency in Sinai, even with the assistance of the Israeli military, recently confirmed by Sisi. Nor has the economic situation stabilized under Egypt's new ruler, with capital flight

---

21 Abdullah Al-Arian, 'Between Terror and Tyranny. Political Islam in the Shadow of the Arab Uprisings', in *Middle East Report Online*, 30 December 2015, https://merip.org/?p=9369.

continuing, along with massive inflation, and currency devaluation at rates once thought unthinkable. The austerity measures Sisi implemented in the hopes of securing the support of international financial institutions have only made things harder on the poorest Egyptians, and could only be enforced through the threat of violence looming over Egyptian society. Meanwhile, all indications suggest that the military's already outsized role in the Egyptian economy has only grown.

Similar narratives have been employed to suggest that the civil conflicts that erupted both in Libya and Yemen resulted from failed democratic transitions. In fact, the worst brutalities of these conflicts, sponsored in large part by the Saudi and Emirati regimes, stem from their efforts to restore authoritarian rule in those respective states. These measures have often been justified primarily as an alarmist response to the presence of Islamist actors within these societies. In the early stages of the uprising, Western observers continuously praised the 'leaderless' and 'non-ideological' nature of the protests, which was celebrated as a sign of social and political maturity on the part of Arab populations that had somehow outgrown their tribal, sectarian, or radical religious ideologies that had doomed them to live under authoritarian rule for so long. But when the opportunity emerged to paint the uprisings with the brush of Islamism, resulting primarily from electoral processes that saw Islamist parties emerge as alternatives to fill the vacuum left by authoritarian rulers, the narrative of instability not only took off, but also became used as a justification for intervention in the name of stability and security.

In fact, a more critical examination of events suggests that many of these crises were actually deliberately enacted to serve as pretexts for action. In the case of Egypt for instance, the artificial fuel shortages that occurred during the brief Morsi era were later revealed to have been deliberately concocted by elements of the counter-revolution to destabilize his presidency and stoke anger at his government.[22]

22 Ben Hubbard and David D. Kirkpatrick, 'Sudden Improvements in Egypt Suggest a Campaign to Undermine Morsi', in *The New York Times*, 10 July 2013, https://nyti.ms/1aLx32A.

Meanwhile, the so-called 'Tamarrod' movement that organized the 30 June 2013 anti-Morsi protests was exposed as a front for Egyptian intelligence agents aiming to shroud the coming military coup beneath the veneer of popular legitimacy.[23] The violent discourse in Tunisia that led to high-profile political assassinations, ostensibly by Salafi extremists, was intended to derail the post-Ben Ali transition. As Tunisia's president during the transition Moncef Marzouki maintained, the efforts to destabilize Tunisia ahead of a crucial parliamentary bill regarding the exclusion of former regime officials 'clearly showed that the intended target of the assassinations was the coalition government itself'.[24] The continued role of Saleh in Yemen, long after he had been supposedly deposed, continued to be used as a wedge to destabilize a transition by dividing Yemen's factions and serving as a vehicle for regional intervention.[25] As Saudi commentator Jamal Kashoggi noted in the year before he too fell victim to Bin Salman's machinations, Saudi Arabia used 'fears of instability on the southern border [...] to orchestrate a leadership change in the country'.[26] While it was the expansion of Houthi control which served as the pretext for counter-revolutionary intervention in the case of Yemen, the Houthis' Shi'a background and alleged allegiances to Iran were highlighted to demonstrate that yet again religious affiliation was deemed a barometer for instability.

---

23 Sheera Frenkel and Maged Atef, 'How Egypt's Rebel Movement Helped Pave the Way for a Sisi Presidency', in *BuzzFeed*, 15 April 2014, https://www.buzzfeednews.com/article/sheerafrenkel/how-egypts-rebel-movement-helped-pave-the-way-for-a-sisi-pre.

24 Oussama Kardi, 'Egypt Coup Plotters Tried to Overthrow Tunisian Democracy, Says Ex-President', in *Middle East Eye*, 11 August 2017, https://www.middleeasteye.net/node/65364.

25 Bruce Riedel, 'Why Did Saudi Arabia Save Yemen's Ex-President Again?', in *Al-Monitor*, 18 October 2017, http://almon.co/2xt3.

26 Jamal Kashoggi, 'With Ali Abdullah Saleh's Death, Saudi Arabia is Paying the Price for Betraying the Arab Spring', in *The Washington Post*, 5 December 2017, http://wapo.st/2jhjjFm.

6.5 Violence vs non-violence

Finally, another false binary that emerges frequently in discussions about insecurity reflects an inherent contradiction in the ways in which violence and non-violence are framed. In their initial stages, the Arab uprisings were lauded in large part due to their non-violent character. This commitment to non-violence conferred on the protest movements a degree of legitimacy that was undeniable even in the eyes of Western states and media that would otherwise seek to discredit mass mobilization as a mode of producing structural change. Nevertheless, those narratives largely broke down around the arming of the Syrian opposition, the descent of Libya and Yemen into civil wars, and the outbreak of political violence in Tunisia and Egypt. In each case, the characterization of violence by non-state actors, particularly those of an Islamist character, differed wildly from the characterizations of regime violence. There was also a tendency to shift the Islamist centre of gravity from movements that professed a non-violent, reformist approach to political change, such as the Muslim Brotherhood, to movements like al-Qaeda and the Islamic State that relied exclusively on the use of violence, thereby delegitimizing the entire revolutionary ambitions of the Arab uprisings in the process.

The subsequent crusade waged against the Muslim Brotherhood and its offshoots by Egypt, Saudi Arabia and in particular the UAE depended entirely on providing a convincing narrative that these parties fit the often nebulous and constantly shifting definition of a 'terrorist organization'. The Muslim Brotherhood was banned in large parts of the Arab world, with members imprisoned, assets seized, publications and online presence erased. In Egypt, even as the Islamic State in Sinai would claim responsibility for a militant attack, the Sisi regime would swiftly ascribe blame to the Muslim Brotherhood anyway. The UAE, in collaboration with the pro-Israel lobby, advocated strongly for a blanket terrorist designation on the Muslim Brotherhood in the UK and the US. The UK government undertook a lengthy review of the Muslim Brotherhood, reportedly under threat of losing lucrative weapons contracts.[27] The Trump administration waffled in its determination to designate the Muslim Brotherhood, due partly to the complex legal implications this would have had on dozens of organizations domestically and around the world, not to mention its diplomatic dealings with states that had Muslim Brotherhood representation in their governments. Bahrain's government was in the unenviable position of banning the organization regionally, while nevertheless recognizing that the local Bahraini branch represented a crucial base of domestic Sunni support in the face of what it considered to be a largely Shia opposition.

Not content with facing down the movement's various non-state offshoots, the emerging regional axis also attempted to take on two regional powers, Turkey and Qatar, for their supposed support of the Muslim Brotherhood, and the Arab uprisings at large. When the blockade of Qatar by the quartet of Saudi Arabia, the UAE, Bahrain and Egypt began in summer 2017, the chief accusation levelled was that it was supporting terrorism, which had not so subtly become the stand-in terminology for supporting the Arab uprisings, and by extension, its leading Islamist actors.

In the final analysis, the current conflict, muddied and mischaracterized by all of the false binaries previously listed, represents two visions for the future of the region that are fundamentally at odds with one another. The counter-revolutionary movement, led by a regional alliance of states, their international backers and their local agents, has defined itself largely in opposition to a constructed Islamist threat that it has used as the facade to mask the deeper demands that ignited the popular uprisings in the first place. It is quite instructive that, in pursuing his reforms, such as lifting the ban on women driving in Saudi Arabia, Bin Salman has also ordered the arrest and torture of female activists who have been advocating for these very same rights.[28] While

27 Randeep Ramesh, 'UAE Told UK: Crack Down on Muslim Brotherhood or Lose Arms Deals', in *The Guardian*, 6 November 2015, https://gu.com/p/4evh3.

28 Patrick Wintour and Bethan McKernan, 'Saudi Female Activists Face Jail Conditions Akin to Torture, Say UK MPs', in *The Guardian*, 4 February 2019, https://gu.com/p/ajzmt.

Western liberals may be aghast at the apparent contradiction, the aim here is actually quite clear: in responding to the challenges posed by the Arab uprisings, Bin Salman has attempted to offer a different model of reform by autocratic decree, one that provides cosmetic appearances of economic and sociocultural change while nevertheless tightening his grip on political power and dramatically increasing the stakes for the widespread demands for a greater role in shaping the political future of the Arab region.

Youssef Cherif

Chapter 7: Dahlan vs Belhaj: The Maghreb in the Arab War of Narratives

One of the most important factors of insecurity in the Middle East and North Africa is the wave of fake news produced by the Gulf states, mainly Saudi Arabia, the United Arab Emirates (UAE) and Qatar. The media and social media outlets funded by these countries have a reach far beyond their respective borders and target the broader Arab hearts and minds, with different perspectives and agendas. The phenomenon increased in the 2000s, after 9/11 and the Iraq war. But it reached its climax with the Arab uprisings of 2011, when Saudi Arabia and the UAE on one side and Qatar on the other entered a period of growing confrontation; the Arab Sunni Cold War. This period also coincided with the social media revolution around the world, which facilitated the mutual use of propaganda. This and fake news went one step further when the Qatar crisis broke out in mid-2017.[1] So what is the language used by the Gulf media outlets? How is it disseminated? And what is its impact on the countries of North Africa?

The war of narratives is an important factor of the Arab Sunni Cold War. This chapter will consist of a qualitative survey of media content, relying on several media outlets, some of them Gulf funded or backed (especially Al-Jazeera, Arabi 21, *Al-Arab* and *Al-Sharq al-Awsat*), and others Tunisian (mainly Kapitalis and Tunisia Now). The choice is tied more to logistical reasons than to the content itself. Search engines are not always efficient: so while it is easy to find all the articles related to a specific keyword on Al-Jazeera's website, this is not the case with Al-Arabiya, which makes using it to retrieve old articles difficult,

---

1 POMEPS, 'The Qatar Crisis', in *POMEPS Briefings*, No. 31 (October 2017), https://pomeps.org/?p=9633.

even though it is between these two competing TV stations that the comparison should take place. Moreover, this is not an exhaustive listing of the Gulf coverage and its effect in North Africa, but rather a selected qualitative observation of some of the most influential outlets. We will focus primarily on Tunisia and to a lesser degree on Libya. Furthermore studying fake news and propaganda usually takes into account Twitter, and the use of bots in the Middle Eastern context is now being scrutinized more frequently.[2] Yet the use of Twitter in North Africa remains limited, being overtaken by Facebook, online content and television news.

7.1 Strategy

Qatar has had a series of historic grievances with its Gulf neighbours, especially Saudi Arabia. The coup of Hamad bin Khalifa Al-Thani against his Saudi-backed father in 1995, the latter's attempted counter-putsch helped by the Saudis, then the launch of Al-Jazeera in 1996, were turning points in the relationship. The programmes and diffusion of Al-Jazeera accelerated a Gulf media race, with Saudi Arabia and the UAE launching their own news networks to counter the Qatari channel (Al-Arabiya in 2003, then Sky News Arabia and Al-Hadath in the following decade). The three countries also tried to undermine each other's local and regional projects and they occasionally resorted to cutting diplomatic ties.

However, it was not until the Arab uprisings of 2011 – and their evolution from 2012 onwards – that the two camps chose clearly distinct paths. Qatar's diplomatic, economic, military and media support to the revolted Arab peoples, especially the Islamists among them, was opposed by Saudi-Emirati assistance to some weakened regimes or newly emerging, anti-Qatari ones, often of authoritarian nature. There were areas where the two camps found a common ground: in Libya against

2 Marc Owen Jones, 'Propaganda, Fake News, and Fake Trends: The Weaponization of Twitter Bots in the Gulf Crisis', in *International Journal of Communication*, Vol. 13 (2019), pp. 1389–415, https://ijoc.org/index.php/ijoc/article/view/8994.

Gaddafi; in Syria against Assad; or in Yemen against Iran's influence. However, the UAE and Qatar quickly felt apart in Libya as the armed groups they were backing started fighting each other. In Yemen, Qatar was supporting the Muslim Brotherhood-affiliated groups, who were not the preferred partners of the Saudis and the Emiratis. Moreover, and since the ostracization of Qatar in 2017, Doha withdrew from the Saudi-led coalition in Yemen and started reaching out to Iran and the Houthis. Even in Syria, the Saudis and especially the Emiratis began to change their positions towards the Assad regime, while Qatar remains firmly opposed to its rehabilitation in the Arab League.

Media was one of the main tools these countries used against one another. Each had a narrative it transmitted to its public, locally and abroad. This Arab war of narratives is not necessarily tied to a particular project. Thus, neither the Saudis nor the Emiratis would like to emulate their model of governance across the Arab world. Nor is that the aim of the Qataris. Their ultimate goals are to survive as they are whilst maximizing their economic gains, countering each other's regional projects and projecting their power outside of their territory. These goals are interlinked. The closer an area is to their geographic immediacy, the more it is impacted by their foreign-policy behaviour. They are therefore very active in the Gulf itself (including Yemen), the Horn of Africa,[3] Egypt and the Levant. This whole area forms a circular belt around their borders.

The Maghreb is of secondary importance to the Gulf countries. Libya, however, is very close to Egypt; it has the potential to destabilize Egypt if the situation degenerates. For Saudi Arabia, an unstable Egypt is a source of problems. Libya is also rich in natural resources and its size makes it a bridge to and from many countries in Africa's Sahel region. Moreover, Libya is now a weak state and it is easy to interfere in its affairs. The Gulf countries are therefore active there, by means

---

3 International Crisis Group (ICG), 'The United Arab Emirates in the Horn of Africa', in *Crisis Group Middle East Briefings*, No. 65 (6 November 2018), https://www.crisisgroup.org/node/8077.

of weapons, money[4] and fake news. Tunisia is of lesser significance, but because of its proximity to Libya, the advent of democracy which makes foreign interference possible, and the Qatari-Turkish influence (facilitated by Ennahda and CPR, the country's most influential parties in 2011–12), it did attract the other Gulf players, although with less intensity than in Libya. In Algeria and Morocco, which are far away from the Gulf immediate sphere of influence and where strong central states are able to limit foreign meddling, the Gulf states are present, but with limited influence. The recent developments in Algeria, however, may change things in the future.

7.2 Language

Generally, the two camps use a pan-Arab language, which goes as follows: Palestine at the core, Israel as the usual harmful element, and the Arab world as a unity. The persistent use of pan-Arabism confirms what Bahgat Korany wrote, that although Pan-Arabism failed from a state-centric perspective, it is very much alive from the people's viewpoint.[5] Pan-Arabism is therefore appealing to the general public even if it is not linked to a unified set of policies or orientations. It only serves, as Marc Lynch noted, as a reference point.[6] Neither the concept of postcolonial nationalism as tested in places like Tunisia or Jordan since the mid-twentieth century, nor Islamism in its softer or radical versions which developed from the 1970s onwards, nor globalization with its values of

---

4 Lipika Majumdar Roy Choudhury (ed.), *Final Report of the Panel of Experts on Libya Established Pursuant to Resolution 1973 (2011)* (S/2018/812), 5 September 2018, https://undocs.org/S/2018/812.

5 Pinar Bilgin, 'Region, Security, Regional Security: "Whose Middle East?" Revisited', in Elizabeth Monier (ed.), *Regional Insecurity after the Arab Uprisings. Narratives of Security and Threats*, Basingstoke/New York, Palgrave Macmillan, 2015, p. 25.

6 Marc Lynch, *Voices of the New Arab Public. Iraq, Al-Jazeera, and Middle East Politics Today*, New York, Columbia University Press, 2006, p. 4.

human rights and liberal democracy which climaxed after the end of the Cold War was able to take the place of pan-Arabism as a unifying and enduring concept that mobilizes the masses.

The message disseminated by the two camps is simple. According to the Saudis and the Emiratis, Qatar is trying to destabilize the Arab world by means of terrorist groups that weaken the nation-states, often in order to serve Israel's interests. According to the Qataris, Israel helps Arab dictatorships, the UAE on top, in order to protect itself; following the same logic, this axis creates or encourages terrorism to give dictators an excuse to stay in power. Both therefore describe each other as an enemy to the common Arab cause. The latter is epitomized in the struggle for the liberation of Palestine and the progress of Arabs as a nation. In the Saudi–Emirati narrative, however, security – authoritarianism – is needed to reach this objective. In the Qatari version, democracy – and the inclusion of political Islam – is key. The means to reach the common goal, therefore, differ.

In the Saudi and Emirati media outlets, the post-2011 Arab tragedy is the result of Qatari policies and its architects are Qatari politicians and their proxies. In the Qatar funded – or backed – outlets, however, everything is to blame on the Saudis and the Emiratis (as well as their allies, proxies, and so on). Egypt is contributing to this conflict on the Saudi-Emirati side using its media empire and symbolic role; Turkey, on the other hand, is siding with Qatar, also using its symbolic role as well as its financial and diplomatic power. As these countries are monopolizing the political narrative in the Arab world, what goes out on their airwaves is echoed in every Arab capital from Nouakchott to Manama. The public sphere of the Arab world is therefore directly affected.

Before the current Arab Sunni Cold War picked, the main target of Gulf media campaigns was Shiite Iran. Sectarian propaganda disseminated by Saudi, Emirati and to a certain extent Qatari media outlets and officials was massive, especially following the 2003 Iraq War and the rise of Iran as a regional power.[7] Gulf Arabs and their clients

---

7 Frederic M. Wehrey, *Sectarian Politics in the Gulf. From the Iraq War to the Arab Uprisings*, New York, Columbia University Press, 2014.

were warning that 'Persian', 'Safavid', 'Shiite' Iran wanted to control the Gulf and by extension the rest of the Arab World, by means of non-state actors such as Hezbollah, and by Shiite proselytism. And although Qatar occasionally bandwagoned with Iran in the last two decades (especially in the period around the Israeli war on Hezbollah, in 2006, and since the Qatar crisis of 2017), its media are equally sectarian. Iranian and Iran-backed media outlets did also use sectarianism to respond. Their main argument was that the Sunni states were fuelling Islamic terrorism. The coverage of post-2011 Syria for instance was largely sectarian, and Shiite activities were scrutinized and shunned on a regular basis by the Saudi, Emirati and Qatari outlets, while Sunnite activism there – including charity actions – was often covered with reference to terrorism in pro-Iran media. Likewise, the coverage of post-2011 Yemen by all sides was largely sectarian, although Qatari media shifted to focusing on human rights violations after Qatar left the Saudi-led coalition.

The case of Syria is interesting as the two levels converge: anti-Iranian sectarianism (and its pro-Iranian response) and intra-Sunni conflict. Saudis, Emiratis, Qataris and Turks would concentrate part of their media coverage on Iran's activities in Syria, from a sectarian perspective. But separately, Saudi Arabia and the UAE would stage accusations against Qatar and Turkey for their alleged support of al-Qaeda or ISIS. Qatar and Turkey, similarly, would wage a campaign against the Emiratis, and to a certain extent the Saudis (they have been especially careful when it comes to criticising Riyadh, until the 2017 crisis), accusing them of equally supporting ISIS or the Assad regime.

The image is less blurry in North Africa. Here, Saudi Arabia and the UAE, and their ally Egypt, are conducting a distinct war of narratives against Qatar and its ally Turkey, and vice versa. It has been the case since the early days of 2011, with Egypt first as a field of contest and since Sisi's July 2013 coup a full player with the Saudi–Emirati axis. The two camps occasionally include Iran[8] or Israel in their North African

8 Amal Raslan, 'Ataya Iran Tafshal fi Shiraa Da'm Shamal Ifriqya li Qatar ...' [Iran's Gifts Fail to Buy North Africa's Support for Qatar], in *Youm7*, 20 June 2017, http://www.youm7.com/3292636.

media campaigns. Israel is a traditional bird banger whose proximity immediately discredits the opponent, and Iran is seen as an evil entity for any brainwashed Sunni Arab. But the inclusion of these two countries in the case of North Africa remains limited.

In North Africa, the two camps are fueling the secularists Vs. Islamists debate, which is now often used as a shortcut to describe politics in places like Tunisia and Libya.[9] On the one hand the Saudi–Emirati axis blames the Qataris for empowering Islamists – and by extension Islamist extremists – for the sake of undermining the nationalist, secular states of North Africa. The Qatari axis, on the other hand, accuses the Saudis and the Emiratis of fostering authoritarianism and threatening democracy – and by extension the Arab-Islamic identity and the existence of Islam in politics. The energy and ferocity applied by the two camps to harm each other in North Africa, using this ideological debate, can be compared to the sectarian campaign they are waging together against Iran in the Middle East and the Gulf.

Because Arabs are interconnected via internet and satellite channels, for almost two decades now,[10] these messages are easily transported from one region to another. In other words, what is produced in Abu Dhabi or Doha does not stay there: it is heard and internalized in the rest of the Arab world. This war of narratives has produced heroes and villains, loved or hated by largely credulous populations across the region. The resulting issue is the securitization of Arab politics,[11] and the delegitimization as well as the othering of political actors. The political opponent becomes a terrorist or a traitor, a foreign agent (to Qatar-Turkey or to the UAE-Saudi Arabia-Egypt, depending on the side), a security threat which should be annihilated – rather than opposed in democratic contest.

---

9 Youssef Cherif, 'Bringing the Economy Back Into Tunisian Politics', in *Sada*, 12 February 2019, https://carnegieendowment.org/sada/78345.

10 Marc Lynch, *Voices of the New Arab Public*, cit.

11 Pinar Bilgin, 'Region, Security, Regional Security', cit., p. 12.

7.3 Bogeymen and conspiracies

Both alliances have their bogeymen. These serve as unifying figures for the public to focus on. It is always easier to give a face to a conspiracy theory, especially when it comes to sulphurous figures with a mysterious past. There is always one chief conspirator who is at the core of the conspiracy web, to whom all the guilt is transferred. For the Saudi-Emirati camp, it is the Libyan Abdelhakim Belhaj, who is described as Prince Tamim's hand in North Africa. For the Qatari camp, it is the Palestinian Mohammed Dahlan, who is portrayed as the henchman of the UAE's de facto leader, Mohammed Bin Zayed.

Abdelhakim Belhadj is a veteran of the Afghan Jihad who fought with the Taliban and al-Qaeda. He is one of the founders of the Libyan Islamic Fighting Group. He was arrested – in a complex operation by the CIA and MI6 – in 2004 in Malaysia and sent back to Libya where he was jailed and tortured. In the late 2000s, Gaddafi's son Saif al-Islam was conducting a reconciliation process with his father's opponents. Belhadj was consequently declared de-radicalized and released from prison in 2010. Yet when the uprising against Gaddafi began, Belhadj assembled a group of armed men, benefiting from Qatari and Turkish support, and led the fight to control Tripoli. By the end of 2011 and after Gaddafi's death, he was said to be the most important military commander in Libya.

He then decided to move into politics, gave up his guerrilla attire and adopted a soft, peaceful rhetoric. Qatari-funded media outlets helped disseminate that image with regular interviews and reports presenting him to the Libyan electorate and the internal community as a reformist politician who turned the page of Jihad and whose political influence makes him the key player in Tripoli. Libyans were encouraged to vote for Belhadj, and Westerners were advised to deal with him. However, he was abducted and physically assaulted by a rival armed group in Tripoli's airport in November 2011, which raised questions about his political and military weight. A few months later, the political party he co-founded, Al-Wattan, had limited results in the first free and fair Libyan elections.

Yet according to the Saudi and Emirati media, his terrorist network spreads across the whole North African region. They portray him as the highest authority of Libya's Islamists, along with the radical Mufti Sadiq al Ghariani. Saudi and Emirati media use the term 'political Islam militias' when mentioning the diverse Islamist groups and militias. Islamists are described as violent, treacherous. Articles and TV reports appearing on these outlets often try to find links between Belhadj and other non-Libyan Islamist leaders such as Tunisia's Rached Ghannouchi. They also frequently mention ties linking Belhadj to the radical Jihadists active in North Africa and the Sahel, be it al-Qaeda or ISIS, and the organized crime networks that are expanding in the region. This is a giant pool where everyone from the anti-Qatar camp is thrown.

By contrasting the Saudi-Emirati media to the Qatari one, a dual portrait of Belhadj emerges. On the Saudi-funded London-based *Al-Sharq Al-Awsat* website, for instance, Abdelhakim Belhadj appears twenty-four times between 1 October 2010 and 1 January 2019, always in relation to Qatar and terrorism, and this narrative accelerated in mid-2017 (with the Qatar crisis). By contrast, he figures 140 times on Qatari-funded Al-Jazeera's website, constantly under a positive light. Belhadj is described as a moderate politician, a reformer, a victim, a revolutionary leader, and so on. He is a global terrorist for one camp, and a rising politician for the other.

Qatari media, On the opposite side, have amplified the image of Palestinian leader Mohammed Dahlan as the UAE's chief conspirator in the Arab world. Dahlan grew up in a Palestinian camp in Gaza and fought against Israeli occupation, like most Palestinian youths of his age in the 1970s and 1980s. He joined Fatah and became one of its leaders. He was jailed several times for his anti-colonial activism, but he then entered the movement's moderate wing and became involved in the peace talks with Israel. Palestinian leader Yasser Arafat appointed him to lead one of the Palestinian Authority's most important security apparatuses, before a fall-out between the two men set them apart. He remained powerful in Gaza though, until the election of Hamas in 2006 when the balance of power began to shift. Dahlan actually worked for years against Hamas and the old rivalry between him and its leaders could not be bridged. His relationship with the Fatah central leadership under Mahmoud Abbas was not good either.

From the late 2000s therefore, Dahlan partly relocated to the UAE where he established business. He forged close ties with the Crown

Prince of Abu Dhabi, Mohamed Bin Zayed. The latter is the actual head of the Emirati army, and Dahlan became his informal advisor. His name was hence linked to numerous shady operations, and his tense relations with both Hamas and Fatah's Mahmoud Abbas made him a regular target of their media outlets. It is nevertheless after 2011, when the UAE took a proactive role in the Arab world, that his international fame – beyond Palestine and the Palestinian camps in the Levant – started.

So for the Qataris, Dahlan is behind every problem that arises in the region. He is, according to their outlets, given unlimited resources by M. Bin Zayed to achieve the regional ambitions of the UAE. So when it comes to supporting authoritarian regimes, fighting political Islam, or countering Qatar, there is usually a link to Dahlan in Qatari outlets: he is hence backing Libyan general Khalifa Haftar, personally monitoring arms and money transfer. He is in charge of the Egyptian dossier in Abu Dhabi. He is said to be paying Tunisian demonstrators to foment rebellion against the Ennahda-backed government. He is leading the Emirati–Israeli plan to destroy Hamas in Gaza, etc.

When applying the same comparison used for Belhadj, we find out that Dahlan figures 110 times on Al-Jazeera's website in articles linking him to the UAE's regional project, between 1 October 2010 and 1 January 2019. During the same period, on the *Al-Sharq al-Awsat* website, Dahlan is mentioned only fourteen times, but always in his capacity as a Palestinian leader. Here again, he is an international spy for one side, and a committed politician for the other.

Another interesting case, from Tunisia, is that of former minister of interior Lotfi Brahem. He was dismissed in June 2018 after disagreements with Prime Minister Youssef Chahed. His dismissal, however, was linked by some to his acquaintance with the Saudi–Emirati camp, and even to a coup-attempt.[12] Brahem is a colonel-major in Tunisia's National Guard force, the second most important armed force in the country after the military. He rose in the ranks during the rule of former dictator Zine el-Abidine Ben Ali. But it was after the revolution that he obtained his most important posts: Director of Public Security, Commander of the

---

12 'Tunisie: Lotfi Brahem se défend de toute tentative de "coup d'État"', in *Jeune Afrique*, 15 June 2018, https://www.jeuneafrique.com/578072/.

National Guard and then Minister of Interior. In this last role, he travelled to Saudi Arabia in February 2018, apparently without informing the prime minister. It remains unclear whether he was sent by the president of the republic, whether he was given a private invitation by the Saudis, or whether he asked to meet with King Salman. He spent one week there, meeting with the Kingdom's most important figures including the king. The three versions persist, but the visit pointed to strong ties with the Saudi kingdom that few Tunisian public figures have had since 2011.

Brahem was largely unknown to the Gulf media before his appointment as minister, in September 2017. But a few weeks after his confirmation by the parliament, the UAE-backed, London-based *Al-Arab* newspaper and e-journal published a laudatory article describing him as a strong securocrat who would tackle the issue of terrorism. They wrote another piece in the same spirit in January 2018, shortly before his Saudi journey. Upon his return from Riyadh in February 2018, *Al-Arab* (and other outlets) were circulating his name as the future prime minister. It was perhaps a trial balloon, as a number of Tunisian outlets began circulating the story too. Related to his sacking, the same newspaper published two articles to his demise, linking it to an alleged deterioration in the security situation (one terrorist attack that targeted Tunisia's security forces in July): his departure, they claimed, resulted in destabilizing the Ministry of Interior, which led to security failures. They also accused Qatar and Ennahda of smear campaigns against Brahem because he allegedly tried to counter their political project. *Al-Arab* was also one of a few media outlets invited to cover a press conference by the Emirati Ambassador to Tunisia Salem Issa al-Zaabi in the days following Brahem's dismissal. In this meeting, ambassador al-Zaabi warned that those linking Brahem to an Emirati coup-attempt wanted to complicate Tunisia's relationship with the UAE, tacitly accusing Qatar.

The picture is completely reversed in the London-based, Qatari-backed Arabi 21 e-journal. Brahem is described under a negative light, often as an obstacle to democracy or an enemy of Islam. In December 2017, three months after Brahem's confirmation, Arabi 21 published an article about a 'Parallel National Security Government' that President Beji Caid Essebsi had initiated in the presidential palace. In Reality, the president created a National Security Council where the ministers of defence and interior, among others, have permanent seats, and where Brahem had a prominent role. Then, when Brahem visited Saudi Arabia in February 2018, Arabi 21 published four articles 'uncovering' counter-revolutionary measures and coup-attempts that were discussed and planned with Saudi leaders during the visit, some of them based on the Saudi, pro-Qatar Twitter handle 'Mujtahid'.[13] After Brahem's sacking, the e-journal published five articles 'confirming' the hypothesis of a Saudi–Emirati coup-attempt that Brahem was accused of. Arabi 21 has also tried to link Brahem to a terrorist attack that occurred after he was removed, almost as a response to the *Al-Arab*'s articles that linked the terrorist attacks to bureaucratic deficiencies following his departure. Lotfi Brahem is, accordingly, a committed and efficient strongman for the Saudis and the Emiratis, and a putschist authoritarian operative for the Qataris.

Furthermore, the two camps use leaks to come up with conspiracy theories. Hence the attacks and counter-attacks that spread in the first year following the Qatar crisis.[14] Once a document or a story is leaked, it is largely spread by the media outlets of one side, but not the other. Hence if the leak is coming from a pro-Qatar outlet, it will be endorsed by Al-Jazeera, Al-Arabi al-Jadid, Arabi 21, for example; but not by Al-Arabiya, Al-Hadath, Sky News Arabia, etc. And vice versa.

On 7 June 2017, two weeks after the hacking of Qatar News Agency and the beginning of the blockade of the peninsula by the Boycott Quartet (Saudi Arabia, the UAE, Egypt and Bahrain), Colonel Ahmed al-Mismari, spokesman for Khalifa Haftar's Libyan National Army and staunch opponent of political Islam – and by extension Qatar – gave a press conference to attack Qatar and accuse it of supporting terrorism in North Africa.[15] He showed documents, pictures and videos, and presented what he claimed were facts. Al-Mismari accused Qatar of

---

13 See Twitter profile: https://twitter.com/mujtahidd.

14 Youssef Cherif, 'The Gulf Crisis Threatens Tunisia's Stability', in *MENASource*, 8 November 2017, https://www.atlanticcouncil.org/blogs/menasource/the-gulf-crisis-threatens-tunisia-s-stability; Youssef Cherif, 'Tunisia, Battlefield of the Gulf Countries', in *OrientXXI*, 12 April 2018, https://orientxxi.info/magazine/tunisia-battlefield-of-the-gulf-countries,2394.

15 'Mismari: Qatar Funds Military Actions on Libyan Soil' (in Arabic), in *Sky News Arabia*, 8 June 2018, https://www.skynewsarabia.com/middle-east/955314.

smuggling money through a Tunisian bank to Libyan terrorist groups. The news was widely publicized by Saudi and Emirati media outlets, but ignored by the Qatari ones.

On 8 June 2017, so almost at the same time as al-Mismari's press conference, Arabi 21 published a 'secret memo' it claimed was internally produced by the Emirates Policy Center (EPC), a think tank close to the rulers of Abu Dhabi.[16] The document, a leak according to Arabi 21 and a forgery according to the EPC leadership, has a three-dimensional outline: countering Ennahda, facing Qatar, and building a local political bloc in Tunisia to secure these two priorities. According to the document, EPC has recommended that the Emirati authorities reach out to a number of Tunisian political and public figures known for their animosity towards Ennahda. It even advised that the UAE foments social troubles in Tunisia. This story was developed by the Qatari outlets, avoided by the Saudi and Emirati ones.

Then, on 3 January 2018, Arabi 21 published another leaked document, this time supposedly from a policy unit inside the UAE's foreign ministry.[17] The memo came after a disagreement occurred between the Tunisian and Emirati authorities Tunisians and Emiratis, over a travel ban that the UAE authorities imposed on Tunisian women flying on Emirati airliners. The document recommended several directions such as the need to push for a public relations strategy linking Ennahda to the terrorism of ISIS and al-Qaeda, including via Tunisian journalists and intellectuals said to be on the UAE's payroll, as the document alleges, as well as the necessity of keeping Nidaa Tounes – Ennahda's previous foe and later ally – unscathed and maintaining its popularity. Similarly, the leak was massively discussed in Qatari outlets, and neglected by the other camp.

These three sets of leaks appeared over a six-month time span. Their order of appearance may point to a tit-for-tat battle. It remains difficult

16 'Hakatha Toukhattitou Al-Emarat li' Istihdaf Tounes wa Thawratiha' [This is how the UAE schemes to target Tunisia and its Revolution], in *Arabi 21*, 21 June 2017, https://arabi21.com/story/1012702.

17 'Hasri: Wathiqa Emaratiya Takshif Khottat Ta'amoul Abu Dhabi ma'a Azmat Tounes' [Exclusive: Memo uncovers the UAE's plan in dealing with Tunisia's crisis], in *Arabi 21*, 3 January 2018, https://arabi21.com/story/1061056.

to discern truth from fiction. But for the recipients in Tunisia and Libya, each side believes its own outlets.

7.4 Effects on the North African public opinion

North Africans are aware of the proactive role the Gulf countries are playing in their region. In the 2018 Euromed Survey of Experts and Actors on the Euro-Mediterranean Relations for instance, respondents said that the Gulf Cooperation Council countries were the second source of instability in the Southern Mediterranean, after the US and more than Russia.[18] However, they still fall for the propaganda campaigns. In fact, when Tunisians or Algerians refer to their suspicion of Gulf countries, it is not regarding the overall Gulf interference, but rather according to which Gulf propaganda they are prey. 'Gulf' means Qatar for the anti-Islamist camp; or the Saudi–Emirati alliance for their foes.

Elements of this propaganda are found in Tunisian and Libyan media outlets, and by extension among the general public, which leads to the problems of othering and securitization. Getting closer to Doha or Abu Dhabi triggers suspicion, and anyone who meets with one of their representatives or accepts their invitations becomes an enemy. So when Ennahda's Rached Ghannouchi meets with Abdelhakim Belhadj, or when Afek Tounes's Yassine Brahim meets with Mohammed Dahlan, that's a scandal, a crime, for different segments of Tunisians.

For Tunisian pro-Ennahda, pro-Qatar e-journal Tunisia Now for instance, the reason behind Afek Tounes' withdrawal from the Ennahda-backed government in September 2017 is a meeting between Yassine Brahim and Mohammed Dahlan. In that meeting, the e-journal claims,

---

18 Xavier Aragall, Ainara Huarte and Silvia Regalón, 'The State of Europe', in Josep Ferré (ed.), *Changing Euro-Mediterranean Lenses. Ninth Euromed Survey of Experts and Actors*, Barcelona, IEMed, December 2018, p. 20, https://www.iemed.org/publicacions-en/historic-de-publicacions/enquesta-euromed/euromed-survey-2018/contents.

the two men discussed Emirati plans to destabilize Tunisia, and Afek's withdrawal was one of the steps needed to reach that goal. Tunisia Now participates in the Qatari campaign against Dahlan, and its articles are shared across Tunisian social media pages.

The same outlet has a positive coverage of Libya's Abdelhakim Belhadj. In its articles, he is described as a respectable civilian politician in Libya without any regional dimension. But for Tunisian anti-Ennahda, anti-Qatar e-journal Kapitalis, however, eleven articles were written about Abdel Hakim Belhadj between January 2011 and January 2019. He is depicted as a terrorist leader with regional ambitions, working for and with Qatar. He is often linked to Ennahda's Ghannouchi, and that is how Kapitalis discredits the latter. The same journal does not say a word about Mohammed Dahlan. Kapitalis and others on the anti-Ennahda side do share Emirati and Saudi news without verifying their accuracy, as long as they serve their political line. Pro-Ennahda media outlets do the same with Qatari sources.

As for former Tunisian interior minister Lotfi Brahem, his dual portrayal is also reflected in Tunisian media and discussions, usually with one side (the pro-Ennahda) sticking by the Qatari scenario and the other (anti-Ennahda) abiding by the Saudi-Emirati scenario. Similarly after Libya's Ahmed Mismari's press conference, Tunisian and Libyan anti-Ennahda newspapers and TV stations reported the accusations and invited guests to analyse them, but pro-Ennahda outlets and figures ignored the story. Also, when it comes to the alleged EPC and Emirati foreign ministry documents that Arabi 21 leaked, they were widely shared in pro-Ennahda newspapers in Tunisia, such as Bab Net. Anti-Ennahda outlets, especially those accused in the documents, avoided commenting on them.

Conclusion

The Arab Sunni Cold War that Saudi Arabia, the United Arab Emirates and Qatar are waging against each other has an important media component.

Because of the media empires that these countries own, their propaganda goes way beyond their national borders and affects the local politics of other Arab states. It is in a way similar to the media campaigns that Washington and some European capitals and organizations use to target Russia, or to Moscow's own fake news strategy to influence Western democracies. This important aspect of Arab politics, however, remains under-studied. The pan-Arab language used by the three Gulf states' media and affiliated media is appealing to the different Arab nations, and the common features they address give them credibility in the eyes of their respective followers. The zero-sum game in their politics is found in their propaganda message: the other becomes a foreign enemy, not a brotherly competitor. A Tunisian sympathiser of Ennahda would see his secular political foes the way Qatar describes the UAE; a Libyan sympathiser of Haftar would also look at his country's Islamists the way the UAE describes Qatar.

A climate of suspicion and fear ensues. This contributes to fueling the ongoing political polarization between Islamist and secularist opponents in Tunisia, and the armed polarization between supporters of Haftar and their foes in Libya. But most importantly it deepens a general fatigue with politics among the population. Political actors are then seen as terrorists, traitors, corrupt, and so on, whose only aims are to spoil and destroy the state, and self-enrichment. Fewer and fewer people go to vote and the results of each election are more contested. Those elected are consequently not seen as representative of the population.

This in turn leads to a growing support for a non-partisan and non-political leadership, which can mean the army and the restoration of dictatorship, as several recent surveys in Tunisia and Libya have showed.[19] Tunisia is heading towards its third free and fair elections by the end of 2019, but due to these reasons and the economic crisis, abstention rates will be high. Moreover, the possibility of picking an authoritarian populist leader exists, if a strong candidate emerges. As for Libya, the country is still divided, but there is a growing importance given to Haftar

19 'Tunisia Summary of Results 2018', in *Afrobarometer*, September 2018, http://afrobarometer.org/node/4270.

and a resilience towards appointing him as the authoritarian governor who can save the country.

Accusing the Gulf states of moving all the pieces in the Arab chessboard is giving them too much weight. However, they are contributing negatively to the current situation, possibly benefiting from the American withdrawal from the region and the geopolitical vacuum it is opening.

Morten Valbjørn

Chapter 8: Dialogues in New Middle Eastern Politics. On (the Limits of) Making Historical Analogies to the Classic Arab Cold War in a Sectarianized New Middle East

The title of this chapter paraphrases one of the most influential works on the role of identity politics in Middle East – or Arab – international relations: *Dialogues in Arab Politics*.[1] From a Constructivist perspective, Michael Barnett examines the construction and transformation of an Arab supra-state identity and its implications for regional politics during the twentieth century with a particular focus on the intense inter-Arab rivalry during the 1950–60s, an era in Arab politics often referred to as the 'Arab Cold War'. In the post-Arab uprisings debates about how to grasp regional politics in a 'sectarianized' new Middle East, this concept – originally coined by Malcolm Kerr[2] – has received renewed attention. Thus, recent years have seen a range of publications, where some directly refer to 'the new Arab Cold War', 'the Arab Cold War redux' or 'the Third Arab Cold War',[3] while others have replaced the

1 Michael N. Barnett, *Dialogues in Arab Politics. Negotiations in Regional Order*, New York, Columbia University Press, 1998.

2 Malcolm Kerr, *The Arab Cold War, 1958–1964. A Study of Ideology in Politics*, London/New York, Oxford University Press, 1965.

3 Curtis Ryan, 'The New Arab Cold War and the Struggle for Syria', in *Middle East Report*, No. 262 (Spring 2012), pp. 28–31; Michael Stephens, 'The Arab Cold War Redux: the Foreign Policy of the Gulf Cooperation Council States since 2011', in Thanassis Cambanis and Michael Wahid Hanna (eds), *Arab Politics Beyond the Uprisings. Experiments in an Era of Resurgent Authoritarianism*, New York, The Century Foundation Press, 2017, pp. 73–104; Raymond Hinnebusch, 'The Sectarian Revolution in the Middle East', in *R/evolutions*, Vol. 4, No. 1 (2016), pp. 120–52, http://revjournal.org/?p=1865; Juan Cole, 'A New Arab Cold War: Saudi Arabia Pressures Qatar on Muslim Brotherhood, American Think Tanks', in *Informed*

'Arab' prefix and instead speak about the emergence of a 'sectarian', 'Iranian–Saudi', 'neo-sectarian', 'Shia–Sunni', 'Islamic', 'Middle Eastern' regional cold war.[4]

The debate is part of a broader discussion triggered by the unexpected region-wide protests in 2011. Since then, Middle East scholars have been occupied by tracing the causes of the Arab uprisings and examining their consequences for (the study of) politics in a (more or less) 'new Middle East'.[5] As for the latter, these discussions have partly revolved around the question of whether it makes sense to speak about the emergence of a genuinely 'new Middle East' or are we rather witnessing a kind of 'return to the past', where dynamics known from previous eras are re-emerging.[6] Another but closely related set of questions concerns how to grasp these

---

Comments, 10 March 2014, http://www.juancole.com/2014/03/pressures-brotherhood-american.html; Steven A. Cook, Jakob Stokes and Alexander Brock, 'The New Arab Cold War', in *Foreign Policy*, 28 August 2014, http://foreignpolicy.com/2014/08/28/the-new-arab-cold-war; Marc Lynch, 'The Arab Cold War', in *The Arab Uprising. The Unfinished Revolutions of the New Middle East*, New York, PublicAffairs, 2012, pp. 29–42; Rola El-Husseini, 'Sectarianism and the New Shiism', in *Tahrir Forum*, 8 May 2016, https://www.thecairoreview.com/tahrir-forum/sectarianism-and-the-new-shiism; Nabeel A. Khoury, 'The Arab Cold War Revisited: The Regional Impact of the Arab Uprising', in *Middle East Policy*, Vol. 20, No. 2 (Summer 2013), pp. 73–87.

4 F. Gregory Gause, 'Beyond Sectarianism: The New Middle East Cold War', in *Brookings Doha Center Analysis Papers*, No. 11 (July 2014), http://brook.gs/2bl1yS3; Ruth Hanau Santini, 'A New Regional Cold War in the Middle East and North Africa: Regional Security Complex Theory Revisited', in *The International Spectator*, Vol. 52, No. 4 (December 2017), pp. 93–111, https://www.iai.it/en/node/8615; Peter Salisbury, 'Yemen and the Saudi-Iranian "Cold War"', in *Chatham House Research Papers*, February 2015, https://www.chathamhouse.org/node/16977; John Turner, 'Great Powers as Client States in a Middle East Cold War', in *Middle East Policy*, Vol. 19, No. 3 (Fall 2012), pp. 124–34; Susanne Koelbl, Samiha Shafy and Bernard Zand, 'The Cold War of Islam', in *Spiegel Online*, 9 May 2016, https://spon.de/aeJUv; Sultan Barakat, 'Is the Iranian-Saudi "Cold War" Heating Up? How to Reduce the Temperature', in *Markaz*, 22 June 2016, http://brook.gs/2auE9QB.

5 Marc Lynch (ed.), *The Arab Uprisings Explained. New Contentious Politics in the Middle East*, New York, Columbia University Press, 2014.

6 Laila El Baradei, 'Back to the Future', in *The Cairo Review of Global Affairs*, No. 15 (Fall 2014), pp. 14–15, https://www.thecairoreview.com/midan/back-to-the-future;

dynamics analytically. Thus, in recent years it has been much discussed whether past theories and analytical approaches to Middle East politics are still useful or whether they have become obsolete through the changes the region has experienced since 2011.[7] In addition, it has been debated whether it analytically is useful to try to grasp the Arab uprisings and their aftermath through historical analogies, and if so whether one should make analogies to, for instance, 1648, 1789, 1848, 1952, 1968, 1979, 1989 or the time of the 'classic' Arab Cold War in the 1950–60s.[8]

This chapter engages in this (self-reflective) debate through an exploration of the question of whether and if so how it analytically makes sense to draw analogies between the 'classic' Arab Cold War and current regional dynamics. It concludes that the value of the exercise depends on what you expect to gain from making historical analogies. On the one hand, the chapter shows that historical analogies are of limited use if one is searching in the past for firm *answers* about the present or future based on an (implicit) assumption that history will repeat itself. Thus, one should not expect some kind of 'replay' of the 'classic' Arab Cold War. On the other hand, historical analogies and studies based on insights from the past may still be useful. They can enrich the current debate by introducing novel (or forgotten) *questions* and through this draw attention to potentially important but ignored aspects of the contemporary situation.

Fawaz A. Gerges (ed.), *The New Middle East. Protest and Revolution in the Arab World*, New York, Cambridge University Press, 2014.

7 Morten Valbjørn, 'Reflections on Self-Reflections. On Framing the Analytical Implications of the Arab Uprisings for the Study of Arab Politics', in *Democratization*, Vol. 22, No. 2 (2015), pp. 218–38; Michelle Pace and Francesco Cavatorta, 'The Arab Uprisings in Theoretical Perspective. An Introduction', in *Mediterranean Politics*, Vol. 17, No. 2 (2012), pp. 125–38; F. Gregory Gause, 'Why Middle East Studies Missed the Arab Spring. The Myth of Authoritarian Stability', in *Foreign Affairs*, Vol. 90, No. 4 (July/August 2011), pp. 81–90.

8 Thomas Carothers, 'Approach Analogies with Caution', in *Alliance Magazine*, 1 December 2011, https://www.alliancemagazine.org/?p=242187; Paul Aarts et al., 'Analogies with Caution. Does History Teach Us Anything?', in *From Resilience to Revolt. Making Sense of the Arab Spring*, Amsterdam, University of Amsterdam Department of Political Science, 2012, pp. 72–9, https://www.wodc.nl/binaries/2119-fulltext_tcm28-72150.pdf.

The chapter unpacks this argument in four steps. Following a brief overview of the debate about the basic features of the 'classic' Arab Cold War, the chapter returns to the discussion about (the limits of) making historical analogies as a way of grasping current regional politics. Then, it discusses why a number of important differences between the past and the present Middle East makes it unlikely that we will witness a return to the 1950/60s Arab politics *as such*. Against this background, the final section turns to an alternative way of using the 'Arab Cold War' analogy and outlines three kinds of takeaway or analytical insights of relevance for the current discussion about dimensions of both continuity and change in regional politics in a 'sectarianized' new Middle East.

8.1 The 'classic' Arab Cold War

In order to evaluate whether and if so how it is useful to make a historical analogy to the 'classic' Arab Cold War in order to grasp key features in regional politics following the Arab uprisings, it is necessary first to establish a basic understanding of some of the key features of regional politics in that era.[9]

While the (Arab) Middle East during the 1950/60s usually is perceived as *the* heyday of Arabism, this did imply neither much inter-Arab harmony nor consensus among Arabs when it came to the implications of the Arabist idea that Arabs belong to the same Arab nation. Quite the reverse, this issue constituted one of the key points of dispute in the Arab Cold War. Despite its simultaneousness with the

---

9 This section is based on Morten Valbjørn and André Bank, 'The New Arab Cold War: Rediscovering the Arab Dimension of Middle East Regional Politics', in *Review of International Studies*, Vol. 38, No. 1 (January 2012), pp. 3–24; and Morten Valbjørn, 'Arab Nationalism(s) in Transformation. From Arab Interstate Societies to an Arab-Islamic World Society', in Barry Buzan and Ana Gonzalez-Pelaez (eds), *International Society and the Middle East. English School Theory at the Regional Level*, Basingstoke/New York, Palgrave Macmillan, 2009, pp. 140–69.

global Cold War, it did in this way hold a distinct *Arab* dimension and should not be reduced to a mere reflection of the rivalry between the two superpowers of that time.

The regional *context* within which the Arab Cold War took place was strictly speaking anarchic – in the sense of the absence of a centralized authority. At the same time, it was also marked by a strong sense of supra-state community. This emerged from a widely held Arabist notion about special bonds between Arab-speaking peoples, who were believed to share common 'Arab interests'. Combined with a high level of interconnectedness at the state and societal levels, this made the Arab world into what Paul Noble has famously depicted as a 'vast sound chamber in which information, ideas and opinions resonated with little regard for state frontiers'.[10] Instead of perceiving them as 'nation-states' in the traditional sense, it would be more accurate to describe these countries as 'territorial states' as their constitutions were often declaring that the Arab-speaking people of the given country form a part of the 'Arab nation'. Due to this state–nation misfit, the classic notion in IR theory of 'the national interest' became an ambiguous behavioural guide as schisms occurred between a narrow '*raison d'état*' and a need to be popularly perceived as being in line with the '*raison de la nation Arabe*'. For instance, it was generally agreed that membership in the Arab nation involved solidarity among Arabs and a commitment to Arab 'core issues' with the defence of Palestine as the most prominent. Apart from such vague notions, it was however highly contested what further implications the idea about special bonds between Arabs had.

Consequently, the *nature of rivalry* in the Arab Cold War largely arose from the question about the political implications of belonging to the same Arab nation. It was concerned with the ability to monopolize the specific meaning of the 'Arab interest' and to define the associated norms for appropriate Arab behaviour.[11] Hence, the *basic cleavage* in the Arab Cold War was less about whether regional politics should hold

---

10 Paul Noble, 'The Arab System: Pressures, Constraints, and Opportunities', in Bahgat Korany and Ali E. Hillal Dessouki (eds), *The Foreign Policies of Arab States. The Challenge of Change*, 2nd edition, Boulder, Westview Press, 1991, p. 56.

11 Michael N. Barnett, *Dialogues in Arab Politics*, cit.

a distinct Arab dimension as such than about whether a '*raison de la nation Arabe*' should always take precedence in situations in which a commitment to 'common Arab interests' was at odds with the narrow self-interest of a particular Arab territorial state. Put differently, whether an Arab state *primarily* should relate to expectations derived from the identity as an *Arab* state or as a *sovereign* state.

One group of *players* included conservative pro-Western monarchies such as the Hashemite Kingdoms in Jordan and Iraq (until 1958) as well as the Kingdom of Saudi Arabia. While projecting an Arab self-image of which support to the Palestinian cause was an integral part, they subscribed to a weak *Political Arabism*[12] similar to the ideas formulated in the Arab League charter about interstate cooperation between sovereign Arab states within an Arab framework of brotherhood, solidarity and coordination. This position was challenged by another group of 'radical' and nominally socialist Arab republics such as Egypt, Syria and after 1958 also Iraq. These states followed the *Pan-Arab* view that the interest of a common Arab nation should take precedence over the individual Arab states. At least in principle, the ultimate goal of this group was the emergence of a single Arab nation-state encompassing all Arabic-speaking territory, including the territory of Palestine, along lines similar to those of the merger between Syria and Egypt in the (short-lived) United Arab Republic.

The *scene of rivalry* between these two Arab blocks was not delimited to the regional level. The Arab Cold War was marked by a complex interplay between the regional and domestic levels, making the Arab world look like 'a set of interconnected organisms separated only by porous membranes, or, alternatively a large-scale domestic system divided into compartments of varying degrees of permeability'.[13] Domestic politics did also take place at the regional level, where Arab regimes lacking electoral legitimacy tried to gain domestic support by presenting themselves in the service of a higher Arab cause. At

12 On 'political Arabism' compared with 'pan-Arabism' and 'cultural Arabism', see Morten Valbjørn, 'Arab Nationalism(s) in Transformation', cit.

13 Paul Noble, 'The Arab System: Pressures, Constraints, and Opportunities', cit., p. 57.

the same time, regional rivalries also involved the domestic level. The interconnectedness of the Arab states and the permeability of their borders thus provided aspiring regional Arab powers a unique opportunity for meddling in the domestic politics of other Arab states based on claims of acting on behalf of the Arab nation. As a consequence, Arab politics during this era was marked by interventions in each other's internal affairs on a scale unseen anywhere else, including other parts of the post-colonial world. A classic expression of this remarkable 'low salience of sovereignty'[14] is Nasser's famous speeches at the Egyptian radio station Sawt al-'Arab (Voice of the Arabs). They resonated throughout the Arab 'sound chamber' allowing Nasser to bypass local leaders and appeal directly to populations in other Arab countries, and these radio speeches did for this reason appear to many other Arab leaders as a greater security threat than the Egyptian military.

Hence, the predominant *means* employed during the Arab *Cold* War were less 'hard' military power than 'soft power' in terms of ideological appeal and the legitimacy derived from being perceived to observe the norms and play the roles grounded in Arab nationalism. Here the Palestine issue constituted a key role as behind the nominal united Arab support for the Palestinians it constituted *the* arena for this inter-Arab rivalry.

While the Arab Cold War seldom evolved into 'hot' warfare like the Arab-Israeli conflict, this did not, however, mean that the conflict had no *impact* on regional politics: the 1950s and 1960s not only saw a series of popular revolts and coup (attempts) by Pan-Arab officers; this era also witnessed a range foreign policy dispositions which from a narrow *raison d'état* perspective would look very puzzling. In order to understand King Hussein's willingness to be dragged into the fatal 1967 war instead of trying to balance the threats from the Egyptian and Syrian Pan-Arab regimes by an open alliance with Israel, one must for instance consider that the likely alternative was popular revolts against

14 Fred Halliday, 'The Middle East and Conceptions of "International Society"', in Barry Buzan and Ana Gonzalez-Pelaez (eds), *International Society and the Middle East. English School Theory at the Regional Level*, Basingstoke/New York, Palgrave Macmillan, 2009, p. 15.

the Hashemite monarchy supported by 'radical' Arab states. Similarly, Egypt's road to the defeat in the 1967 war has been interpreted as Nasser being trapped by his own rhetoric, which was part of an outbidding spiral among competing 'radical' Pan-Arab states that all aspired to being the true defender of 'the Arab cause'.

8.2 'This is like . . .' Historical analogies in the debate on the Arab uprisings and its aftermath

In most accounts, the 'classic' Arab Cold War reached its end following the 1967 Arab debacle. To some observers, this marked the 'end of Arabism' *as such*, whereas others prefer to talk about a transformation of Arabism into new forms.[15] In discussions about regional politics, the notion about an 'Arab Cold War' did not ever disappear completely,[16] and in the debate about the 2006 Summer War the notion about a 'new Arab Cold War' gained new attention.[17] Yet, it was not before the Arab uprisings that the concept really gained traction, as reflected in the aforementioned surge of publications using the 'Arab Cold War' as an analytical lens to grasp dynamics of regional politics in the aftermath of the Arab uprisings.

In order to understand the renewed interest in this specific era of inter-Arab politics, it is useful to see it in the context of all the confusion the unexpected Arab uprisings triggered among observers of Middle East politics. Thus, in situations where one lacks a 'script' to understand

---

15 Fouad Ajami, 'The End of Pan-Arabism', in *Foreign Affairs*, Vol. 57, No. 2 (Winter 1978/79), pp. 355–73; Morten Valbjørn, 'Arab Nationalism(s) in Transformation', cit.

16 Hilal Khashan, 'The New Arab Cold War', in *World Affairs*, Vol. 159, No. 4 (Spring 1997), pp. 158–69.

17 Morten Valbjørn and André Bank, 'Signs of a New Arab Cold War. The 2006 Lebanon War and the Sunni-Shi'i Divide', in *Middle East Report*, No. 242 (Spring 2007), pp. 6–11.

what is going on, it is quite common to turn to historical analogies as an analytical strategy for providing some order and meaning to the unexpected events and clues about their causes and consequences.[18] In addition to the analogy to the 1950–60s Arab Cold War, the debate on the Arab uprisings and their aftermath was for instance also full of statements about 'how this is like …' 1648, 1789, 1848, 1952, 1968, 1979, 1989, and so on.[19]

While historical analogies have been very popular in this debate about the Arab uprisings and their aftermath, the exact purpose of making such analogies has seldom been specified or accompanied with reflections of what kind of (implicit) assumptions the exercise is based on.[20] Thus, the existing broader literature on the (mis)use of historical analogies has in general only received very limited attention. It is a pity, as this might have brought attention not only to how historical analogies carry both promises and pitfalls but also to how they come in various

18 This reaction was also common at the time of the unexpected end of the Cold War, where for instance Mearsheimer was drawing analogies to the pre-WWII era in European politics in his discussion about how Europe would be impacted by the end of the superpower rivalry. See John J. Mearsheimer, 'Back to the Future. Instability in Europe After the Cold War', in *International Security*, Vol. 15, No. 1 (Summer 1990), pp. 5–56.

19 Amr Adly, 'The Problematic Continuity of Nasserism', in *Jadaliyya*, 31 March 2014, http://www.jadaliyya.com/Details/30469; Steven A. Cook, 'The Banality of Abdel Fattah al-Sisi', in *Foreign Affairs Snapshots*, 8 June 2014, https://www.foreignaffairs.com/articles/egypt/2014-06-08/banality-abdel-fattah-al-sisi; Richard N. Haass, 'The New Thirty Years' War', in *Project Syndicate*, 21 July 2014; Michael D. Kennedy, 'Arab Spring, Occupy Wall Street, and Historical Frames: 2011, 1989, 1968', in *Jadaliyya*, 11 October 2011, http://www.jadaliyya.com/Details/24493; Thomas Carothers, 'Approach Analogies with Caution', cit.; Laila El Baradei, 'Back to the Future', cit.; Marwan Muasher, *The Second Arab Awakening. And the Battle for Pluralism*, New Haven, Yale University Press, 2014; Robert Springborg, 'Whither the Arab Spring? 1989 or 1848?', in *The International Spectator*, Vol. 46, No. 3 (September 2011), pp. 5–12, https://doi.org/10.1080/03932729.2011.609357.

20 Among the exceptions Thomas Carothers, 'Approach Analogies with Caution', cit.; Paul Aarts et al., 'Analogies with Caution. Does History Teach Us Anything?', cit.

forms and can serve different kinds of purpose.[21] In some ways, the use of historical analogies can be a productive and worthwhile exercise, but at the same time, it is necessary to pay attention to a number of issues. As illustrated in the debate on the Arab uprisings and their aftermath, it is rarely given exactly which year/era it is most obvious to draw analogies to. However, this is important to consider, as an analogy to, say, 'Europe 1989' or 'Iran 1979' will steer our attention and imagination in quite different directions. Moreover, it is useful to ponder whether an analogy is more useful to enlighten some rather than other dimensions or aspects of the current era, for example is the Arab Cold War analogy better to enlighten dynamics among 'Sunni actors' than the nature of the current Iran–Saudi rivalry? Last but not least, it is also important to consider whether the purpose of drawing historical analogies is to search in the past for firm *answers* about the present or future, based on an (unacknowledged) assumption that history repeats itself. Or is the purpose rather to enrich a debate by introducing novel, or forgotten, *questions* and through this draw attention to potentially important but ignored aspects of the present – but without expecting that the outcome today necessarily will be the same as in the past?

Such questions have rarely been explicitly addressed, when historical analogies have been employed as a way of grasping dynamics of regional politics in the aftermath of the Arab uprisings. The following two sections will therefore discuss how the utility of making analogies to the 'classic' Arab Cold War very much depends on how you position yourself in relation to these basic questions.

---

21 On the use of historical analogies more generally see among others Markus Kornprobst, 'Comparing Apples and Oranges? Leading and Misleading Uses of Historical Analogies', in *Millennium*, Vol. 36, No. 1 (2007), p. 29–49; Yuen Foong Khong, *Analogies at War. Korea, Munich, Dien Bien Phu, and the Vietnam Decisions of 1965*, Princeton, Princeton University Press, 1992; Ernest R. May, *'Lessons' of the Past. The Use and Misuse of History in American Foreign Policy*, New York, Oxford University Press, 1973; Jørgen Møller, 'Composite and Loose Concepts, Historical Analogies, and the Logic of Control in Comparative Historical Analysis', in *Sociological Methods & Research*, Vol. 45, No. 4 (November 2016), pp. 651–77.

8.3 The Arab Cold War redux? Searching for firm answers about the present in the past

The most straightforward, but at the same time also least useful, way of using the 'Arab Cold War' analogy is by claiming that the Middle East is moving 'forward to the past' in the sense that the region in some sense is returning to the 1950/60s and is almost replaying the Arab Cold War.

This approach is visible in more or less explicit versions in the current debate. In the article 'Back to the Future' (a direct reference to the famous movie where a time machine accidentally catapults Michael J. Fox thirty years into the past), Laila El Baradei for instance concludes, after having highlighted similarities between Egypt during Nasser and Sisi, that 'we Egyptians are traveling backwards in a time capsule. Lately, we seem to have arrived in the 1960s'.[22] While Egypt during Nasser often figures prominently in the most explicit versions of this first way of using historical analogies, as already mentioned references to the 'classic' Arab Cold War are also common in broader discussions about dynamics in current regional politics, in particular regarding the Saudi–Iranian rivalry. Often, however, it is anything but clear whether past dynamics as such are expected to be replicated in the present and to what extent and in which way the past is supposed to provide answers about the present and future. This ambiguity is also reflected in the aforementioned popularity of making 'Arab Cold War' analogies. Sometimes the 'Arab' prefix is replaced with 'sectarian', 'Iranian–Saudi', 'neo-sectarian', 'Shia–Sunni', 'Islamic', 'Middle Eastern',[23] but this is rarely accompanied with any explicit reflections about whether this carries any implications as regards the utility of drawing analogies between the 1950/60s inter-Arab rivalries and today. The change of prefix does however deserve attention as it points to one of more reasons why this first way of using the analogy to the 'classic' Arab Cold War seems problematic. Thus, it is possible to

22 Laila El Baradei, 'Back to the Future', cit., p. 14.

23 See footnote 4.

outline at least four reasons why some kind of straightforward return to the time of the 'classic' Arab Cold War is unlikely.

First, while the Arab Cold War should not be perceived as a mere reflection of the global cold war between the US and USSR, it is important to notice how the global context of today is fundamentally different from that within which the regional rivalries of the 1950/60s took place. Instead of a bipolar global order with two superpowers representing a capitalist and a communist system, regional politics of today is played out in the context of a global change from American unipolarity to what some observers describe as a 'post-Western' multipolarity, which does not have an ideological dimension similar to the past. While global powers in the past were far from absent in the Middle East, the time of the Arab Cold War marked an era when the European powers were withdrawing and the superpowers had not yet entered the regional scene to the extent they later did, in particular the United States, which despite of all the talk about a 'post-American' Middle East is still the dominant military power in the region.[24]

Second, the regional gravity and the composition of key regional players have also changed. Egypt is hardly any longer an important regional player and Iraq has completely lost its regional influence and has almost become an arena for rivalries among other actors. In turn, the Gulf states, in particular Saudi Arabia, Qatar and the UAE, have entered the regional scene together with non-Arab states such as Iran and Turkey.

This change in the composition of key regional players also points to a *third* reason why a genuine 'return to the past' is unlikely. There is a long tradition of depicting the Middle East as a region 'dripping with identity politics',[25] which in Middle East scholarship has been reflected in a long-standing debate on the relative – and changing – importance of

24 Morten Valbjørn, 'Global/Regional IR and Changes in Global/Regional Structures of Middle East International Relations', in 'Shifting Global Politics and the Middle East', in *POMEPS Studies*, No. 34 (March 2019), pp. 18–22, https://pomeps.org/?p=10700.

25 Shibley Telhami and Michael Barnett, 'Introduction: Identity and Foreign Policy in the Middle East', in Shibley Telhami and Michael Barnett (eds), *Identity and Foreign Policy in the Middle East*, Ithaca/London, Cornell University Press, 2002, p. 3.

supra-state identities compared to territorial-state identities.[26] While the 1950/60s marked the heyday of *Pan-Arabism*, the Arab uprisings triggered a new round of the classic debate about (the myth of) the end of Arabism. Initially, this debate revolved around the question of whether the presence of only Egyptian flags at the Tahrir Square in early 2011 indicated that territorial state identities had gained prominence over supra- or sub-state identities or whether the resonance of the Arab uprisings across the 'Arab sound chamber' instead marked the rise of a 'new Arabism'.[27] Soon, however, this discussion was replaced by growing attention paid to how a fragmentation of the 'Arab public sphere'[28] and a weakening of the Arab dimension of Arab politics did not necessarily have to result in a strengthening of territorial state identities. In line with Lynch's statement that 'a number of deeper trends have come together in recent years to give frightening new power to identity politics writ large',[29] various kinds of sub- and supra-state identities other than the Arab instead began to receive increasing attention. Some scholars focused on sub-state identities based on tribe or ethnicity, while others suggested that the defining feature of identity politics in a 'new Middle East' would be what Geneive Abdo coined the 'new sectarianism',[30] and others have described as a process of 'sectarianization'.[31] While Shia/Sunni sectarianism also had been

---

26 Morten Valbjørn, 'Introduction: The Role of Ideas and Identities in Middle East International Relations', in Morten Valbjørn and Fred Lawson (eds), *International Relations of the Middle East, Vol. 3: The Role of Ideas and Identities in Middle East International Relations*, London, Sage, 2015, pp. vii–xxiii.

27 Leon T. Hadar, 'Burying Pan-Arabism', in *The National Interest*, 1 March 2011, https://nationalinterest.org/node/20173; Youssef Mohamed Sawani, 'The "End of Pan-Arabism" Revisited: Reflections on the Arab Spring', in *Contemporary Arab Affairs*, Vol. 5, No. 3 (2012), pp. 382–97.

28 Marc Lynch, 'The Rise and Fall of the New Arab Public Sphere', in *Current History*, Vol. 114, No. 776 (December 2015), pp. 331–6.

29 Marc Lynch, 'The Entrepreneurs of Cynical Sectarianism', in 'The Politics of Sectarianism', in *POMEPS Studies*, No. 4 (13 November 2013), p. 3, https://pomeps.org/?p=3888.

30 Geneive Abdo, *The New Sectarianism. The Arab Uprisings and the Rebirth of the Shi'a-Sunni Divide*, New York, Oxford University Press, 2017.

31 Nader Hashemi and Danny Postel (eds), *Sectarianization. Mapping the New Politics of the Middle East*, London, Hurst, 2017.

debated in the decade before 2011, in the post-Arab uprisings debate also previous sceptics now acknowledged that sectarianism had become 'a real factor in politics'.[32] Regional polls made in the wake of the Arab uprisings did at the same time report a growing concern across the region about sectarianism along with an increasing identification with sect-centric identities contrary to similar polls made before 2011.[33] This trend is also reflected in the scholarly debate. Instead of discussing whether sectarianism was a 'myth or reality',[34] the debate on sectarian politics has in recent years largely revolved around questions about why the Middle East became 'sectarianized' and what implications this would have for various dimensions of regional politics.[35] In other words, the Middle East may still be 'dripping with identity politics', but the exact composition

32 F. Gregory Gause, 'Sectarianism and the Politics of the New Middle East', in *Up Front*, 8 June 2013, http://brook.gs/2bpJ2oW.

33 Zogby Research Services, *Looking at Iran. How 20 Arab and Muslim Nations View Iran and Its Policies*, 2012, https://www.wilsoncenter.org/sites/default/files/iranpollresultsreport.pdf; Zogby Research Services, *Middle East 2016. Current Conditions & the Road Ahead*, November 2016, http://www.zogbyresearchservices.com/new-gallery-5; Michael Lipka, 'The Sunni-Shia Divide: Where They Live, What They Believe and How They View Each Other', in *FacTank*, 18 June 2014, https://www.pewresearch.org/?p=260523; Jacob Poushter, 'The Middle East's Sectarian Divide on Views of Saudi Arabia, Iran', in *FacTank*, 7 January 2016, https://www.pewresearch.org/?p=276590. More recently, it has been debated whether the 'sectarian surge' of recent years is in retreat (in parts of the region). See for instance Fanar Haddad, 'The Waning Relevance of the Sunni–Shia Divide. Receding Violence Reveals the True Contours of "Sectarianism" in Iraqi Politics', in *TCF Reports*, 10 April 2019, https://tcf.org/content/report/waning-relevance-sunni-shia-divide.

34 Moshe Ma'oz, 'The "Shi'i Crescent": Myth and Reality', in *Saban Center Analysis Papers*, No. 15 (November 2007), http://brook.gs/2bPAojA.

35 Raymond Hinnebusch, 'The Sectarian Revolution in the Middle East', cit.; Frederic M. Wehrey, *Sectarian Politics in the Gulf. From the Iraq War to the Arab Uprisings*, New York, Columbia University Press, 2014; Geneive Abdo, *The New Sectarianism*, cit.; Morten Valbjørn and Raymond Hinnebusch, 'Exploring the Nexus between Sectarianism and Regime Formation in a New Middle East: Theoretical Points of Departure', in *Studies in Ethnicity and Nationalism*, Vol. 19, No. 1 (April 2019), pp. 2–22.

of regional (supra-state) identities seems to be quite different from the time of the 'classic' Arab Cold War.[36]

This brings us to the *fourth* and final reason, which is related to the aforementioned question of whether the exact identity of the prefix in the *Arab* Cold War matters. While supra-state identities may still play a role in regional politics, the nature of what one might call the ideational cleavages appear to be different today compared to in the past. As explained above, the regional politics during the 'classic' Arab Cold War of the 1950/60s was defined by two quite different forms of cleavage: the first concerned the *Arab-Israeli conflict*, which to a large extent was played out as conventional 'hot' military conflicts between actors, which did not claim to share the same (supra-state) identity.[37] The other cleavage concerned the *inter-Arab rivalry* between regional players subscribing to the same Arab supra-state identity. The main focus in the traditional literature about the Arab Cold War has been directed towards how this gave rise to a distinct kind of identity politics concerning the ability to monopolize what it meant and implied to be Arab. As explained above, this gave rise to a rivalry taking place in a complex interplay between domestic and regional theatres, where 'soft power' derived from ideological appeal and from being perceived as protecting Arab interests (including supporting the Palestinian cause) often constituted a much more important commodity than 'hard' military power.

---

36 For an elaboration, see Morten Valbjørn, 'Studying Identity Politics in Middle East International Relations Before and After the Arab Uprisings', in Raymond Hinnebusch and Jasmine Gani (eds), *Routledge Handbook on the Middle East State*, London/New York, Routledge, forthcoming.

37 For the present debate, the important point here is that Israel did not consider itself as sharing the same Arab identity as its counterparts. Whether it also in the Israeli case makes sense speaking about a tension between an (Israeli) territorial state identity and some kind of (Jewish) supra-state identity is another question to be debated elsewhere. See also Michael N. Barnett, *The Star and the Stripes. A History of the Foreign Policies of American Jews*, Princeton/Oxford, Princeton University Press, 2016; and Michael N. Barnett (ed.), *Israel in Comparative Perspective. Challenging the Conventional Wisdom*, Albany, State University of New York Press, 1996.

While supra-state identities also constitute an important dimension in today's Middle East, the ideational cleavages are in more ways different. The regional rivalries are no longer dominated by mainly Arab players and the former distinctly Arab dimension of Arab politics is today far less visible. Compared to the 1950/60s, the Arab-Israeli conflict has for instance become less Arab than Palestinian and does not any longer seem to have the same mobilization potential in the Arab world, where some Arab states such as Saudi Arabia and the UAE are now instead seeking an open rapprochement with Israel. This trend can be traced all the way back to the Camp David accord in 1978, but the classic 'Arab norm' against such unilateral moves has subsequently been further weakened and violations of the norm do not any longer trigger regional popular protests among the Arab public or sanctions from the other Arab states like those Sadat experienced after the Egyptian-Israeli peace treaty. Instead of the ideational cleavage structure of the 1950/60s, which is hard to trace in today's regional politics, the aforementioned frequent references to not only to an 'Iran–Saudi' but also a 'sectarian' or 'Shia–Sunni' regional cold war point to a different kind of cleavage structure, where supra-state identities may still matter for how regional rivalries are played out, but in a quite different way than in the past. While most agree that Shia/Sunni divisions are not the main drivers for the Iranian–Saudi rivalry,[38] it is widely acknowledged that recent years' aforementioned growing sectarianization of various parts of the Middle East has also left its mark on how this rivalry is played out.[39] That said, it is at the same

38 For an overview of the evolution of the Iran–Saudi relations, see Simon Mabon, *Saudi Arabia and Iran. Soft Power Rivalry in the Middle East*, new edition, London, I.B. Tauris, 2016.

39 On how sectarianism influences this rivalry, Daniel Byman, 'Sectarianism Afflicts the New Middle East', in *Survival*, Vol. 56, No. 1 (2014), pp. 79–100; Afshon Ostovar, 'Sectarian Dilemmas in Iranian Foreign Policy: When Strategy and Identity Politics Collide', in *Carnegie Papers*, November 2016, https://carnegieendowment.org/publications/?fa=66288; Suzanne Maloney, 'The Roots and Evolution of Iran's Regional Strategy', in *Atlantic Council Issue Briefs*, September 2017, https://www.atlanticcouncil.org/publications/issue-briefs/the-roots-drivers-and-evolution-of-iran-s-regional-strategy; Danny Postel and Nader Hashemi, 'Playing with Fire: Trump, the Saudi-Iranian Rivalry, and the Geopolitics of Sectarianization in the Middle East', in *IEMed Mediterranean Yearbook 2018*, pp. 58–63, https://www.

time also clear that the ideational dimension of the Iranian–Saudi rivalry is very different from the inter-Arab rivalries during the time of the 'classic' Arab Cold War. The rivalry between Iran and Saudi Arabia can hardly be said to be about monopolizing the meaning. The behavioural implications of a *shared* identity and the logic according to which they in their rivalry are 'playing the (sectarian) identity card', for instance in proxy conflicts across the region, must therefore also be assumed to be quite different from the 'classic' Arab Cold War, where adversaries all claimed to act in the service of the same common 'Arab interest'.

In view of these differences between the 1950/60s Arab politics and the present as regards the global context, regional players, the nature of supra-state identities and associated ideational cleavages, the 'classic Arab Cold War' appears to be of limited use, if the purpose is to search in the past for firm answers about the present and future based on the assumption that history will repeat itself.

8.4 Three takeaways: searching for novel or forgotten questions

Before throwing 'the classic Arab Cold War baby out with the bathwater', it is however useful to recall that there are more ways of using historical analogies. Instead of searching for firm answers in the past, they can also be used to enrich a debate by introducing novel – or forgotten – *questions* and through this draw attention to potentially important but ignored aspects of the present – but without expecting that the outcome today necessarily will be the same as in the past. Moreover, historical analogies can sometimes be more useful to cast light on some rather than other aspects of the current era. These reminders are relevant in the present context. While the Middle East may not be moving 'forward to

---

iemed.org/publicacions-en/historic-de-publicacions/anuari-de-la-mediterrania/sumaris/anuari-iemed-de-la-mediterrania-2018.

the past', in at least three ways some of the insights from the traditional literature on the 'classic' Arab Cold War still seem to be of relevance for current discussions about dimensions of both continuity and change in regional politics in a 'sectarianized' new Middle East.

First, the literature on the 'classic' Arab Cold War can to some extent be perceived as part of a larger literature on cold wars and how they constitute a specific kind of conflict in international relations. The very term 'cold war' can allegedly be traced all the way back to the time of the Spanish Reconquista, where the Christian campaign to reconquer the Iberian Peninsula from Islamic power was described as a cold war or *guerra fria*.[40] It was not before the end of the Second World War, however, that the term gained broader traction. Here it referred to the emerging global rivalry between the superpowers of the United States and the USSR, which George Orwell had already in 1945 coined as a 'cold war'.[41] Basically, the notion of a 'cold war' refers to a state of conflict between powers not involved in *direct* military confrontation, hence 'cold'. Instead, their conflict is played out through *indirect* means, such as economic and political action, propaganda, espionage or proxy warfare often via local 'clients' in domestic theatres. Usually the struggle is less about military conquest than domestic influence in the areas where these proxy wars are fought (and through this wider regional influence). Military strength is therefore often less important than 'soft power', financial power and not least access to local proxies.

To some extent these basic features of the (Arab) *cold war* analogy provides a useful lens through which to highlight a number of important traits of, for instance, the current Iranian–Saudi rivalry: despite the absence of a direct 'hot' military confrontation, there is an intense rivalry between the two regional powers. However, it takes place in terms of an indirect rivalry, often through proxies in weak and permeable states such

40 Adda B. Bozeman, *Politics and Culture in International History. From the Ancient Near East to the Opening of the Modern Age*, 2nd edition, New Brunswick, Transaction Publishers, 1994, p. xxxviii.

41 George Orwell, 'You and the Atom Bomb', in *Tribune*, 19 October 1945, https://www.orwellfoundation.com/?p=3495.

as Syria, Iraq, Lebanon and partly Yemen and the purpose has less to do with territorial conquest than the ability to shape the regional order.

Second, while the literature on the classic *Arab* Cold War can be seen as part of a broader debate on cold wars as such, as indicated in the identity prefix, it also carries more distinct features. Arabism as well as the associated Arab identity may play a far less important role today compared to the 1950/60s. Yet the identity prefix still serves as a reminder both of how the ideational dimension of international relations may involve other identities than the territorial state identity and how this may carry implications for some of the general cold war dynamics.

As already mentioned, the traditional literature on the 'classic' Arab cold war has usually stressed how the presence of a strong Arab supra-state identity in a region with young and quite weak post-colonial states made the 1950/60s Arab world into what Noble famously described as a 'vast sound chamber in which information, ideas and opinions have resonated with little regard for state frontiers'.[42] This blurriness between the domestic and the regional provided a fertile ground for aspiring Arab powers' interference and mingling in domestic politics in other Arab countries and contributed to a complex interplay between regional and local actors during the 'classic' Arab Cold War. The presence of a strong Arab supra-state identity did, furthermore, constitute an important tool for external players to gain access to local 'clients' and mobilize the broader public by appealing to a shared 'Arab cause'. At the same time, local players were also using the 'Arab card' not only to achieve domestic legitimacy but also to attract external support in their own local rivalries.

Despite the limited role of an Arab supra-state identity in current regional politics, it is still possible to draw some parallels to today, where the presence of 'sectarianized' supra-state identities, the rise of new media (this time social media rather than Nasser's radio) and the 'return of the weak Arab state'[43] once again have contributed to the blurring

---

42 Paul Noble, 'The Arab System: Pressures, Constraints, and Opportunities', cit., p. 56.

43 Bassel F. Salloukh, 'Overlapping Contests and Middle East International Relations: The Return of the Weak Arab State', in *PS: Political Science & Politics*, Vol. 50, No. 3 (July 2017), pp. 660–3.

of the line between the domestic and the regional. Thus, the notion of a regional 'sound chamber', where ideas and information resonate across the region and weapons, fighters and money flow across borders, also seems useful for an understanding not only of how protests in the periphery of Tunisia in 2011 turned into the Arab uprisings, but also of how, for instance, the Syria conflict became sectarianized and at the same time contributed to a growing sectarianization in other parts of the region. Like before, supra-state identities, though more frequently of sectarian rather than Arab nature, do also today seem to play a role in how regional actors try to mingle in domestic theatres and gain access to local 'clients', who at the same time appeal to shared identities to attract external support.[44]

Drawing such a parallel to the 'classic' *Arab* Cold War can in more ways be useful for the current debate on regional politics in the aftermath of the Arab uprisings. Besides serving as a general reminder of how supra-state identities can influence cold war dynamics, it can also bring attention to novel questions that have not received much attention in past or current debates on regional cold wars. For instance, while it might still make sense to speak about a kind of 'regional sound chamber' mediated by, among others, social media and satellite television, it is at the same time clear that it has become much more fragmented compared not only to the 1950/60s, but also to the 'new Arab public sphere' that rose just before and around the beginning of the Arab uprisings.[45] Yet, it is still not entirely clear how, for instance, 'sectarian Twitter wars'[46] influence regional politics and how a more fragmented 'regional sound chamber' influences cold war dynamics. Another question concerns whether different supra-state identities work in similar or different ways. Much of the existing literature on identity politics in the Middle

---

44 Morten Valbjørn, 'Unpacking a Puzzling Case: On How the Yemeni Conflict Became Sectarianised', in *Orient*, Vol. 59, No. 2 (2018), pp. 65–73.

45 Marc Lynch, *Voices of the New Arab Public. Iraq, al-Jazeera, and Middle East Politics Today*, New York, Columbia University Press, 2006; Marc Lynch, 'The Rise and Fall of the New Arab Public Sphere', cit.

46 Alexandra Siegel, 'Sectarian Twitter Wars. Sunni-Shia Conflict and Cooperation in the Digital Age', in *Carnegie Papers*, December 2015, https://carnegieendowment.org/publications/?fa=62299.

East has focused on the relative importance of territorial-state identities compared with supra-state identities and how the latter influence regional politics. However, far less attention has been devoted to the question of whether it makes a difference whether supra-state identities are based on religion, nationality, ethnicity or sect. This relates to an even more basic question: should identities (including supra-state identities) be considered as 'empty' in the sense that they can be treated as alike based on the assumption that their relevance is limited to being a marker useful for the drawing of borders between in- and out-groups, or do identities have some kind of 'content' in the sense that they inform how we see and understand the world, for which reason it is crucial to distinguish not only between territorial-state identities and supra-state identities but also different kinds of, for instance, supra-state identities?[47] So far, these questions have largely been ignored in the current analogy debate. However, they are closely related to the aforementioned confusion about whether it makes a difference if you replace the 'Arab' prefix with 'sectarian', 'Iranian–Saudi', 'neo-sectarian', 'Shia–Sunni', 'Islamic', 'Middle Eastern' when speaking about some kind of regional cold war.

Third, if historical analogies sometimes are more useful for casting light on some rather than other aspects of the current era, it is natural to consider whether the Arab Cold War analogy has more to offer when it comes to other dimensions of today's regional politics than the Iranian-Saudi rivalry or the kind of sectarian politics that emphasises some sort of Shia–Sunni schism.

As already discussed in the previous section, there are some fundamental differences between today's Iranian–Saudi rivalry and the 'classic' Arab Cold War, which in addition to the prominent role assigned to the Palestine issue concerned relations between actors subscribing to the *same* supra-state identity. As suggested above, this does not mean that some of the more general lessons from the Arab Cold War analogy are without any value in examinations of the current Iranian–Saudi rivalry and the role of the Shia–Sunni divide. Yet, some of the more

47 Christopher Phillips and Morten Valbjørn, '"What Is in a Name?" The Role of (Different) Identities in the Multiple Proxy Wars in Syria', in *Small Wars & Insurgencies*, Vol. 29, No. 3 (2018), pp. 414–33.

subtle insights from the literature on the 'classic' Arab Cold War may be more relevant for another aspect of current regional politics. More specifically, the one concerning relations among actors subscribing to the same supra-state identity. Contrary to the 1950/60s, where Arabism constituted the frame of reference for a shared supra-state identity, recent years' sectarianization of regional politics has made sect-centric identities more salient. By moving attention from the prevalent focus in the current sectarianism literature on Shia versus Sunni in favour of intra-Shia and Sunni relations, it turns out that Barnett's aforementioned seminal work on *Dialogues in Arab Politics* serves as a useful reminder of how a shared supra-state identity – as being Arab, Shia or Sunni – can impact dynamics among regional players in quite ambiguous ways.[48]

On the one hand, a common identity can inform actors about who are likely friends and enemies and make some kind of cooperation more or less likely or costly. In the past, an Arab identity, for instance, did constitute the key selection criteria for whether one could become a member of the Arab League. Likewise, it could be costly to cooperate with actors with similar 'real politics' interests but different identities – the classic examples would be Egypt's peace treaty with Israel or Jordan's decision in the 1960s not to ally with Israel, which according to a 'realist' logic would have been the most natural way of balancing the overt threats from pan-Arabist Syria and Egypt. Today, any talk about some sort of 'Arab front' has vanished. Instead Saudi has (without much success) tried to build what it has presented as a 'Sunni block', to which also non-Arab but Sunni actors such as Pakistan were invited.[49] At the same time, Iran has in recent years tried to mobilize various Shia militias across the region; not because Iran does not want to engage with Sunni actors – contrary to Saudi Arabia, Iran usually tries to tone down the picture of the region as divided between Sunnis and Shias – but because in a sectarianized context it has become increasingly difficult for Iran to get access to the 'Sunni scene' compared to in the past. As noted by Byman, this very process has paradoxically meant that Iran in the

48 Michael N. Barnett, *Dialogues in Arab Politics*, cit.

49 Hussein Ibish, 'Saudi Arabia's New Sunni Alliance', in *The New York Times*, 31 July 2015, https://nyti.ms/1VRbClM.

end has contributed to the kind of sectarianization which in many ways runs counter to its own regional interests in downplaying the sectarian question.[50]

On the other hand, and maybe even more importantly, Barnett's seminal work does also serve as a reminder of how a common identity does not have to lead to harmony and coexistence. Thus, sharing the same supra-state identity can also spur, at times subtle, disagreements about the normative implications of having a certain identity. It can give rise to intense rivalries between aspiring leaders, which may take the form of attempts at discrediting the other as being at odds with the norms of proper behaviour for a given identity. In the past, this kind of rivalry constituted an important part of the Arab Cold War, which was played out both between 'radical' and 'conservative' Arab players (for example Nasser's Egyptian pan-Arabism vs Saudi Arabia's weak political Arabism) and among 'radical' players (for example Syrian Baath vs Iraqi Baath vs Egyptian Nasserism, which subscribed to various forms of pan-Arabism). Moreover, one would see much lip service paid to the 'common cause' without any real action (for example the Arab League's inefficiency). Thus, relations between actors subscribing to the same supra-state identity do not have to be more harmonious, but the nature of their rivalry and conflicts may differ from actors that do not share a common identity. Even a cursory look at the recent years' *intra*-Sunni relations confirms this point.[51] There has been much talk about the need for Sunni cooperation, for example Saudi's call for a 'Sunni block', in order to balance the 'Shia threat'. Just like the Arab League in the past, it has however mainly been limited to 'talk' without resulting in

50 Daniel Byman, 'Sectarianism Afflicts the New Middle East', cit. See also Christopher Phillips and Morten Valbjørn, '"What Is in a Name?", cit.; Suzanne Maloney, 'The Roots and Evolution of Iran's Regional Strategy', cit.

51 Hussein Agha and Robert Malley, 'The Middle East's Great Divide Is Not Sectarianism', in *The New Yorker*, 11 March 2019, https://www.newyorker.com/news/news-desk/the-middle-easts-great-divide-is-not-sectarianism. See also the chapter by Youssef Cherif in this volume.

much real cooperation.[52] Instead, the 'Sunni scene' has been marked by considerable internal disagreement and rivalry among state actors – such as Saudi Arabia, the UAE, Qatar, Turkey and Egypt as well as non-state actors, including the Muslim Brotherhood, various Salafist groups, Islamic State, al-Qaeda, and so on – and part of this rivalry has revolved around competing notions about what it means to be Sunni.[53]

The Arab Cold War analogy may usually have been applied to the Saudi–Iranian rivalry, but some of the more subtle points in the traditional literature on Arab politics during the 1950/60s seem more useful for discussions about relations among actors sharing the same supra-state identity. Again, the point is not that one should expect that, for instance, intra-Sunni relations would turn out to be a mere replay of the past inter-Arab relations. Rather, the analogy should serve as a reminder of how dynamics among actors with a shared identity might be different from those marked by other kinds of ideational structures, but that they can nevertheless be very ambiguous and not necessarily harmonious.

Concluding remarks

The aim of this chapter has been to contribute to the current discussion about how to grasp regional politics in the aftermath of the Arab uprising and in particular discuss whether, and if so how, historical analogies constitute a useful analytical strategy. In order to do so, the chapter has examined the renewed interest in the 'classic' Arab Cold War, which has become a popular analytical lens through which to grasp regional dynamics in a 'sectarianized' new Middle East. This use of historical analogies, for instance to inter-Arab politics in the 1950/60s, has seldom been accompanied by specification of the exact purpose of making such

52 F. Gregory Gause, 'Ideologies, Alignments, and Underbalancing in the New Middle East Cold War', in *PS: Political Science & Politics*, Vol. 50, No. 3 (July 2017), pp. 672–5.

53 Marc Lynch, 'The War for the Arab World', in *Marc Lynch's Blog at Foreign Policy*, 23 May 2013, https://foreignpolicy.com/2013/05/23/the-war-for-the-arab-world.

analogies, or reflections on what kind of assumptions they are based on. This is problematic, because the value of making historical analogies very much depends on what you expect to gain from this exercise.

The most straightforward, but at the same time least useful, way of using the 'Arab Cold War' analogy is by claiming that the Middle East is moving 'forward to the past' in the sense that the regional politics of today will resemble those of the 1950/60s. Due to a number of important differences between that era and today, such a 'replay' of the 'classic' Arab Cold War appears very unlikely. While the past may not provide firm answers about the present or the future, this does not mean, however, that one should throw the 'Arab Cold War baby out with the bathwater'. Thus, historical analogies and studies based on insights from the past can still be useful in discussions about continuity and change in today's regional politics. They can introduce novel (or forgotten) questions and through this draw attention to potentially important but ignored aspects of the contemporary situation. In order to illustrate this, the chapter has pointed to how the traditional literature on the 'classic' Arab Cold War offers at least three takeaways. In addition to serving as a reminder of some of the basic features of 'cold wars' as such, the Arab Cold War analogy can also draw attention to how the ideational dimension of cold wars may involve identities other than the territorial state identity. Even more importantly, it raises the question of whether different kinds of supra-state identity are influencing cold war dynamics in similar ways. Finally, the Arab Cold War analogy can also bring attention to how a shared supra-state identity can have a quite ambiguous and not necessarily harmonious implications for the relations between regional actors. All in all, these three takeaways illustrate how historical analogies in principle can contribute to and enrich the current discussions about regional political in today's Middle East. In order to realize this analytical potential, it is however necessary that more effort is devoted to specifying when and, not least, how historical analogies can be useful in discussions about current affairs.

Lorenzo Kamel

Chapter 9: Whose Stability? Assessing the 'Iranian Threat' Through History

It is estimated that around 7 per cent of the French population took part in the French Revolution (1789–99). Over a century later, approximately 9 per cent of the Russian population participated in the 1917 Russian Revolution. It is, however, necessary to wait another six decades (1979) to encounter the most 'popular' revolution of modern times: about 11 per cent of Iranians took part in the revolution of 1979,[1] the one that more than any other shaped present-day Iran and, more in general, the contemporary Middle East.

Despite such a high participation rates, the regime led by the *'āyatollāh al-'uẓma* (the great ayatollah) Ruhallah Khomeynī represented an immediate paradox: in his eyes, the very concept of popular sovereignty was to be stigmatized as a sort of colonial imposition created for the purposes of undermining the concept of *umma* (the Muslim community). The presence of empowered citizens, thus, was not deemed as necessary: there was, in fact, only space for 'subjects' in need of guidance.

Islam, or more precisely a peculiar interpretation of its main dictates, represented the 'guide' invoked by Khomeynī. Until the rise of the *Velāyat-e faqih* (government of the jurisconsult), the totalizing doctrine conceived by Khomeynī, local Shiite clerics largely agreed on the need to limit their influence to the spiritual sphere. It was Khomeynī who gave the clerics the right and legitimacy to govern the state: 'it was

---

1 See Abbas Milani, 'The Three Paradoxes of the Islamic Revolution in Iran', in *MEI Articles*, 29 January 2009, https://www.mei.edu/publications/three-paradoxes-islamic-revolution-iran.

precisely over this point', in Laurence Louër's words, 'that Khomeini would prove to be "revolutionary"'.[2]

These considerations and the historical processes that underlie them remain – forty years after the outbreak of the Iranian Revolution – more relevant than ever, and still exert direct repercussions on the (in) stability and (in)security of a large part of the contemporary Middle East. With the aim of analysing and placing them within a broader analytical perspective, this chapter intends to investigate some of the dynamics that have influenced the most the nexus between religion and politics in the Iranian context, providing a long-term historical overview of the political involvement of the country's clerics. To this end, the first part examines the 1891–2 Tobacco Protest which prepared the ground for the outbreak of the Persian Constitutional Revolution (1905–11), creating the conditions for 'the emergence of Shi'ism as an insurrectionary movement against colonialism'.[3] The section that follows throws light on the dynamics which prompted London to back the rise of Reza Shah (1921) as the last but one Persian Shah and the first in the Pahlavi dynasty, a key piece in the puzzle of the processes triggered in the three decades which followed. This same section also analyses the causes and medium- to long-term consequences of the operation with which the CIA and MI6, taking advantage of internal dynamics, overthrew the democratically elected Mohammed Mossadeq government (1953). The genesis of the 'most popular' revolution in modern and contemporary history, generally known as the 'Islamic Revolution' of 1979, was directly related to these events, and its causes and consequences are still clearly visible in the fractures that affect large part of the region. Fernand Braudel noted that even an apparently minor event 'can mirror a long term situation or "structural" circumstances'.[4] The four 'moments' on which this chapter focuses are themselves components of a wider and more complex 'structure' that has much to do with the 'security' and the

2 Laurence Louër, *Shiism and Politics in the Middle East*, London, Hurst, 2012, p. 6.

3 Hamid Dabashi, *Islamic Liberation Theology. Resisting the Empire*, London/ New York, Routledge, 2008, p. 77.

4 Cited in Rashid Khalidi, *Brokers of Deceit. How the U.S. Has Undermined Peace in the Middle East*, Boston, Beacon Press, 2013, p. xi.

'stability' of the Middle East. Each of them continues to reverberate in various ways and forms, both in Iran and in the broader region.

9.1 Colonialism and tobacco

If Michel Foucault had lived at the time of the 1891–2 Tobacco Protest he would probably have described it as a watershed, 'the point of inflexion of a curve'.[5] It was, in fact, the first form of organized resistance designed to combat Western expansionism in Persia and, more specifically, the agreements that the European powers had drawn up with the local elite to guarantee certain advantageous concessions. Local women, particularly in the area of Tabriz, played an active and central role in the protests.[6]

Shiism's Twelver branch was an integral part of Persian power until 1501 when it was proclaimed the official religion of the Safavid dynasty at the expense, in particular, of other Shiite branches. At the time, as in the bulk of the Qajar era (1794–1925), the influence of the Twelver clerics was, however, largely limited to the religious, educational and legal spheres. A sort of unwritten agreement thus existed according to which the Qajar left the Twelver clerics free rein in each of these fields in exchange for recognition of the legitimacy of its rule.[7]

A more concrete and organized political role for the Shiite clerics began to emerge clearly only in the second half of the nineteenth century when Persia, like mutatis mutandis the Ottoman Empire, attempted to respond to its endemic and growing internal weakness by centralizing the state administration and opening up to European capitals. These were the years of the Crimean War (1854), an epochal event which, on the

5 Michel Foucault, *The Archaeology of Knowledge and the Discourse on Language*, New York, Pantheon Books, 1972, p. 9.

6 See M. R. Alam, Sousan Z. Razavi, 'Study of Women's Role in Tobacco Protest', in *Woman and Culture*, Vol. 4, No. 15 (Spring 2013), pp. 71–8.

7 Abdellatif al-Zain, *LilBahth 'an Tārīkhanā fi Lubnān* [In Search of Our History in Lebanon], Beirut, n.d., 1973, pp. 481–3.

one hand, sanctioned the inclusion of the lion's share of the region in the world economy, and, on the other, represented the greatest war in which Great Britain took part in the time frame stretching from the Napoleonic Wars to the outbreak of World War I.

It is important to highlight that it was precisely to the Crimean War that some of the first movements and proto-democratic reforms introduced in Muslim-majority countries are to be linked. In 1861 the *bey* (lord) of Tunis brought in the Islamic world's first written constitution. Five years later the first elections were held in Egypt and in 1876 the first Ottoman constitution was drawn up – all events which can at least partially be linked with the fact that the Crimean War was the first war in which Ottoman and European soldiers fought side by side against a common enemy.[8] In addition, it was the first war in which news from the front arrived by telegraph and was printed virtually live by the era's newspapers. Also thanks to the first photographs taken on the battlefield, this novelty generated unprecedented echoes of the victories registered by the (still incomplete) Western democracies at the expense of the despotic Russian Empire.

Finally, it should also be mentioned that, during that very same years, a plethora of missionaries were extremely active in distributing the Scriptures. Edmund Hornby (1825–96), nominated head judge of the British Supreme Court in Constantinople in 1857, pointed out that during the Crimean War 'British and French bible societies and a great many missionary corps were extremely active in distributing the New Testament to Turkish soldiers [...] when these soldiers ended their military service period a great many bibles thus ended up in the homes of Turkish families scattered around the country'.[9]

Whatever the consequences of the Crimean War and other episodes that occurred at the time, what is interesting here is to note that the second half of the nineteenth century was the phase in which the interests

8 Specifically, it was the first war in history in which a Christian power (Britain) fought alongside a Muslim Empire (Ottoman) and against a Christian Empire (Tsarist Russia).

9 The National Archives (TNA), FO 78/1851, Hornby to the then Foreign Minister John Russell (1792–1878), Constantinople, 26 July 1864.

of the great powers – Great Britain, France and Russia primarily – and in relation to the Dardanelles Straits in particular, began to exert a growing influence in the context of a region and, more specifically, an area (Persia) which had long seemed impermeable to outside penetration.

Persian Shah Nāsir al-Dīn (1831–96), the first Persian monarch to have visited Europe (in 1873 and again in 1879 and 1889), made protracted attempts to exploit these rivalries to his own advantage with results which were, however, in many ways the reverse of his intentions. The increase in political and economic interference by the great powers in contexts which had for centuries been subject to direct or indirect Persian influence was the most tangible evidence of this. This, for example, is the case of the decisive role played by Great Britain in the context of the annexation of Herat to Afghanistan, a country which London saw as functional to its goal of limiting Russian expansion in Central Asia. For its part, in addition to conquering modern-day Uzbekistan and Turkmenistan, Russia succeeded in breaking the bonds uniting Persia and other strategic historic cities in the Samarkand area.

The straw which broke the camel's back, of determinant influence in triggering the subsequent Tobacco Protest, dates to late 1890 when Nāsir al-Dīn granted English Major Gerald F. Talbot a fifty-year monopoly over tobacco production, sales and exports – a widely consumed product in Iran. It was not, however, the first grant made by Nāsir al-Dīn. In 1872, German businessman (naturalized British) Paul Reuter (1816–99) had already succeeded in obtaining from the Shah 'exclusive and definitive' rights to extract everything he could from Persia's 'coal, iron, copper, lead' and oil mines and also in obtaining road and other public works building rights.[10]

In both cases, these grants were greeted with great hostility by local people. The latter, in particular, triggered a national boycott prompting immediate withdrawal of the grant, a process which in many ways coincided with the first phase in modern Iranian nationalism.

---

10 Firuz Kazemzadeh, *Russia and Britain in Persia. Imperial Ambitions in Qajar Iran*, new edition, London, I.B. Tauris, 2013, p. 107.

It is precisely to the phase which coincided with the 1891-2 revolt – still today considered a great success[11] – that it is possible to trace the first concrete involvement in politics by Shiite clerics in modern Iran. More specifically, the revolt 'symbolized the alliance that matured between powerful bazaaris in Iran and senior mujtahids in the shrine cities'.[12]

The alliance between the clerics and social classes linked to the 'bazaar' – 'the place of prices',[13] which echoes the concept of souq/market in Arabic – was the backbone of the main historical phenomena which had occurred in the country since the end of the nineteenth century (including the Tobacco Protest, the 1905–11 Constitutional Revolution, and the 1979 revolution). This alliance was not, however, an inevitable outcome of the country's internal dynamics but rather the culmination of a series of failed attempts – by local *tujjār* (merchants) – to combat, in a structured and organized way, the concessions granted to the Western powers. A significant example of this is the Council of the Representatives of the Merchants of Iran (*Majlis-i Vukalā-yi Tujjār-I Iran*), a sort of organized pressure group founded in Tehran in 1883 and led by a famous merchant of the day, Hāj Muhammad Hasan Amīn al-Zarb, whose objective was to assert its right to 'a voice in the affairs of the country'.[14] The council was soon dismantled, primarily because

---

11 Between 1890 and 1980, according to Ali Pirzadeh, 'only the Tobacco Protest of 1891 and the 1978 Islamic Revolution can be considered as successful'. Ali Pirzadeh, *Islam Revisited. Exploring the Historical Roots of Culture, Economics, and Society*, Cham, Springer, 2016, p. 145.

12 Yitzhak Nakash, *The Shi'is of Iraq*, Princeton, Princeton University Press, 1994, p. 210.

13 For centuries, as Keshavarzian has noted, the very nature of the bazaar represented 'the necessary foundation for communal allegiance, with its confined nature fostering long-term and face-to-face interactions among bazaaris'. See Arang Keshavarzian, *Bazaar and State in Iran. The Politics of the Tehran Marketplace*, Cambridge, Cambridge University Press, 2007, pp. 71–2.

14 Vanessa Martin, *Iran between Islamic Nationalism and Secularism. The Constitutional Revolution of 1906*, London/New York, I.B. Tauris, 2013, p. 22. Mahdawi has noted that the Shah initially gave his full support to the council. See Shireen Mahdawi, *For God, Mammon, and Country. A Nineteenth-century Persian Merchant, Haj Muhammad Hassan Amin al-Zarb, 1834–1898*, Boulder, Westview Press, 1999.

it was seen as incompatible with the interests of the absolute monarchy, opening the way to a historic phase in which the great merchants began to present their protests in religious terms.

A central role in this process was played by Mīrzā Shīrāzī (1814–96), an eminent *mujtahid* (Islamic law judge) originally from Shiraz, who had also distinguished himself for his consolidated bonds with traders active in Southern Iran. Urged on by Jamāl al-Dīn al-Afghānī (1838–97) – possibly the most influential ideologist in the Muslim world during the late nineteenth century – Shīrāzī[15] acted as spokesman for the assertion of rights which were increasingly deeply felt by the local population, first and foremost its traders. The concessions granted by the Shah to the European powers – including the one regarding tobacco – effectively constituted a serious threat to merchant wealth in the country's largest towns and cities, from Isfahan to Fars by way of Tabriz and Tehran. As noted by Nakash:

> The interdependency that began to mark the relations between the bazaaris and senior mujtahids in the shrine cities reinforced the strong orientation of the latter toward Iran. The bazaar emerged as the major source of credit for senior mujtahids in Iraq while the latter became both the superior authority for arbitration between bazaaris and mujtahids in Iran, as well as a counterpoise against the government.[16]

---

15 Al-Afghānī wrote a letter to Shīrāzī in which he urged the latter to 'save and defend' Iran from the 'criminal' concessions granted to the great powers. Ideologically speaking, Al-Afghānī, native to Iran, held that Islam and progress were entirely compatible. His ideas were taken on board by a great many intellectuals including Egyptian jurist Muḥammad ʿAbduh (1849–1905), one of the key figures in Islamic modernism as well as a direct witness to the British occupation of Egypt (1882). Al-Afghānī's thesis was promoted in a historic phase in which a growing number of scholars were questioning whether Islam and modernity were compatible: this questioning undermined well-established certainties and fostered the ideological conditions necessary to the penetration of nationalist and/or secular ideologies and concepts. See Muḥammad ʿAbduh and Muḥammad 'Imarāh (eds), *al-A'mal al-kamilah* [The full works of the Imam Muḥammad ʿAbduh], Vol. 3, Beirut, al-Mu'assasat al-Arabīyya, 1972; and Muḥammad ʿAbduh and Muḥammad 'Imarāh (eds), *Al-Islam wa al-mar'ah* [Islam and Woman in the Opinion of the Imam Muḥammad ʿAbduh], Cairo, Al-Qāirah li al-Thaqāfa al-'Arabīyya, 1975.

16 Yitzhak Nakash, *The Shi'is of Iraq*, cit., p. 210.

It is significant to note that each of these elements contributed to preparing the ground for the 1905 Constitutional Revolution, the first constitutional revolution in the whole of Asia. As in the case of the 1979 revolution, a wide spectrum of local people were involved (including merchants, intellectuals and clerics)[17] and it was significantly influenced also by an exponential rise in the prices of primary goods – wheat prices shot up 90 per cent in the first three months of 1905, largely as a consequence of the Russian Revolution and a cholera outbreak – as well as the fears expressed by merchants and clerics alike about growing and pervasive 'external interference'.[18] It was precisely in the excitement of the protests, which resulted in the promulgation of the new constitution, that the expression '*Mellat-i Iran*' ('the Iranian nation') was first heard on the streets of Tehran.[19]

9.2 The 1921 and 1953 coups d'état

The origins of the Pahlavi dynasty can be traced to the 1921 coup d'état in which the Reza Khan regime emerged, thanks in particular to the

17 It is significant that the central role played by the clerics in the 1905–11 revolution notwithstanding, this latter generated a markedly Western-style constitution and form of government. However, the 1979 revolution, in which secular elements in the population also played a significant part, led to an Islamic revolution whose constitution accords religion a totalising role.

18 These include the (pro-Russian) policies implemented by Belgain consultant Joseph Naus (1897) to whom Iranian Prime Minister Amin ad-Dauleh had turned for assistance. Afshin Matin-Asgari has noted that during World War I 'the entire [Iranian] constitutional experiment was suspended as British and Russian occupation forces put an end to the country's independence. Moreover, the occupying armies requisitioned food and other vital resources, causing enormous economic devastation, famine, and millions of deaths'. Afshin Matin-Asgari, 'The Pahlavi Era Iranian Modernity in Global Context', in Touraj Daryaee (ed.), *The Oxford Handbook of Iranian History*, Oxford, Oxford University Press, 2012, p. 347.

19 Ervand Abrahamian, *Iran between Two Revolutions*, Princeton, Princeton University Press, 1982, p. 82.

support assured by the British authorities present in the country. His son, Mohammad Reza Pahlavi, came to the throne via a further coup d'état three decades later, in 1953. The deposition of the last Qajar dynasty sovereign was not the outcome of planned and organized military action (Iran did not have a full-blown army). It was actually a sort of 'one man show',[20] largely triggered and implemented by the British authorities in order to get a strong man capable of combating the covert ambitions of post-Bolshevik Russia into power. The individual chosen for this purpose, a 'violent'[21] and 'illiterate'[22] army officer known as Reza Khan, immediately suppressed all forms of opposition in order to consolidate his personal power.

Inspired by the policies adopted by Kemal Atatürk (1881–1938) in Turkey, Reza Shah adopted an ambitious modernization programme and succeeded in a short time in presenting himself convincingly as a reformer, a modern statesman. Appearances notwithstanding, his frequently counterproductive methods did not go unnoticed by the British authorities present in Iran either: 'The fact that the Shah alone has policies and drives them through', noted the British legation in Tehran, 'increases his prestige and strength politically, but this political predominance is apt to interfere in business and in the long run the effect cannot be beneficial'.[23]

It is thus reasonable to question why he chose not to follow in the footsteps of the great 'modernisers' of his era (including Atatürk), opting for a Republican- rather than monarchist-style government. The answer to this is largely to be found in his desire not to make an enemy of

---

20 Hazem Kandil, *The Power Triangle. Military, Security, and Politics in Regime Change*, New York, Oxford University Press, 2016, p. 35.

21 Citing Kandil: 'Always a violent man, Reza cursed his generals, struck them with his cane, and ordered court-martials all around'. Ibid., p. 41.

22 Andrew Scott Cooper, *The Oil Kings. How the U.S., Iran, and Saudi Arabia Changed the Balance of Power in the Middle East*, New York, Simon & Schuster, 2011, p. 417.

23 British Library Manuscript Collection (BLMC), India Office Records, Coll. 28/39, v. 1, f. 117, British legation in Tehran to Foreign Minister Anthony Eden (1897–1977), 27 June 1936.

the clerics whose main representatives Reza Shah himself consulted in March 1924 in the holy city of Qom.

To this is to be added the fact that a 'monarchist framework' fitted more naturally with the process of 'racialization' which marked out Reza Pasha's regime right away. As Adib-Moghaddan has noted, 'Reza Shah imagined grandeur exactly in psycho-nationalistic terms: Iranian identity was racialised and Iranian superiority was thus inscribed in the syntax of the emerging Pahlavian national narrative.'[24]

An instrumental role was played in this sense by 'Aryanism', an ideology inspired by a self-attributed sense of the superiority of the 'Aryan race' which prompted Reza Shah to change the nation's name from Persia to Iran, that is, 'Land of the Aryans', in 1935. Reza Shah's attempt to 'purify' the country culturally and 'racially' speaking also took the form of a marked attention to the presumed cultural affinities between Iran and Nazi Germany (then on the rise) as well as via the systematic suppression of a large number of 'foreign' words, primarily Arabic, present in the Farsi language, a goal which was achieved thanks to the creation and strengthening of specific institutes and research centres including *Farhangistan* (1935).

Both Aryanism and the concomitant emphasis on the great pre-Islamic Persian empires constitute two aspects of great importance: those which more than any other bind together Reza Shah and his son and heir, Mohammad Reza Pahlavi. The latter laid claim, twenty-two years after (1965) the defeat of the Nazi regime, to the title of *Aryamehr* ('the light of the Aryans'), an expression chosen to assert 'his leadership of a racially defined ethnic group'.[25] Fascinated, as his father had been, by Napoleon, like the latter he had himself crowned monarch in an opulent ceremony in 1967. Reza Pahlavi went as far as to cancel out or downplay all traces of Islam's influence over the country and declared that Iran's history and culture were 'more akin

24 Arshin Adib-Moghaddam, *Psycho-nationalism. Global Thought, Iranian Imaginations*, Cambridge, Cambridge University Press, 2018, p. 54.

25 Ali M. Ansari, *The Politics of Nationalism in Modern Iran*, Cambridge, Cambridge University Press, 2012, p. 174.

to that of the West'.[26] In his opinion, Persian culture was 'the oldest continuous one racially and linguistically linked to that of the West'.[27]

It is thus hardly surprising that the repression set in motion under Reza Pahlavi's dictatorship had an immediately identifiable and well-defined target. It struck, in particular, at two specific sectors of the population, those which had acted as the backbone to the great historical processes which had occurred in the country in previous decades: 'the bazaar' and the 'ulema'.[28] The Rastakhiz (Party of Rebirth), a party founded in the 1970s, represented the latest and most effective incarnation of a series of tools adopted for this purpose. According to the Shah, those who did not agree to join Rastakhiz fell into two categories: either they were members of the Tudeh (Communist party), and thus liable for imprisonment, or they were traitors and thus to be exiled from the country. Repression went well beyond this, however. Note that in June 1977 the Red Cross confirmed that 900 of the 3,000 political prisoners present in Iranian jails had been tortured.[29] In the words of Michael Axworthy: 'It appeared that quiet dissent was no longer an option: the regime was intent on erasing all dissent. It was not just Tudeh and extremists that were threatened – large sections of Iranian society became anxious that their interests were in danger.'[30]

---

26 Cited in Zhand Shakibi, *Revolutions and the Collapse of the Monarchy. Human Agency and the Making of Revolution in France, Russia, and Iran*, London/New York, I.B. Tauris, 2007, p. 86.

27 Ibid.

28 Michael Axworthy, *Revolutionary Iran. A History of the Islamic Republic*, New York, Oxford University Press, 2013, p. 91. More than the bazaars – the corporations were reformed and placed under direct regime control – it was, however, the 'ulema who were subjected to the greatest repression. This aim was pursued by means of the creation of repressive bodies set up for this purpose. A new calendar was also established – to substitute the Islamic calendar – calibrated to match the date of the rise to the throne of Cyrus the Great.

29 See Andrew Scott Cooper, *The Fall of Heaven. The Pahlavis and the Final Days of Imperial Iran*, New York, Henry Holt, 2016, p. 237; Afshin Matin-Asgari, 'Twentieth Century Iran's Political Prisoners', in *Middle Eastern Studies,* Vol. 42, No. 5 (September 2006), pp. 689–707.

30 Michael Axworthy, *Revolutionary Iran*, cit., p. 92.

How had things gone this far? To respond to this question it is necessary to take a step back in time and look at the frantic months of 1953 and thus the historical processes which led to the downfall of the democratically elected government of nationalist leader Mohammad Mossadeq, and the return to power of Reza Pahlavi.

Between 16 September 1941 – when, following on from the Anglo-Soviet invasion of the country,[31] Reza Pahlavi succeeded his father Reza Shah to the throne – and 1953, thirty-one cabinets and 140 ministers succeeded one another in office, a much higher figure than the ten cabinets and fifty ministers who had occupied the highest state offices in the previous sixteen years.[32] The last of the sixteen cabinets was led by Mohammad Mossadeq, who had won more votes than any other member of Tehran's key council. Arrested in the early 1920s for his opposition to Reza Shah's rise to power, Mossadeq had devoted much of his life to defending Iran's national integrity. His policies were especially unfavourable to Western interests in the area. The nationalization of Iranian oil was, in fact, seen by the London establishment above all as a serious threat to British interests in the area.[33] Washington, for its part,

---

31 The purpose of the invasion was to undermine a possible support by the Reza Pahlavi regime for the Axis powers. It also aimed to create a safe supply route by which British help could be sent to the Soviet Union. A new book by Ashley Jackson confirms the thesis according to which a sort of unwritten pact was in place at the time which was well summarized by the words of the man who was soon to be the British ambassador to Tehran, Reader Bullard (1885–1976): 'The Persians expect that we should at least save them from the Shah's tiranny as a compensation for invading their country'. Cited in Ashley Jackson, *Persian Gulf Command. A History of the Second World War in Iran and Iraq*, New Haven, Yale University Press, 2018, p. 183. On Bullard's point of view, including discriminatory judgements on Iran's Kurdish community, see also TNA FO 624/28/152, a dispatch signed by R. Bullard, Tehran, 28 October 1942.

32 Bahman Baktiari, *Parliamentary Politics in Revolutionary Iran. The Institutionalization of Factional Politics*, Gainesville, University Press of Florida, 1996, p. 28.

33 It was defined 'a heavy blow to our prestige' in a memorandum signed by Under-Secretary of State, Roger Makins (1904-94), 11 August 1951 (TNA FO 371/124968/ZP24/2).

primarily feared that the country's powerful Communist party, Tudeh, might take control.[34]

When, in late 1951, Mossadeq succeeded in getting parliamentary approval for his oil nationalization law proposal – closing down the Anglo-Iranian Oil Company (AIOC) and inspiring what happened later in Algeria and Libya in the 1960s and 70s respectively – the British authorities responded by blocking Iranian oil exports and appealing to the Hague Court of Justice. Despite this latter coming down clearly on the side of the Iranians, London reacted by tightening its embargo on Iran and exerting growing diplomatic pressure on its allies to do likewise. Iranian oil exports only restarted from 1954 onwards, after the creation of the Consortium for Iran led by British Petroleum (ex-AIOC), together with Gulf Oil, Shell, Mobil, Texaco, Standard Oil of California and Standard Oil of New York: the famous (in Enrico Mattei's definition) 'seven sisters'.

It is certainly true that, in the three years between the nationalization of Iranian oil and the August 1953 coup which led to the removal of Mossadeq – replaced by General Fazlollah Zāhedī (1892–1963) – this latter became the object of growing hostility by a significant segment of the country's public opinion (the collapse of the local economy played a front-rank role in this process as did the growing hostility of the clerics). It is, however, clear that the role played by the United States and Great Britain in implementing this coup d'état exerted an enormous influence, directly or indirectly, on the country's subsequent history.[35] In the words of Mark J. Gasiorowski and Malcolm Byrne:

34 This does not imply that Washington had no other aims. On 23 April 1951 the future (from 1953) president of the United States, Dwight Eisenhower (1890–1960), then Supreme Commander of NATO's Allied Forces noted the following in his diary: 'Lord knows what we'd do without Iranian oil'. Cit. in Louis Galambos (ed.), *The Papers of Dwight David Eisenhower, Vol. 12: NATO and the Campaign of 1952*, Baltimore, John Hopkins Press, 1989, p. 239.

35 According to Paul R. Pillar, 'it's impossible to say what directions Iran would have taken if Britain and the United States had not pushed out Mossadegh. But it's a safe bet that, with the Cold War having come and gone, we wouldn't be talking today about what was the main worry in 1953: a communist Iran'. Paul R. Pillar, 'Sixty-Five Years On: Iran Regime Change Advocates Haven't Learned from Coup', in

> The Anglo-American operation interrupted the Iranian drive to affirm its own sovereignty over its own resources and helped to bring an intense period in the history of the country's nationalist and democratic movement to an end. These consequences came dramatically back to haunt Iran in the years which followed. The fall of the Shah in 1979 brought back memories of 1953 US action as it had made possible the subsequent increasingly unpopular monarchy and intensified the anti-American nature of the revolution in the minds of many Iranians in the intervening twenty-five years.[36]

9.3 The rise of the clerics and the 'twilight' of the bazaars

In a famous speech given in June 2009 at Cairo's Al-Azhar University, President Barack Obama admitted that 'the United States played a role in the overthrow of a democratically-elected Iranian government' at the peak of the Cold War.[37] The three decades which followed – inaugurated by Reza Pahlavi's return to Tehran with the director of the CIA, Allen Dulles (1893–1969), as his escort[38] – also marked a watershed in what

---

IranSource, 15 August 2018, Available online: http://www.atlanticcouncil.org/blogs/iransource/sixty-five-years-on-iran-regime-change-advocates-haven-t-learned-from-coup. It should, however, be highlighted that the general opinion of the day was very different. On 16 June 1932 the apostolic delegate in Iran, Egidio Lari (1882–1965), made known to Cardinal (and future pope) Eugenio Pacelli (1876–1958) that 'the Russians are very active in Persia especially in the primary schools, hospitals [. . .] and trade but the Bolsheviks have the upper hand and are flooding Persia with their products. In this they have beaten their rivals, the English'. Vatican Secret Archives (ASV), Arch. Deleg. Apostolica in Iran, fasc. 24, b. 10, f. 201.

36 See the book abstract of Mark J. Gasiorowski and Malcolm Byrne (eds), *Mohammad Mosaddeq and the 1953 Coup in Iran*, Syracuse, Syracuse University Press, 2004.

37 White House, *Remarks by the President at Cairo University*, 4 June 2009, https://obamawhitehouse.archives.gov/the-press-office/remarks-president-cairo-university-6-04-09.

38 For years Dulles played an active role as arms sales middleman, including for the Nazi regime.

Ahmad Ashraf called 'the two inseparable twins' of the Iranian context, the bazaars and the mosques.[39]

Whilst he was also an expression of the Iranian conservative oligarchy, Mossadeq came down decisively against repeated attempts by the militant Shiite clerics to impose the use of the full face veil as well as to legally ban alcohol. He also immediately undertook to improve the country's health system and ensure a minimum of social insurance. A convinced secularist, Mossadeq embodied the spectre of a Turkish Atatürk-style secular republic in the eyes of the more hardline religious groups – including the Quietist Shiite hierarchy based in the holy city of Qum. It was precisely this strata of the population – the one that ultimately had benefited the most from the interference of external players – which represented one of the foundation stones of the events which occurred three decades later. Darioush Bayandor went as far as to argue that 'the core group in the Islamic Revolution [1979] was in effect of direct ideological lineage to the clerics who played a key part in Mosaddeq's downfall'.[40] In this sense it is certainly not a coincidence that it was some of the Mossadeq's most fervid enemies, including Ayatollāh Abu'l-Qāsem Kāshāni (1882–1962) and Navvab Safavi (leader of the Fadā'iyān-e Islam movement), who emerged as 'icons of the new order' in the aftermath of the 1979 revolution.

Just as the 1890 revolt coincided with the first Shiite clerical intervention in modern Iranian politics, so the events of 1953, and Mossadeq's failed attempt to establish his sovereignty over the country's energy resources, directly or indirectly ushered in the definitive pre-eminence of the clerics in the country's political life. In this context it should be underlined that many scholars have recently downplayed the United States and British roles in the events which led to the overthrow of Mossadeq. Bayandor, for example, noted in a 2010 book based largely on US and British sources that 'internal political dynamics more than

39 Ahmad Ashraf, 'Bazaar-Mosque Alliance: The Social Basis of Revolts and Revolutions', in *International Journal of Politics, Culture, and Society*, Vol. 1, No. 4 (Summer 1988), p. 538.

40 Darioush Bayandor, *Iran and the CIA. The Fall of Mosaddeq Revisited*, Basingstoke, New York, Palgrave Macmillan, 2010, p. 2.

foreign intrigues were responsible for the ultimate blow'.[41] The role played by the country's internal dynamics have, indeed, for long been underestimated or ignored. Plenty of archival sources published for the first time in the last five years have, however, confirmed beyond any reasonable doubt that it was, to a considerable extent, Washington's interference which triggered the process which ultimately led to Mossadeq's fall and the strengthening of the Iranian Shiite clerics. More specifically, the strategies implemented by the US 'resulted in literal revolt of the population'.[42] The British establishment, at the same time, was and remained aware of 'some very embarrassing things about the British'[43] in the context of the 1953 coup d'état.

What has been argued thus far does not intend to suggest that the 1979 revolution, whose primary slogan was *Istiqlāl, Āzādī, Jomhūri-e Eslāmī* ('Independence, Liberty, Islamic Republic'), was exclusively related to the involvement and initiative of the clerics. It is enough to mention that even a figure like Ali Shariati (1933–77), a firm oppositor of the Shah and considered by many as the 'Revolution's ideologue', was largely influenced by the anti-imperialist policies of the global left and perceived Islam as a theological tool serving a purpose ('the liberation').[44] It should also be added that the lay and secular component of the revolution was present right from the start while its (however

41 Ibid., p. 155.

42 Central Intelligence Agency (CIA), DDO Files, Job 80–01701R, box 3, file 11, Misc. TPAJAX Correspondence. The file is available online: *Summary, Campaign to Install a Pro-Western Government in Iran*, https://nsarchive2.gwu.edu/NSAEBB/NSAEBB435/docs/Doc%202 %20-%201954-00-00 %20Summary%20of%20 Wilber%20history.pdf.

43 TNA PRO FCO 8/3216, B.L. Crowe to R.S. Gorham, 'Iran: release of confidential records, US State Department papers for 1952-1954', 12 October 1978. The file is available online: *Minute, B.L. Crowe to R.S. Gorham, Anglo-American Planning Talks: Iran*, https://nsarchive2.gwu.edu/NSAEBB/NSAEBB435/docs/Doc%20 23 %20-%20October%2012.pdf.

44 Shirali wrote: 'Shariati transported religious discourse onto the ground of the Marxists, the progressives, and the liberals, that is, the ground of ideology in the full meaning of the term'. Mahnaz Shirali, *The Mystery of Contemporary Iran*, New Brunswick, Transaction Publishers, 2015, p. 135.

prevalent) 'Islamic' character became an all-encompassing element only later, in particular as a consequence of the occupation of the American Embassy in Tehran (4 November 1979–20 January 1981) and the outbreak of the war with Iraq (22 September 1980): two historical events which played a crucial role in paving the way to the most extremist of the revolutionary groups. In the words of Mohammad Ayatollahi Tabaar, 'revolution came first, and "Islam" followed'.[45]

In the context of these arguments, a further aspect would appear to be especially significant. By means of the Savak, Iran's terrible secret police whose power Mossadeq had attempted unsuccessfully to weaken, for years Reza Pahlavi engaged in brutal repression of any (be it 'timid' and/or clandestine) form of opposition, adopting his infamous 'torture rooms', particularly from 1963 onwards.[46] To this it should be added, citing Benjamin Smith, that 'most "old" social institutions in Iran were destroyed or significantly weakened during the Pahlavi dynasty (1926–79)',[47] a process which peaked in 1965[48] and 1975, the year the single party was founded (Hezb-e Rastakhiz, Party of Rebirth), imposed by the Shah.[49] The wide-ranging anti-monarchical sentiments – within which

45 Mohammad Tabaar, *Religious Statecraft. The Politics of Islam in Iran*, New York, Columbia University Press, 2018, p. 5.

46 In 1963 the Iranian economy became de facto bound to what Ibrahim M. Oweiss has called the 'petrodollar'. Katouzian was referring to the post-1963 period – when the autocratic character of the dictatorship headed by Reza Shah reached its apex – using the concept of 'petrolic despotism'. See Homa Katouzian, *The Political Economy of Modern Iran. Despotism and Pseudo-Modernism, 1926-1979*, New York, New York University Press, 1981.

47 Benjamin Smith, 'Collective Action with and without Islam: Mobilizing the Bazaar in Iran', in Quintan Wiktorowicz (ed.), *Islamic Activism. A Social Movement Theory Approach*, Bloomington/Indianapolis, Indiana University Press, 2004, p. 185.

48 Katouzian has noted that 'the long-term origins of the revolution [1979] may be said to go back to the 1960s when the upper and modern social classes were eliminated from politics and so the state lacked a social base'. Homa Katouzian, *Iran. Politics, History and Literature*, Abingdon/New York, Routledge, 2013, p. 100.

49 Chehabi noted that 'the bazaaris resented the creation of the Rastakhiz party, whose totalitarian tentacles threatened to reach into the farthest corners of civil society and take away the last vestiges of Bazaar autonomy [. . .] Their anger and hostility contributed greatly to the close cooperation between the Bazaar and Khomeni

the militant clerics[50] represented just one of many components – were thus solid and deeply rooted. It should not come as a surprise, thus, that also the bazaaris (a significant proportion of whom were ideologically close to the Khomeyni's ideology),[51] in common with thousands of workers, students and intellectuals with Marxist–Leninist tendencies (many of whom belonged to parties and groups such as Tudeh and Fadai'i), played a prominent role within the revolutionary body which enabled the 1977–9 revolutionary movement.[52]

Many among those workers, students and intellectuals were also bound by a firm opposition toward the privileges granted by the regime to a growing number of foreign entities, American first and foremost. It has been estimated that around 8,000 Americans lived in Iran in 1970. Just eight years later, in 1978, this number had risen to 50,000. Many of these lived separated off from the rest of the population enjoying benefits, including in the hospitals, which were out of reach to the bulk of Iranians. James Bill has noted that 'the very best and the very worst of America were on display in the cities of Iran'.[53]

Without prejudice to these and other potential considerations, it is, however, worth bearing in mind that the definitive affirmation of the Shiite clerics, favoured by the events of 1953 and which came to full fruition twenty-six years later, coincided precisely with a reduction in the historical role played by the bazaaris, perceived by Reza Pahlavi as a

during the years that led up to the revolution'. H. E. Chehabi, *Iranian Politics and Religious Modernism. The Liberation Movement of Iran under the Shah and Khomeini*, London, I.B. Tauris, 1990, p. 94.

50 The clerics initially opposed the social reform ('White Revolution') enacted by the Shah. The same can be said for agricultural reforms by means of which many goods controlled by the religious authorities (mortmain) were expropriated.

51 According to Keddie, 'the "traditionalist" bazaar attitude, along with the close family, financial, and cultural ties of the bazaar with the ulama, help explain the bazaar-ulama alliance that has been responsible for so much revolutionary activity in Iran since 1891'. Nikki R. Keddie, *Modern Iran. Roots and Results of Revolution*, updated edition, New Haven, Yale University Press, 2006, p. 227.

52 James A. Bill, *The Eagle and the Lion. The Tragedy of American-Iranian Relations*, New Haven, Yale University Press, 1988, p. 381.

53 Ibid.

'crowd of fanatics'.[54] This progress was given a determinant boost under the Reza Pahlavi dictatorship and then reached full fruition in the wake of the 1979 revolution. In the words of Arang Keshavarzian:

> When the Pahlavi regime stepped in to directly restructure the Bazaar in 1976, these functions were politicized and directed resources toward mass politics. However, the shifting institutional setting and location of networks that transformed the Bazaar structure after the Islamic Revolution also inhibited its potency.[55]

The Islamic Republic was easily able to implement a series of policies which (also) shaped the ways in which the bazaar operated with evident repercussions for the bazaaris' own potential to have their say in the country's political mobilization context.[56] To this it should also be added that, in post-1979 Iran, both the imposition of the monopolies and a more interventionist management of licences and the growing co-optation of the more influential business people into the state apparatus (public administration included) undermined the bazaaris' power and scope for action at the roots, effectively leaving the militant Shiite clerics an empty field.

Conclusions: Qablan, Alan, Ayandeh

Regular elections, monitored by international institutions, are held every four years in Iran. Yet, the country's power structure (ultimate power is

---

54 For the Shah the 'bazaaris were a crowd of fanatics, highly resistant to any change as a result of the fact that their status guaranteed them a lucrative monopoly'. Mohammad Reza Pahlavi, *Answer to History*, New York, Stein and Day, 1980, p. 156.

55 Arang Keshavarzian, *Bazaar and State in Iran*, cit., p. 23.

56 Zahedi noted that 'the theocracy has proved itself to be just as harsh, even more severe, than the monarchy in controlling and repressing segments of the bazaari community'. Dariush Zahedi, *The Iranian Revolution Then and Now. Indicators of Regime Instability*, Boulder, Westview Press, 2000, p. 47.

in the hands of a non-elected religious leader[57]) is criticized and/or seen with suspicion by many, in particular amongst the younger segments of the population.[58] Torture, unregulated arrests and extra-judicial killings are well-documented.[59] Despite this, a large proportion of public opinion in Iran is aware of the long-term processes which led to the 1979 revolution (the 'rise of the mullahs') and looks with a mixture of concern and disillusion to the potential consequences of fostering a new power structure.

---

57 The current Supreme Leader of Iran, ʿAlī Ḥoseynī Khāmeneī, substantially performs a guarantor and intermediary role within the system. In this sense it is important to bear in mind that the *Velāyat-e faqih* ('rule of the jurisconsult') principle, a totalitarian doctrine conceived by Khomeynī in accordance with which the task of a Muslim jurist is to oversee parliament's action in order to ensure that it conforms to what a jurist (*faqih*) would consider suitable, has changed significantly over the last four decades. See Mojtaba Mahdavi, 'Ayatollah Khomeini', in John L. Esposito and Emad El-Din Shahin (eds), *Key Islamic Political Thinkers*, New York, Oxford University Press, 2018, pp. 104–39.

58 See Maral Karimi, *The Iranian Green Movement of 2009. Reverberating Echoes of Resistance*, Lanham, Lexington Books, 2018.

59 On the summary executions common since the earliest days of Khomeynī's rise to power, see Payam Akhavam, 'Is Grassroots Justice a Viable Alternative to Impunity? The Case of the Iran People's Tribunal', in Rebecca Barlow and Shahram Akbarzadeh (eds), *Human Rights and Agents of Change in Iran*, Singapore, Palgrave Macmillan, 2018, pp. 85–6. To this it should be added that women's status, whilst better than that of many other countries in the region (Saudia Arabia first and foremost), has taken substantial steps backwards from the days of the Reza Pahlavi regime. Axworthy has noted that, since 1979, 'Iranian women have been subject to one of the most restrictive dress codes in the Islamic world, yet partly in consequence, Iranian families have released their daughters to study and work in unprecedented numbers'. Michael Axworthy, *A History of Iran. Empire of the Mind*, New York, Basic Books, 2008, p. 20. It should also be noted that, certain reforms implemented notwithstanding, Reza Pahlavi always demonstrated a disdain for women. An example is the following declaration during an interview in English with Oriana Fallaci: 'In a man's life, women count only if they're beautiful and graceful and know how to stay feminine and... This Women's Lib business, for instance. What do these feminists want? What do you want? Equality, you say? Indeed! I don't want to seem rude, but... You may be equal in the eyes of the law, but not, I beg your pardon for saying so, in ability. Oriana Fallaci, 'The Shah of Iran: An Interview with Mohammad Reza Pahlevi', in *The New Republic*, 1 December 1973, https://newrepublic.com/article/92745.

This is made even more evident by a widespread awareness that the two 'inseparable twins', bazaar and mosque, are further apart than ever before. In this sense, the imbalance in favour of the 'mosques' would now seem irreversible. The little that has remained of the economic power and historic role played by the bazaaris – including their political mobilization ability – has been swept away in recent years, last but not least by a series of markedly neo-liberal policies implemented by former president Rafsanjāni (in the 1990s) and Ḥasan Rūḥānī (in office since 2013). The 'alliance' which was the backbone of the great historical phenomena which cut through the whole of Iran's history from the second half of the nineteenth century onwards represents now a sort of vestige of the past: a fact which would make any attempt to undermine the current leadership even more vulnerable and uncertain.

In other respects, however, little seems to have changed. Various actors, for the most part external to the region, are in fact committed, in more or less direct ways, to reinforcing the country's most conservative and extremist elements[60] or, in other cases, to hing on a series of strategies and pressure groups in order to trigger regime change. These attempts have grown to an unprecedented extent in the last decade, and in particular in the wake of Iraq's implosion (and thus that of Pan-Arab party Ba'th, hostile to Tehran), a geographical area and, later, a state which had always constrained Persian/Iranian influence in the region.

The Trump administration, in particular, has identified growing economic sanctions and groups/parties such as Mujahedin-e Khalq

60 The protests which began in January 2017 in Mashhad, an area in which the most militant and extremist clerics are concentrated, were largely triggered by a strengthening in the more conservative elements in the country as well as by the concurrent failure of the economic policies adopted in recent years by the regime's more moderate and pragmatic wing. Supported by the cultured elite, the bourgeoisie and the urban middle classes, President Hassan Rūhānī had, in fact, implemented a policy of moderation in internal affairs and greater Iranian integration into the international economy. Washington's unilateral abandonment of the so-called 'Iran deal' (the nuclear weapons agreement signed in 2015 by the 5 plus 1 countries, the European Union and Iran) was the factor which undermined the success of these objectives to the greatest extent.

(MEK)[61] as the key to constraining Iran's growing influence in the region and/or promoting regime change in the country. Whilst it has as yet no effect on public opinion in Iran, groups such as MEK embody, in some respects, what General Fazlollah Zahedi represented at the time of the 1953 coup d'état. As the current US National Security Advisor John Bolton noted during a meeting organized by MEK in Paris in July 2017, 'there is a viable opposition to the rule of the ayatollahs, and that opposition is centered in this room today'.[62] The political actors who contributed most to fostering – primarily as a consequence of the invasion of Iraq in 2003[63] – the structural conditions for Tehran's rise to power in the region are thus the same that are now prompting the international community to act against the 'regime of the āyatollāhs'.

The past, as is frequently the case, thus does not seem to have passed. For some eminent observers this represents even a sort of cause and structural responsibility for the region's current troubles. In the words of a recent work by Thomas Friedman, the Middle East 'made itself poor by repeatedly letting the past bury the future'.[64] Rather than facing up to

61 Set up in 1965 in Tehran and included by the US State Department in its list of terrorist groups until September 2012, MEK has been involved in various assassination attempts in Iran (causing the deaths of a large number of civilians). In the 1980s the movement's leadership took shelter in Paris. Its militias were, however, in Iraq (at the time of the war with Iran), becoming loyal allies of Saddam Hussein, thus significantly tarnishing their reputation in large swathes of Iranian public opinion.

62 'John Bolton on Iran', in *The Iran Primer*, 22 February 2018, https://iranprimer.usip.org/node/4796. Rudolph Giuliani, former mayor of New York and great Trump supporter, went even further: 'I say to the Iranian government, you must truly be afraid of being overthrown'. Cited in 'Trump Attorney Rudy Giuliani: US Sympathizes with Iran Regime Change', in *The Guardian*, 23 September 2018, https://gu.com/p/9enjg.

63 Five of the 19 terrorists involved in the 11 September 2001 massacre were Saudi citizens. Despite this, the Bush government reacted by attacking Iraq and Afghanistan.

64 Thomas L. Friedman, 'Crazy Poor Middle Easterners', in *The New York Times*, 4 September 2018, https://nyti.ms/2Nfb9xx.

the weight of history, a widely held current of opinion, well embodied by Friedman himself, has thus chosen to burn its bridges with the past, promoting an approach which is as widespread as it is short-sighted: the *qablan* (before), *alan* (now) and *ayandeh* (future) of Iran – as well as of the rest of the region – are and will remain inextricably bound together.

Contributors

Arshin Adib-Moghaddam is professor in Global Thought and Comparative Philosophies at SOAS, chair of the Centre for Iranian Studies at the London Middle East Institute, and series editor for Cambridge University Press ('The Global Middle East').

Abdullah Al-Arian is an associate professor of History at Georgetown University in Qatar, editor of the 'Critical Currents in Islam' page on the Jadaliyya e-zine, and a frequent contributor to the Al-Jazeera English network and website.

Youssef Cherif runs the Columbia Global Centers in Tunis. He is a member of Carnegie's Civic Activism Network and a Valdai Club expert. He is North Africa's political analyst for several international think-tanks and media outlets.

Nader Hashemi is director of the Center for Middle East Studies and associate professor of Middle East and Islamic Politics at the University of Denver's Josef Korbel School of International Studies.

Waleed Hazbun is Richard L. Chambers professor of Middle Eastern Studies at the University of Alabama. He previously taught at the American University of Beirut, where he served as director of the Center for Arab and Middle East Studies (CAMES).

Lorenzo Kamel is associate professor of History at the University of Turin, director of the Research Studies of the Istituto Affari Internazionali (IAI), and scientific director of the New-Med Research Network.

Elijah J. Magnier is the chief international correspondent at *Al Rai* and a veteran war correspondent and political risk analyst with over 35 years' experience covering Europe, Africa and the Middle East.

Nicolò Russo-Perez is the coordinator of the International Affairs Program at the Compagnia di San Paolo foundation. Previously he worked at the European Commission, at the International Labour Organisation and was a senior associate fellow at the EUISS in Paris.

Coralie Pison Hindawi is associate professor of International Politics and Law at the Department of Political Studies at the American University of Beirut, and a member of the Critical Studies on Security in the Arab Region network (Beirut Collective).

Morten Valbjørn is associate professor at the Department of Political Science, Aarhus University, and director of the interdisciplinary research project 'SWAR: Sectarianism in the Wake of the Arab Revolts'.

Abbreviations

ACSS	Arab Council for the Social Sciences
AIOC	Anglo-Iranian Oil Company
AQ	al-Qaeda
AQAP	al-Qaeda in the Arab peninsula
AQIS	al-Qaeda in the Indian Subcontinent
AUB	American University of Beirut
BDS	Boycott, Divestment and Sanctions
CAAT	Campaign Against Arms Trade
CIA	Central Intelligence Agency
CPR	Congress for the Republic (Tunisia)
CTC	Counter-Terrorism Coordinator
EPC	Emirates Policy Center
EU	European Union
FJP	Freedom and Justice Party
IR	International Relations
ISIS	Islamic State of Iraq and Syria
JCPOA	Joint Comprehensive Plan of Action
MEK	Mujahedin-e Khalq (People's Mujahedin of Iran)
MIT	Massachusetts Institute of Technology
NATO	North Atlantic Treaty Organization
NGO	Non-governmental organization
R2P	Responsibility to Protect
RELAC	Religion and Armed Conflict
SIPRI	Stockholm International Peace Research Institute
SOAS	School of Oriental and African Studies
UAE	United Arab Emirates
UK	United Kingdom

UN	United Nations
UNSC	UN Security Council
US	United States
USSR	Union of Soviet Socialist Republics
WMD	Weapons of mass destruction

www.ingramcontent.com/pod-product-compliance
Ingram Content Group UK Ltd.
Pitfield, Milton Keynes, MK11 3LW, UK
UKHW021849100926
8556IPUK00020B/1132

9 783034 338769